The TRAVELS of
MARCO POLO

THE COURT OF KUBLAI KHAN

The TRAVELS of MARCO POLO
[THE VENETIAN]

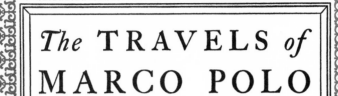

Revised from MARSDEN'S *Translation and Edited with Introduction by* MANUEL KOMROFF

LIVERIGHT PUBLISHING CORP. - NEW YORK

For information about permission to reproduce selections
from this book, write to Permissions, Liveright Publishing Corporation,
500 Fifth Avenue, New York, NY 10110

ISBN 0-87140-657-8

ISBN 0-87140-184-3 pbk.

Liveright Publishing Corporation
500 Fifth Avenue, New York, N.Y. 10110
www.wwnorton.com

W. W. Norton & Company Ltd.
Castle House, 75/76 Wells Street, London W1T 3QT

2 3 4 5 6 7 8 9 0

INTRODUCTION

AFTER AN ABSENCE OF twenty-six years, Marco Polo and his father Nicolo and his uncle Maffeo returned from the spectacular court of Kublai Khan to their old home in Venice. Their clothes were coarse and tattered; the bundles that they carried were bound in Eastern cloths and their bronzed faces bore evidence of great hardships, long endurance, and suffering. They had almost forgotten their native tongue. Their aspect seemed foreign and their accent and entire manner bore the strange stamp of the Tartar. During these twenty-six years Venice, too, had changed and the travellers had difficulty in finding their old residence. But here at last as they entered the courtyard they were back home. Back from the Deserts of Persia, back from the lofty steeps of Pamir, from mysterious Tibet, from the dazzling court of Kublai Khan, from China, Mongolia, Burma, Siam, Sumatra, Java; back from Ceylon, where Adam has his tomb, and back from India, the land of myth and marvels. But the dogs of Venice barked as the travellers knocked on the door of their old home.

The Polos had long been thought dead, and the distant relatives who occupied the house refused admittance to the three shabby and suspicious looking gentlemen. After **much** questioning, finally, the travellers took advantage of a moment when the bolt was drawn and beat their way into the house, dragging their bundles with them. Other relatives were brought from various parts of Venice and after much discussing, the three Polos, who had long been counted among the dead, finally succeeded in convincing their own kindred that they were not impostors. The news soon spread and great excitement reigned.

A day or two later a grand feast was arranged to which all the old friends and relatives were asked. The three travellers were clothed in long robes of crimson satin, but these they removed before they sat down to the feast and they put on other robes of crimson damask, while the first were cut up and the cloth divided among the servants. Once, during the course of the meal, the travellers left the room and came back, this time in long robes of crimson velvet and the damask garments were presented to some of the guests. When the dinner was finished the robes of velvet were removed and the travellers appeared dressed in the ordinary fashion of the day; and the velvet robes were likewise distributed to the guests in strict accordance with the Mongol custom.

This performance caused much wonder. But when the table had been cleared, and all the servants had been asked to retire from the hall, Marco Polo produced the coarse, shabby costumes which the three travellers had worn on their arrival. Then taking sharp knives they ripped the seams and pleats and let fall to the table quantities of rubies, carbuncles, sapphires, diamonds, emeralds, pearls and other jewels of great value. Amazement bewildered and dumbfounded the guests; but if a shadow of doubt had remained in the minds of some regarding the identity of the travellers, it was now wholly dispersed. And all paid honour to the three gentlemen, agreeing that they could be no other than those of the merchant family. The year was now 1295.

This story of the return of Marco Polo with his father and uncle comes from his very first editor, John Baptist Ramusio, who, in his *Collection of Voyages and Travels* says: "This story I have often heard when I was a young-ster from the illustrious Messer Hasparo Malpiero, a gentle-man of very great age, and a Senator of eminent virtue and integrity, whose house was on the Canal of Santa Marina; . . . and he said he had heard the story from his own father and grandfather, and from other old men among the neighbours."

How Marco Polo Went to China

Marco Polo was born in Venice in the year 1254. His father, Nicolo, and his uncle, Maffeo, were merchants who had seats in the great council and were enrolled with the noblemen of Venice. Marco also had another uncle who lived in Constantinople and Crimea and was engaged in commerce.

The first great eastern journey of the Polos began in 1260. Nicolo Polo and his brother, Maffeo, first visited Constantinople and from there started out on a trading expedition to the Crimea. From here the quest of profits drove them far north along the Volga and then east to Bokhara. They were now well within the domain of the Great Kublai Khan, Emperor of the Tartars, and it was here that the merchants met an ambassador who was pro-ceeding to the court of Kublai Khan and were invited to accompany the party. In the prologue to his book of travels Marco Polo tells about the arrival of his father and uncle at the court of the Great Khan, who was highly pleased with these gentlemen from Europe and showed them great honour.

The Emperor heard all that the merchants had to tell him about their native land and Christianity and very soon decided to send them back to the Pope as his ambassadors, with messages of peace and a request for a hundred educated missionaries to come to China and convert them all to Christianity. The motives that prompted this plan were not wholly religious; a craftier design was in the background, as we shall soon learn when we look into the story of Kublai Khan. At any rate, when the brothers returned in 1269 the Pope, Clement IV, who is known to posterity as the benefactor and protector of the English philosopher, Roger Bacon, had already been dead a year and his successor had not yet been elected. When they arrived in Venice Nicolo found that his wife, too, had died during his absence, but that his son, Marco, was now quite grown, a fine lad of fifteen.

The merchants remained in Venice for two years, and as a new Pope had not yet been elected, they decided to keep their promise, return to Kublai Khan and report the reason of their failure. Large profits from trade with these distant parts also, no doubt, prompted the brothers to return; and on this journey they took Marco with them.

At Acre they procured letters from the Archdeacon of Liège, who was then accompanying Edward of England on a crusade, explaining the reason for the failure of the mission. With these documents in hand, the Polos started on the long journey eastward. They had, however, not travelled very far when they were overtaken by messengers informing them that their friend the Archdeacon of Liége, had been elected Pope and requested their return. To carry

out the mission of Kublai Khan they returned to Acre, but
the new Pope, Gregory X, was able to supply the Emperor
of the Tartars with only two Dominican Friars. To these
ill-educated monks was entrusted the spiritual destiny
of a domain that reached from the borders of Poland to the
Yellow Sea, from the Siberian Steppes to India. Two friars,
for the whole of Mongolia, China, Tibet, Siberia, Turkestan, Persia and Turkey! And they themselves seemed
but lightly inspired with their mission, nor were they accustomed to the hardships of a long journey. They soon
lost courage, and before they had taken the first step of the
journey, pretended that they were ill, made their excuses to
the Venetians, and took the very first opportunity to return
home.

The three Polos went on alone, forcing their way across
the perilous deserts of Persia. It was here that Marco
contracted a dangerous fever and was led to record in his
travels the great joy that they experienced when they reached
the cool, fragrant climate of Balkh, in what is now northern
Afghanistan. Here they remained a whole year, recovering
from the illness contracted in Persia and, taking advantage
of their time, studied the native languages.

From this point they ascended to the plateau of Pamir,
often referred to as the top of the world. This land was
wholly unknown to Europe and the name Pamir unheard
until it was described by Marco Polo; and for many hundreds of years this and other regions further east towards
Kashgar and Yarkand, remained almost entirely closed to
our knowledge. In fact, parts of it still remain uncharted.

The Gobi Desert now lay between the Venetians and
Kublai Khan. It is interesting to note that Marco Polo's
account of the difficulties and terrors, as well as of the
strange superstitions of tribes living on its borders, had been

independently described by a Chinese Pilgrim six hundred years earlier.

As they neared the capital the Emperor Kublai was informed, through the well organized post system described by Marco Polo, of the approach of the Venetians, and when they were still forty days from the court sent orders ahead providing for their comfort. At last, after travelling for three and a half years, the ambassadors returned to the court and bowed low before the Emperor. Instead of the hundred learned men, they had with them a few letters from the new Pope, a little sacred oil from the Holy Land, and Marco. By this time Marco was twenty-one and the year was 1275.

The Emperor of Asia

Kublai Khan was born in 1216 and was therefore fifty-nine years old when young Marco arrived at his court. His youth had been spent in war, his middle life was devoted to ambitious schemes of conquest, and after the death of his brother, during a siege in the invasion of China, he proclaimed himself emperor. He was then forty-four years old; and after reorganizing his army he resumed the invasion of China. At the same time he established himself and his court in a city that he selected for the future capital of his Empire and which is now known as Peking. This was only ten or eleven years before Marco arrived and the splendour and pomp of his court was already at its height.

With the downfall of the degenerate Sung dynasty, after fifty years of wars, the Mongols became lords of the East. The deciding battle was fought a year after Marco Polo's arrival in China. But "China is a sea that salts all rivers that flow into it." Before the conquest was complete, before Kublai had founded his Mongol dynasty, symptoms of

decline were evident. Discontent and revolt were brewing;
a certain social twitching and uneasiness were already apparent. The decline had begun before the height had been
reached. The vast domain that stretched from the sea
westward into Europe and from Arctic lands south to India,
Burma and Siam was now falling apart, bit by bit, while on
the throne Kublai, more powerful than any other Emperor
the world had ever seen, surrounded by great splendour and
pomp, still dreamed of further conquest.

But how did Kublai become lord of so extensive a domain?
Let us go back for a moment and trace briefly the rise of the
Mongol dynasty which at one very critical moment threatened to overrun the entire world. The dynasty began with
the grandfather of Kublai, who was born in 1162, the son
of the chief of a petty Mongolian tribe. It was he who was
the master conqueror, not Kublai. Before his career was
ended Jenghiz Khan lived to see his armies victorious to the
very banks of the Dnieper. But his invasion of Europe was
unpremeditated and was the outcome of a minor bit of
treachery.

At the early age of thirteen Jenghiz Khan began his wars,
after the death of his father had made him chief of the
Mongol tribe. At once secession was demanded by several
Tartar clans that had owed allegiance to the Mongols. They
said, "The deepest wells are sometimes dry, and the hardest
stone is sometimes broken; why should we cling to thee?"
But the young chief, with the aid of his mother, subjugated
them in battles and succeeded in holding in check all hostile
neighbouring tribes. He was forty-four years old before he
felt himself strong enough, or his enemies weak enough,
to proclaim himself ruler of an empire. Having vanquished
his last enemy on the Mongol steppes, he turned his attention to an invasion of the Tartars in northern China. Several

pitched battles followed. Jenghiz Khan entered the Great
Wall of China, and establishing himself there, divided his
troops into three great armies.

The first army, commanded by three of his sons, marched
south; the second, commanded by his four brothers, marched
eastward, while he himself with his youngest son, Tule,
went in a south-easterly direction. Complete success followed and a vast sector was encompassed. Jenghiz Khan
was satisfied and wanted no more; he wrote to Mohammed
the Shah: "I send thee greeting; I know thy power and
the vast extent of thine empire; I regard thee as my most
cherished son. On my part thou must know that I have
conquered China and all the Turkish nations north of it;
thou knowest that my country is a magazine of warriors, a
mine of silver, and I have no need of other lands. I take
it that we have an equal interest in encouraging trade between our subjects." This proposal was well received, but
was followed by an unfortunate occurrence. The very first
trading mission was seized and put to death by an ignorant
governor. Jenghiz sent envoys who demanded the surrender of the offending governor, but in reply the chief
ambassador was beheaded and the others were returned by
Mohammed to Jenghiz without their beards. War followed
this insult.

Again the Khan's troops were divided into three large
armies; and Jenghiz with his youngest son Tule, father of
Kublai, went into battle. The armies were marched across
the continent and over the mountainous barriers of Tibet.
. . . Tashkent surrendered, Bokhara fell, and here he organized two flying columns to pursue Mohammed and harry
him from all directions. Slaughter followed; cities were
sacked, burned and the inhabitants massacred. Jenghiz
Khan controlled a war machinery unprecedented in the his-

tory of the world. The city of Herat withstood for six
months a siege from an army of 80,000 men, who were
fighting thousands of miles from their homes. At last it
was taken by force and the entire population of over a million and a half was massacred by the soldiers of Jenghiz
Khan. Vengeance was now complete and Jenghiz Khan
was satisfied to return to Mongolia.

In the meantime, however, the two flying battalions drove
a horde of Ottoman Turks into Europe and had gained so
much momentum that all fell before them. The presence
of the "terrible Turk" in Europe may be said to be the outcome of this Tartar invasion, prompted by an indiscreet act
of treachery. In the spring of 1222 the Mongols advanced
into Georgia; and at this time the Russians made the same
mistake and put to death several envoys from the Mongol
camp. The Mongols replied: "We have done you no
harm, but as you wish for war you shall have it." Once
more the invaders swept across the country, this time into
Great Bulgaria, which they looted, ravaged and gouged.
The empire of Jenghiz Khan was in this way extended to
the borders of Poland.

A second invasion of Europe followed ten years later,
but Jenghiz Khan was now dead and his son was emperor.
Pope Innocent IV, uneasy at this threatening horde, endeavoured to induce all European nations to rise in mass and
save the Christian name from destruction. The Dukes of
Austria and Carinthia and the King of Bohemia assembled
their meagre forces to check the invasion. These armies
would have been tissue to the Mongol tooth were it not for
the sudden death of the Emperor, the son of Jenghiz Khan.
The Mongol armies retired from Hungary, Poland and
Kiev, encamped on the eastern bank of the Dnieper and
here waited for word from the East. Europe was saved.

The Pope felt that the victory was entirely his and sent several friars as envoys to the Mongols, asking them to be baptised and embrace the Christian faith. To one of these requests a grandson of Jenghiz replied: "The series of your letters contained advice that we ought to be baptised and to become Christians; we briefly reply, that we do not understand why we ought to do so. . . . You inhabitants of the West believe that you only are Christians, and despise others; but how do you know on whom God may choose to bestow His favour. We adore God, and, in his strength, will overwhelm the whole earth from the East to the West. But if we were not men strengthened by God, what could we do?"

Again, some years later, three Dominican friars, describing themselves as ambassadors of the Pope, entered the Mongol domain and sought an audience with one of the princes. They were indiscreet enough to ask the Mongols to repent their past wickedness, especially the evil they had done by killing Christians, and to promise to cease annoying the people of God.

Once more in 1253, Friar William de Rubroquis acted as ambassador of the Pope and travelled eastward to convert the Emperor and all his subjects. He was sent from the prince of one province to that of another until finally he received the answer: "Fools say there is one God, but wise men say there are many." The country was then ruled by Mangu Khan, grandson of Jenghiz and elder brother of Kublai. As Rubroquis originally came from France, inquiries were made as to the wealth of that country and the friar was led to believe that an invasion of the whole of Europe was contemplated. Mangu died in 1259 and his brother, Kublai, assumed the throne. He is considered the founder of the Mongol dynasty, because he gave the finishing stroke to the defeat of the House of Sung. But his downfall was already under way. Savage tribes at the north, mutiny among his troops in the south, discontent among the conquered races and lastly the failure of ventures at sea against Japan, all contributed to a great uneasiness. These were symptoms that he well recognized and took steps to overcome. He believed this could be stayed by education and that peace would follow in the patient steps of learning.

When the two gentlemen merchants arrived from Venice, Kublai was very favourably impressed and under the pretext of embracing the Christian faith asked the Pope for a hundred men of learning. In the back of his mind, undoubtedly, lodged other schemes. But regardless of the sinister motives of Kublai Khan, the Pope cannot be forgiven for having lost so welcome an opportunity; an opportunity for wisdom, if not for virtue. Had he sent a thousand men instead of a hundred, little impression would they have made in so vast a territory. A new religion might have resulted; for inasmuch as China has altered Buddhism, probably it would have distorted Christianity also.

While this might have been little or no consolation to the Pope its effects would have been far-reaching. Even though Christianity in China had degenerated, it certainly would not have sunk to the level of the faith of the Nestorian Christians, who were banished from Syria in the fifth century, and were so frequently encountered by Marco Polo in various sections of China. The benefits might well have been enormous. A thousand, or even a hundred, cultured men living in China at this time and returning home at various periods would have changed the course of human events. Europe was just awakening from a long, barbaric sleep, while China was already cultured in many fields. Marco Polo came to exchange merchandise, while a hundred cultured men would have returned to exchange ideas. It is the traffic of ideas that is of greater profit to humanity.

Kublai Khan Beats His Drums

What was the civilisation of China at the time Marco Polo arrived? In what way was it above that of Europe? The first observation to be made in this direction came from Rubroquis who, prior to Marco Polo's visit, had acted as envoy of the Pope. In a record of his impressions he wrote: "Another circumstance, equally opposite to preconceived ideas, was the polish, courtesy, and respectful familiarity, which distinguished their social intercourse. Quarrels, blows, combats, and bloodshed, then so frequent in Europe, were not witnessed, even amid their deepest potations. Honesty was everywhere conspicuous; their wagons and other property were secure without locks or guards; and if any of their cattle strayed, arrangements were made by which they were speedily recovered. Notwithstanding the frequent scarcity of victuals, they were generous in relieving those in greater want than themselves." The spirit of tolerance can be noted on almost every page of Marco Polo's record. Jews and Christians had complete religious freedom, and their temples were exempt from taxation.

Two outstanding engineering marvels had already been completed before Marco Polo arrived. One was the Great Wall of China and the other the Grand Canal, the last 600 miles of which was finished by Kublai Khan. This canal runs from Peking to Canton and to this day remains the longest waterway constructed by man. Land communications by post riders were developed to a high degree and are fully described by Marco Polo.

In the various arts China was already mature. Painting, engraving, bronze casting, sculpture, the making of porcelain and architecture were already very highly developed. Literature, too, was greatly respected. The invention of paper came as early as A.D. 105 and books were printed from wood blocks in 932. About fifty years later the large Encyclopædia, consisting of a thousand different sections, was ordered printed under the personal supervision of the Emperor. Marco Polo could have found books already in circulation dealing with political economy, philosophy, religion, warfare, agriculture, painting, music and other arts. Movable type first made its appearance in China in the form of baked clay blocks at the early date of 1043 and paper money, spoken of with such wonder by Marco Polo, was the currency in many sections of the empire.

Mechanical devices were not lacking. Water clocks were found on bridges, astronomical instruments were in constant use, metals and coal were mined and salt extracted from brine.

It was in this world of wonders that Marco Polo, an impressionable youth of twenty-one, found himself. Kublai Khan took very kindly to the young man, who at once applied himself to the written and spoken languages of the country; and the Emperor, seeing that he was both clever and tactful, very soon began to employ him on public missions. Chinese records show that a certain Polo was, in the year 1277, nominated as commissioner attached to the imperial council.

Before his public missions carried him to various distant parts of the country Marco Polo had observed that the Emperor was often bored by the dry reports of his commissioners but that he took great delight in hearing about the manners and oddities of people in strange parts. He soon acquired the habit of taking notes in small books of those strange facts that were likely to amuse and interest Kublai Khan. And these marvels he related to the Emperor on his return to court.

Marco, it seems, did all he could to please the Khan and rose high in the Emperor's esteem and favour. At one time he was commissioned governor of the great city of Yang-chow and at various times held many other important posts. During one of the battles the Polos rendered the Emperor aid by constructing from lumber a huge artillery engine capable of hurling 300-pound stones into the ranks of the enemy. At another time Marco distinguished himself by speaking the truth against a favourite, but treacherous, minister.

The fascinating descriptions of the Emperor's hunting parties could not have been written by anyone but an eye witness. The great masses of detail recorded in these chapters could come only from a well-trained observer who had accompanied the Great Khan and was apparently quite close to his person. It is in these pages that we learn of the ingenious lost-and-found system conducted by appointed officers who followed the hunt and established their headquarters in conspicuous places to take care of unclaimed property. "If, on the other hand," Marco Polo concludes, "a person finds any article that has been lost, and fails to carry it to the proper depository, he is punished as a thief. . . . The effect of this regulation is, that no articles are ultimately lost."

The minute detail in the thrilling description of how Kublai Khan went to battle could have been recorded by no one but a participant. These descriptions form the most complete records known of the war machine of a mediæval Asiatic emperor. Read what he says about the great drums

of the emperor: "As soon as the order of battle was arranged, an infinite number of wind instruments of various
kinds were sounded, and these were succeeded by songs,
according to the custom of the Tartars before they engage in
fight, which commences upon the signal given by the cymbals
and drums, and there was such a beating of the cymbals and
drums, and such singing, that it was wonderful to hear.
This signal, by the orders of the Great Khan, was first given
to the right and left wings, and the great drums of Kublai
Khan began to sound. Then a fierce and bloody conflict
began."

The Polos prospered in the court of the Emperor. Marco
tells of the many places he visited and of some of the things
that occupied his time. They remained in China for twenty
years. As the Emperor was already middle-aged when they
arrived, he was, by this time, quite an old man. Fearing
that his death might place them in the hands of one of
Kublai's enemies, and thus endanger their lives, the Polos
tried to gain permission to return to their native land. But
Kublai had by this time become attached to the Venetians
and would not consent to their departure.

The opportunity, however, came, as Marco Polo records
in his prologue, when the Khan of Persia, grandson of
Kublai's brother, lost his favourite wife and desired that
another be sent him of the same Mongol tribe from which
she had come. As the journey overland was considered
most perilous, the Polos, who were expert navigators, proposed to Kublai that they be allowed to pilot the ships that
would carry the bride and the returning envoys to Persia.
He consented, but not without a good deal of reluctance.
After equipping the party in the best manner at his disposal,
he said farewell to the Venetians and at the same time gave

them friendly messages to be delivered to the Christian kings of France, Spain, England, as well as to the Pope.

The Polos exchanged their acquired possessions for jewels and other precious objects that were easily carried and with these concealed in their clothes set sail on a long and dangerous voyage through southern waters, touching at the islands of Sumatra, Java, Ceylon and at points along the coast of India. It took them more than two years to reach Persia where, alas, the Khan was already dead and the bride was delivered to his son instead. Within another year they were home; but before they arrived in Venice, although they knew it not, Kublai Khan, he who could command the great battle drum of the East to be beaten, had already passed away.

How the Travels Came to Be Written

There are few actual records of Marco Polo's existence after the return of the travellers to their home in Venice, but what records do remain seem quite definite and authentic.

As the Polos were merchants, they at once set themselves up in business again and no doubt began trade with some of the merchandise brought from the Far East. Great rivalry existed between the merchants of Venice and those of Genoa and Pisa. Commercial jealousies between these three independent Italian communities soon grew to resentment and bitterness. Many years before, Venice had taken an important part in the conquest of Constantinople and a very valuable trade had resulted from the venture. This prosperity was envied by the Genoese, who, on the other hand, had done very well in Acre and Syria and were developing a galley fleet that blocked the trade of their competitors in several directions. In the early part of 1298, as the result of the seizure of three Genoese vessels sailing in Grecian waters, war between Venice and Genoa became unavoidable. In the records of this conflict we find the name of Marco Polo recorded as a "Gentleman-Commander" of a galley.

The war galleys of the time were equipped and maintained by rich merchant families for the protection of their harbours and trading ships from both pirates and truculent rivals. Records show that the Polo family had at one time built and maintained such a galley in the Venetian fleet but it is not likely that Marco Polo was at this time in command of that particular vessel. The vessels were timber, built on a narrow beam, and had probably a hundred oars on each side. The crews numbered about 250 and included some forty or fifty men armed with mechanical cross-bows, two carpenters, two caulkers, two attendants, one cook and the Captain with his staff of quartermasters. Every ship had also a "Gentleman-Commander" who was on deck ready to be consulted by the Captain when occasion demanded. He acted in an advisory capacity and shared the responsibility with the master of the boat.

A galley fleet often consisted of about sixty or more vessels under the command of an admiral and two assistants. Besides the crew already mentioned, a personnel was augmented by physicians, surgeons, fletchers, armourers, cross-bar makers, a council of gentlemen, officers of supplies and arms, and last, but not least, twenty or more musicians capable of making much clamorous noise, thus rousing the blood of the crews to fighting pitch.

With coloured banners gaily floating in the wind and with hundreds of oars beating step to the kettle drums and fifes, the Venetian fleet met the Genoese on September 7, 1298, just three years after Marco Polo's return from the east.

In the battle that followed the entire Venetian fleet was captured. Marco Polo and 7000 of his countrymen were taken prisoners. According to the custom of the time the gay banners of the defeated galleys were torn down and allowed to drag in the water while the vessel itself was towed to port backwards. The commander of the Venetian fleet, unable to bear the humiliation of defeat, put an end to himself by dashing his head against a bench.

Marco Polo's father and uncle no doubt made attempts to gain the prisoner's release by paying ransom or entering into some form of exchange. In fact, some of the Venetians obtained their liberty in this way, but for some reason or other the Genoese would not consent to the release of Marco Polo.

During the three years that Marco Polo had been home in Venice he had many times been called upon to relate the story of his travels and tell of the oddities and curious things he had experienced in unheard-of lands. To his listeners it all seemed incredible. The vastness of the distances and the great numbers mentioned by Marco Polo led the people to nickname his house the "court of the millions." Marco himself is often referred to in records of the time as "Marco Polo of the Millions."

There is, indeed, no record to prove that a single one of his contemporaries really believed much of the story he told. But now in prison his opportunity was before him. He sent for the notebooks he had kept for the entertainment of Kublai Khan, and with the aid of a scribe called Rusticien, who was a fellow prisoner from Pisa, the travels were dictated and written down on parchment.

The work was done very quickly, all probably completed within several months, for before a year was over a truce was signed between Venice and Genoa and Marco Polo, freed, returned home.

At about this time Marco Polo married a woman called Donata, and three daughters were born to him. They were named Fantina, Bellala, and Moreta. But very little else is known of his family life. While he was still engaged in trade his fame as a traveller continued, for in 1307, twelve years after his return from China, we learn that he presented a copy of his travels to a French nobleman. This data is contained in a note in one of the Marco Polo manuscripts, now in the Paris Library. The note states that the copy was requested of Marco Polo, "a very honourable person, of high character and respect in many countries, because of his desire that what he had witnessed should be known throughout the World. . . ." Marco Polo presented this volume and expressed pleasure that it would be taken to France.

The extent of the precious merchandise brought home from the East must have been considerable, for sixteen years after his return Marco Polo still had some of the goods on his hands. Some of the sweet-scented musk that came from Tibet was given to a commission merchant for disposal and a law-suit resulted over one-sixth of an ounce of this reddish-brown powder and a half-pound that was sold and not paid for. The judge ruled in favour of Marco Polo and ordered the commission merchant to pay with costs or suffer imprisonment.

The final document is in the form of a will, now in St. Mark's Library. It is dated 1324 and Marco Polo was then seventy years old. Disease had taken hold of him and finding himself growing feebler each day he sent for a priest and notary and gave them detailed instructions regarding the disposal of his property. The will appointed his wife and three daughters, two of whom were by this time married, as his trustees.

On his death-bed his friends pleaded with him, for the peace of his soul, to retract some of the seemingly incredible statements he made in his book; but to this his only reply was, "I have not told half of what I saw." He was buried in the church of San Lorenzo.

"It's a Marco Polo"

Soon after the death of Marco Polo a comic figure appeared in every Venetian carnival. The ruffian was dressed like a clown and represented Marco of the Millions. His pranks consisted of gross exaggerations expressed by gestures and his only object was to amuse the crowds. In this he well succeeded. At the same time some of the scribes who made copies of the Marco Polo book felt called upon to express the opinion that while the document was highly interesting they did not at all vouch for its truthfulness. It took many hundreds of years to break down this strong popular belief. The discoveries of Columbus that followed two centuries later and the wonders that came with the opening of a new world had little effect on the established opinion. In fact, even in our own century, school boys in England use the phrase, "It's a Marco Polo," to describe a falsehood.

It seems easier to maintain a belief once established than to reject it. From time to time proofs even were brought forward to discredit some of the statements made by Marco Polo. A missionary named Magaillans, who was also a Chinese scholar of parts, returned from the Orient about two hundred years ago and denied that paper money was ever used as currency in China. Fortunately some of the banknotes of the old Ming Dynasty have since been located and are now preserved. It was also difficult for Europeans to believe that certain black stones found in China could be broken up and used as fuel, but this we now know was nothing but coal. The same was true of the Indian nuts described by Marco Polo as being as large as a man's head. These we now know to be cocoanuts. And it is only in very recent times that the existence of the great sheep of Pamir, described by our traveller and since named after him, Ovis Poli, has been confirmed. A long catalogue could be made of the true statements contained in this volume that were at one time believed incredible. It was many years before the travels as a whole took their place as an authentic account of Mediæval Asia.

Marco Polo was the first traveller to cross the entire continent of Asia and name the countries and provinces in their proper consecutive order. Yet, owing to the early rejection of his book of travels, his work had little or no influence on the geographical conception of the world. Nor did the map makers of the time make very many changes in their charts to accord with the careful descriptions contained in Marco Polo's book. Even after America had been discovered the attempts to draw the position of China in relation to other lands were most feeble. On the other hand explorers during the last century have been able to trace Marco Polo's footsteps across vast stretches of the continent and follow his route from the descriptions contained in his book. In most cases the distances roughly recorded by Marco Polo were found quite accurate by recent explorers who visited these parts for the purpose of charting the areas.

Many of the sections traversed by Marco Polo over six hundred years ago were revisited by European explorers in quite recent years. In our own time Sven Hedin, Sir Aurel

Stein, Colonel Henry Yule, Dr. Paul Pelliot, Colonel Koslov
and Major Sykes have all made extensive journeys along
the itineraries first laid down by the Venetian Traveller.

This should be quite enough to establish Marco Polo's
fame, but even more may be added. He was the first traveller to record the perilous deserts of Persia, the first to
visit the jade-bearing streams of Khotan, which have since
been seen by only one man of our own race, Sven Hedin.
Marco Polo was also the first traveller to describe accurately
the life of the people in China, Tibet, Burma, Siam, Ceylon,
India and the hundred other places that he visited or heard
about. He gave us the very first hint of the existence of
the dark land of Siberia, of Zanzibar and its black races
and white ivory, of Christian Abyssinia and cannibal
Sumatra. He pointed north to the Arctic Ocean with its
white bears, dog-sledges and reindeer and he also pointed
south and recorded the fierce heat of India and its mines of
diamonds, beds of pearls and strange myths. He described
the dazzling court of Kublai Khan and the organization of
the Mongol Army that came perilously near conquering the
entire world; and he also described strange little birds and
animals unknown in his own land and temples that had
golden roofs, and odd customs, strange sights, historical and
allegorical legends and many, many other things. No
volume has ever contained a richer magazine of marvels.

Plan of the Present Edition

Marco Polo dictated the travels to his fellow prisoner in
Genoa many years before the development of printing. The
volumes were copied in manuscript, fashioned by hand, and
variations in wording and even more serious changes often
crept into the work. About eighty-five manuscripts of Marco

Polo's book are preserved in various museums and libraries. No two are exactly alike. Some are in Italian, some in Latin and some in French.

One of the earliest printed editions on record is that made by Marco Polo's first editor, Ramusio. This was published in 1559. Marsden's classical English edition was translated from this Italian version and published in 1818. In 1854 an edition was prepared by Thomas Wright for Bohn's Library. Marsden's translation was used for this text with the addition of several chapters and an abridgment of the original notes. This edition was later republished in the Everyman's Library and is at present the one most known to the English reading public.

The French Geographical Society printed a most important Marco Polo text in 1824. This was from a manuscript written in Old French, and after careful examination and discussion by eminent scholars it is quite well established today that this text is the most nearly authentic. It is quite probable that Marco Polo even dictated the manuscript in the colloquial French used by merchants of his time. This edition was later revised by a most capable French scholar, M. Pauthier, and published in France in 1865.

It was this French edition that was used by the famous English scholar Henry Yule. Before undertaking an English translation of the work Henry Yule made a personal examination of a great many of the original Marco Polo manuscripts and decided that the French text, in spite of its deficiencies and crudities, was by far the most accurate.

For many years Henry Yule had been resident in India and after contributing a number of valuable volumes on the Orient, began in about 1863 to make researches into Mediæval travellers. In 1866 he published his *Cathay and the Way Thither* and the following year, on his return to London, began systematically working on the Travels of Marco Polo. To this task he passionately devoted a great portion of the remainder of his life. He used the crude and awkward French text as his basis and to this added erudite notes upon notes from every known available source. In 1871 the work was ready for publication and was printed in two volumes. This he corrected, revised and enlarged for a new edition, which appeared in 1875. Still he did not rest, for another enlarged edition was well under way when he died in 1889. The completion of the work was entrusted to a distinguished French scholar, Henri Cordier, who made many valuable contributions to the present edition, published in 1902. Without the many years of painstaking effort and devotion that Henry Yule put into his researches any present edition would be poverty-stricken.

Henri Cordier continued the researches and in 1920 published an addenda to Henry Yule's last edition, forming a third volume to the set containing the results of recent explorations, research and discovery.

Since Marsden's classical Marco Polo in 1818 all editions have laid stress upon the notes substantiating the observations of the traveller—researches, expeditions, mediæval historical material, geological observations and the results of explorations. Not one edition has appeared treating the entire work as a classical travel narrative with Marco Polo's complete text.

The tendency of the present edition is in this direction. Prompted by a desire to give the reader the entire spectacular travel narrative of Marco Polo in as accurate a manner as possible, the editor has discarded all encumbering notes and material that would tend to check the progress of the narrative. Several problems presented themselves, the most serious being the choice of translation. While the Yule translation was the most accurate, its language was awkward; on the other hand, Marsden's English translation, which had grown into a classic, was done in splendid style, but filled with errors. It seemed simpler to correct the mistaken than to polish the translated French text. Not only was the text corrected by a careful comparison with Yule's edition but long sentences were adjusted, archaic words and expressions were removed and their equivalent substituted, all with one object in view: to make Marco Polo more readable. Only here and there did the text seem to require an occasional short note and these have been supplied. The old names used in Marco Polo's time have been kept throughout but occasionally, where possible, the modern equivalent has been inserted after the original name, thus: Kanbalu [Peking]. Beside this, missing paragraphs and a whole chapter found in the French version have been added in order to make the present volume as complete as possible.

On examination it will be found that the numbers of the chapters are entirely different from those used by Marsden. Many long chapters will be found divided into several short ones. This was done in order to make the numbering correspond with the French version used by Yule. Students desiring to refer to Yule's famous notes on any given chapter may, by this plan, readily turn to the corresponding place in the large three-volume work.

The Man Marco Polo

We have spoken of Marco Polo the traveller and we have seen him in many situations, but his entire record is impersonal. What manner of man was he? What was his character?

We know first of all that Marco Polo was a merchant,

born in a merchant family and that he travelled to China
with his father and uncle.   It is therefore not surprising
to hear him constantly speak of trade, money, risks and
profits.   His eye was trained to appraise in these directions
and examples of this type of observation may be found
throughout the entire narrative.   But Marco Polo also had
an eye for nature.

In the first section of the travels he makes twenty signifi-
cant references to birds.   Throughout the volume he uses
a good deal of detail in describing animals, trees and various
forms of vegetation.   He also talks about different fruits,
nuts and seeds.   The keenness of these observations leaves
us in no doubt regarding his love of nature.   This is further
borne out in the treasures he brought home.   In one place
he tells of getting some wool from a wild yak to take home
with him; in another place we hear that he is taking home
the head and feet of the musk-producing gazelle; then
seeds of the Brazil plant, and finally a few cakes made from
the pith of the sago tree.   These things interested him and
all were related to nature rather than to other sides of life.
He does not speak of bringing home samples of the strange
paper money he found in circulation in China, neither does
he speak of taking with him any of the art objects he
mentions.

In his book he fails to speak about the great Wall of China
in definite terms, or about tea or the bound feet of the
women, but he does not lose an opportunity to describe the
length of the tail-feathers of certain birds or how the Khan's
falcons were marked with silver rings on their feet.

In many situations we find him frank, brave, tactful and
anxious to be in the current of life.   His speech is unpoetic
and concerns itself with matter-of-fact things closely related
to the business of living.   He is without poetic imagination

or vision and in this unfortunate respect resembles the ordinary business man of all ages.

He was, however, very loyal to Kublai Khan and speaks with great enthusiasm about him and the splendours that he found in the court. He offers no word of protest in the description of the annual selection of vast numbers of girls for the Khan's harem, but on the other hand, when speaking of the wandering life of the Tartars, he says that it is admirable to observe the loyalty of the husbands towards their wives.

Marco Polo also shows an almost prudish dislike for those who use offensive language and speaks of gambling as another form of cheating. At all times he is serious and without a grain of humour. Nothing seems to disturb his equilibrium; the greatest oddity or the most ridiculous custom is described in a plain matter-of-fact business manner.

It should also be noted that the traveller must have possessed a fair amount of mechanical aptitude. Marco Polo and his father and uncle made an artillery engine for the Khan and there are many other cases where the construction of things is carefully noted. But throughout the narrative the merchant in Marco Polo is predominant; his love of nature takes second place and his enthusiasm for sport ranks third.

Kublai Khan was, however, not the fine, upstanding Emperor that Marco Polo would have us believe. It is true that he gave generously to charity but from Chinese accounts he was hated by many of his subjects and only held the throne by sheer force. He was a crafty schemer and did not hesitate to resort to treachery. All means were fair if they furthered his designs.

One of the generals of the House of Sung, when captured by Kublai Khan and thrown into prison, wrote: "My

dungeon is lighted by the will-o'-the-wisp alone; no breath
of spring cheers the murky solitude in which I dwell. Exposed to mist and dew, I had many times thought to die; and
yet, through the seasons of two revolving years, disease
hovered around me in vain. The dank, unhealthy soil to me
became Paradise itself. For there was that within me which
misfortune could not steal away; and so I remained firm,
gazing at the white clouds floating over my head, and bearing in my heart a sorrow boundless as the sky."

This was written while Marco Polo was with Kublai
Khan. But let us return now to the battle between Genoa
and Venice and to Genoa, where Marco Polo is himself a
prisoner as the result of the defeat of the Venetian fleet.
He is weary of the confinement and is anxious once more to
travel. He, too, feels the murkiness and the prison damp.
He has no poetry in his nature and he has no passion to
record. But he has the truth to tell. He has wonders and
unknown marvels of far-away lands to chronicle. His notes
are beside him and his fellow prisoner is ready to act as
scribe. Once more he tells his story. The scribe writes;
and now the one unique record in all travel literature begins.

MANUEL KOMROFF

CONTENTS

(

LIST OF ILLUSTRATIONS

LIST OF ILLUSTRATIONS

The T R A V E L S *of*
MARCO POLO

BEGINNING OF THE JOURNEY

THE TRAVELS OF
MARCO POLO

PROLOGUE

Y e E m p e r o r s, K i n g s, Dukes, Marquises, Earls, and Knights, and all other people desirous of knowing the diversities of the races of mankind, as well as the diversities of kingdoms, provinces, and regions of all parts of the East, read through this book, and ye will find in it the greatest and most marvellous characteristics of the peoples especially of Armenia, Persia, India, and Tartary, as they are severally related in the present work by Marco Polo, a wise and learned citizen of Venice, who states distinctly what things he saw and what things he heard from others. For this book will be a truthful one.

It must be known, then, that from the creation of Adam to the present day, no man, whether Pagan, or Saracen, or Christian, or other, of whatever progeny or generation he may have been, ever saw or inquired into so many and such great things as Marco Polo above mentioned. Who, wish-

3

ing in his secret thoughts that the things he had seen and heard should be made public by the present work, for the benefit of those who could not see them with their own eyes, he himself being in the year of our Lord 1298 in prison at Genoa, caused the things which are contained in the present work to be written by master Rustigielo, a citizen of Pisa, who was with him in the same prison at Genoa; * and he divided it into three parts.

Chapter 1

HOW THE TWO BROTHERS POLO SET FORTH FROM CONSTAN-TINOPLE TO TRAVERSE THE WORLD

It should be known to the reader that, at the time when Baldwin II. was emperor of Constantinople † where a magistrate representing the doge of Venice then resided, and in the year of our Lord 1260, Nicolo Polo, the father of the said Marco, and Maffeo, the brother of Nicolo, respectable and well-informed men, embarked in a ship of their own, with a rich and varied cargo of merchandise, and reached Constantinople in safety. After mature deliberation on the subject of their proceedings, it was determined, as the measure most likely to improve their trading capital, that they should prosecute their voyage into the Euxine or Black Sea. With this view they made purchases of many fine and costly jewels, and taking their departure from Constantinople, navigated that sea to a port named Soldaia, from whence they travelled on horseback many days until they reached the court of a powerful chief of the Western Tartars, named Barka, who dwelt in the cities

---

* A truce between Genoa and Venice, signed in July 1299, undoubtedly released both Marco Polo and his scribe Rustigielo. (*See Sir Henry Yule's introduction to his great scholarly work Ser Marco Polo.*)

† Baldwin II. reigned from 1237 to 1261.

of Bolgara and Sarra, and had the reputation of being one of the most liberal and civilized princes hitherto known amongst the tribes of Tartary. He expressed much satisfaction at the arrival of these travellers, and received them with marks of distinction. In return for which courtesy, when they had laid before him the jewels they brought with them, and perceived that their beauty pleased him, they presented them for his acceptance. The liberality of this conduct on the part of the two brothers struck him with admiration; and being unwilling that they should surpass him in generosity, he not only directed double the value of the jewels to be paid to them, but made them in addition several rich presents.

The brothers having resided a year in the dominions of this prince, they became desirous of revisiting their native country, but were impeded by the sudden breaking out of a war between him and another chief, named Alaù, who ruled over the Eastern Tartars. In a fierce and very sanguinary battle that ensued between their respective armies, Alaù was victorious, in consequence of which, the roads being rendered unsafe for travellers, the brothers could not attempt to return by the way they came; and it was recommended to them, as the only practicable mode of reaching Constantinople, to proceed in an easterly direction, by an unfrequented route, so as to skirt the limits of Barka's territories. Accordingly they made their way to a town named Oukaka, situated on the confines of the kingdom of the Western Tartars. Leaving that place, and advancing still further, they crossed the Tigris [Volga], one of the four rivers of Paradise, and came to a desert, the extent of which was seventeen days' journey, wherein they found neither town, castle, nor any substantial building, but only Tartars with their herds, dwelling in tents on the plain.

Having passed this tract they arrived at length at a well-built city called Bokhara, in a province of that name, belonging to the dominions of Persia, and the noblest city of that kingdom, but governed by a prince whose name was Barak. Here, from inability to proceed further, they remained three years.

It happened while these brothers were in Bokhara, that a person of consequence and gifted with eminent talents made his appearance there. He was proceeding as ambassador from Alaù before mentioned, to the Great Khan * supreme chief of all the Tartars, named Kublai, whose residence was at the extremity of the continent, in a direction between north-east and east. Not having ever before had an opportunity, although he wished it, of seeing any natives of Italy, he was gratified in a high degree at meeting and conversing with these brothers, who had now become proficients in the Tartar language; and after associating with them for several days, and finding their manners agreeable to him, he proposed to them that they should accompany him to the presence of the Great Khan, who would be pleased by their appearance at his court, which had not hitherto been visited by any person from their country; adding assurances that they would be honourably received, and recompensed with many gifts. Convinced as they were that their endeavours to return homeward would expose them to the most imminent risks, they agreed to this proposal, and recommending themselves to the protection of the Almighty, they set out on their journey in the suite of the ambassador, attended by several Christian servants whom they had brought with them from Venice.

---

* Khan = Lord. Kublai was also called the Great Kaan. Kaan = Supreme Sovereign (Lord of Lords). Polo always referred to Kublai in writing as the Great Kaan and to lesser princes as Khan.

The course they took at first was between the north-east and north, and an entire year was consumed before they were enabled to reach the imperial residence, in consequence of the extraordinary delays occasioned by the snows and the swelling of the rivers, which obliged them to halt until the former had melted and the floods had subsided. Many things worthy of admiration were observed by them in the progress of their journey, but which are here omitted, as they will be described by Marco Polo, in the sequel of the book.

Chapter 2

HOW THE GREAT KHAN SENT THE TWO BROTHERS AS HIS ENVOYS TO THE POPE

BEING introduced to the presence of the Great Khan, Kublai, the travellers were received by him with the condescension and affability that belonged to his character, and as they were the first Latins who had made their appearance in that country, they were entertained with feasts and honoured with other marks of distinction. Entering graciously into conversation with them, he made earnest inquiries on the subject of the western parts of the world, of the Emperor of the Romans, and of other Christian kings and princes. He wished to be informed of their relative consequence, the extent of their possessions, the manner in which justice was administered in their several kingdoms and principalities, how they conducted themselves in warfare, and above all he questioned them particularly respecting the Pope, the affairs of the Church, and the religious worship and doctrine of the Christians. Being well instructed and discreet men, they gave appropriate answers upon all these points, and as they were perfectly acquainted with the Tartar language, they expressed themselves always in becoming terms; insomuch that the Great Khan, holding them in high estimation, frequently commanded their attendance.

When he had obtained all the information that the two brothers communicated with so much good sense, he expressed himself well satisfied, and having formed in his mind the design of employing them as his ambassadors to the Pope, after consulting with his ministers on the subject, he proposed to them, with many kind entreaties, that they should accompany one of his Barons, named Khogatal, on a mission to the See of Rome.

His object, he told them, was to make a request to his Holiness that he would send to him a hundred men of learning, thoroughly acquainted with the principles of the Christian religion, as well as with the seven arts,* and qualified to prove to the learned of his dominions by just and fair argument, that the faith professed by Christians is superior to, and founded upon more evident truth than, any other; that the gods of the Tartars and the idols worshipped in their houses were only evil spirits, and that they and the people of the East in general were under an error in reverencing them as divinities.† He, moreover, signified his pleasure that upon their return they should bring with them, from Jerusalem, some of the Holy Oil from the lamp which is kept burning over the Sepulchre of our Lord Jesus Christ, whom he professed to hold in veneration and to consider as the true God. Having heard these commands addressed to them by the Great Khan they humbly prostrated themselves before him, declaring their willingness and instant readiness to perform, to the utmost of their

---

* The seven arts of the time were: Rhetoric, Logic, Grammar, Arithmetic, Astronomy, Music, and Geometry.

† ". . . and that if they would prove this, he and all under him would become Christians and the Church's liegmen" (*from Yule's translation*).

ability, whatever might be the royal will. Upon which he caused letters, in the Tartarian language, to be written in his name to the Pope of Rome, and these he delivered into their hands.

He likewise gave orders that they should be furnished with a golden tablet displaying the imperial cipher, according to the usage established by his majesty; in virtue of which the person bearing it, together with his whole suite, are safely conveyed and escorted from station to station by the governors of all places within the imperial dominions, and are entitled, during the time of their residing in any city, castle, town, or village, to a supply of provisions and everything necessary for their accommodation.

Being thus honourably commissioned they took their leave of the Great Khan, and set out on their journey, but had not proceeded more than twenty days when the officer, named Khogatal, their companion, fell dangerously ill, and unable to proceed further, he halted at a certain city. In this dilemma it was determined, upon consulting all who were present, and with the approbation of the man himself, that they should leave him behind. In the prosecution of their journey they derived essential benefit from being provided with the royal tablet, which procured them attention in every place through which they passed. Their expenses were defrayed, and escorts were furnished. But notwithstanding these advantages, so great were the natural difficulties they had to encounter, from the extreme cold, the snow, the ice, and the flooding of the rivers, that their progress was unavoidably tedious, and three years elapsed before they were enabled to reach a sea-port town in the lesser Armenia, named Laiassus.

Departing from thence by sea, they arrived at Acre in the month of April, 1269, and there learned, with extreme concern, that Pope Clement the Fourth was recently dead. A legate whom he had appointed was at this time resident in Acre, and to him they gave an account of what they had in command from the Great Khan of Tartary. He advised them by all means to wait the election of another pope, and when that should take place, to proceed with the object of their embassy. Approving of this counsel, they determined upon employing the interval in a visit to their families in Venice. They accordingly embarked at Acre in a ship bound to Negropont, and from thence went on to Venice, where Nicolo Polo found that his wife, whom he had left with child at his departure was dead, after having been delivered of a son, who received the name of Marco, and was now of the age of fifteen years. This is the Marco by whom the present work is composed and who will give therein a relation of all those matters of which he has been an eye-witness.

Chapter 3

HOW THE TWO BROTHERS AGAIN DEPARTED FROM VENICE ON THEIR WAY BACK TO THE GREAT KHAN ❦ AND THEY TOOK WITH THEM MARCO THE SON OF MESSER NICOLO

IN the meantime the election of a pope was retarded by so many obstacles, that they remained two years in Venice, continually expecting its accomplishment; when at length, becoming apprehensive that the Great Khan might be displeased at their delay, or might suppose it was not their intention to revisit his country, they judged it expedient to return to Acre; and on this occasion they took with them young Marco Polo. Under the sanction of the legate they made a visit to Jerusalem, and there provided themselves with some of the Oil belonging to the Lamp of the Holy

Sepulchre, conformably to the directions of the Great Khan. As soon as they were furnished with his letters addressed to that Prince bearing testimony to the fidelity with which they had endeavoured to execute his commission, and explaining to him that the Pope of the Christian Church had not as yet been chosen, they proceeded to the before-mentioned port of Laiassus.

Scarcely however had they taken their departure, when the legate received messengers from Italy, despatched by the college of cardinals, announcing his own elevation to the Papal Chair; and he thereupon assumed the name of Gregory the Tenth. Considering that he was now in a situation that enabled him fully to satisfy the wishes of the Tartar sovereign, he hastened to transmit letters to the King of Armenia, communicating to him the event of his election, and requesting, in case the two ambassadors who were on their way to the court of the Great Khan should not have already quitted his dominions, that he would give directions for their immediate return. These letters found them still in Armenia, and with great alacrity they obeyed the summons to repair once more to Acre; for which purpose the King furnished them with an armed galley; sending at the same time an Ambassador from himself, to offer his congratulations to the Sovereign Pontiff.

Upon their arrival, his Holiness received them in a distinguished manner, and immediately despatched them with letters Papal, accompanied by two friars of the Order of Preachers, who happened to be on the spot; men of letters and of science, as well as profound theologians. One of them was named Friar Nicholas of Vicenza, and the other, Friar William of Tripoli. To them he gave licence and authority to ordain priests, to consecrate bishops, and to grant absolution as fully as he could do in his own person.

He also charged them with valuable presents, and among these, several handsome vases of crystal, to be delivered to the Great Khan in his name, and along with his benediction. Having taken leave, they again steered their course to the port of Laiassus, where they landed, and from thence proceeded into the country of Armenia.

Here they received intelligence that the soldan of Babylonia, named Bundokdari, had invaded the Armenian territory with a numerous army, and had overrun and laid waste the country to a great extent. Terrified at these accounts, and apprehensive for their lives, the two friars determined not to proceed further, and delivering over to the Venetians the letters and presents entrusted to them by the Pope, they placed.themselves under the protection of the Master of the Temple, and with him returned directly to the coast.*

Nicolo, Maffeo, and Marco, however, undismayed by perils or difficulties—to which they had long been inured—passed the borders of Armenia, and prosecuted their journey. After crossing deserts of several days' march, and passing many dangerous defiles, they advanced so far, in a direction between north-east and north, that at length they gained information of the Great Khan, who then had his residence in a large and magnificent city named Clemeinfu † [Shangtu]. Their whole journey to this place occupied no less than three years and a half; but, during the winter months, their progress had been inconsiderable. The Great Khan having notice of their approach whilst still remote, and being aware of how much they must have suffered from

---

* "But this abortive mission was only one of a number of attempts to communicate, and always they were feeble and feeble-spirited attempts, with nothing of the conquering fire of the earlier Christian missions." H. G. Wells, *The Outline of History*.

† Clemeinfu became Kublai's favorite summer residence and ir. 1256 was named Shangtu or "Upper Court."

fatigue, sent forward to meet them at the distance of forty days' journey, and gave orders to prepare in every place through which they were to pass, whatever might be requisite to their comfort. By these means, and through the blessing of God, they were conveyed in safety to the Royal Court.

Chapter 4

HOW MESSER NICOLO AND MESSER MAFFEO POLO AND MARCO PRESENTED THEMSELVES BEFORE THE GREAT KHAN

Upon their arrival they were honourably and graciously received by the Great Khan, in a full assembly of his principal officers. When they drew nigh to his person, they paid their respects by prostrating themselves on the floor. He immediately commanded them to rise, and to relate to him the circumstances of their travels, with all that had taken place in their negotiation with his Holiness the Pope. To their narrative, which they gave in the regular order of events, and delivered in perspicuous language, he listened with attentive silence. The letters and the presents from Pope Gregory were then laid before him, and, upon hearing the former read, he bestowed much commendation on the fidelity, the zeal, and the diligence of his ambassadors; and receiving with due reverence the Oil from the Holy Sepulchre, he gave directions that it should be preserved with religious care.* Upon his observing Marco Polo, and inquiring who he was, Nicolo made answer, "This is your servant, and my son"; upon which the Great Khan replied, "He is welcome, and it pleases me much," and he caused him to be enrolled amongst his attendants of honour. And on account of their return he made a great feast and

---

* Kublai later became an ardent Buddhist, and lost a good deal of his tolerance, for, while he paid honours to Confucius he caused, in 1281, all Taoist literature to be burnt. See Giles, *Chinese Biographical Dictionary.*

rejoicing; and as long as the said brothers and Marco remained in the court of the Great Khan, they were honoured even above his own courtiers. Marco was held in high estimation and respect by all belonging to the court.

He learnt in a short time and adopted the manners of the Tartars, and acquired a proficiency in four different languages, which he became qualified to read and write. Finding him thus accomplished, his master was desirous of putting his talents for business to the proof, and sent him on an important concern of State to a city named Karazan, situated at the distance of six months' journey from the Imperial Residence; on which occasion he conducted himself with so much wisdom and prudence in the management of the affairs entrusted to him, that his services became highly acceptable. On his part, perceiving that the Great Khan took a pleasure in hearing accounts of whatever was new to him respecting the customs and manners of people, and the peculiar circumstances of distant countries, he endeavoured, wherever he went, to obtain correct information on these subjects, and made notes of all he saw and heard, in order to gratify the curiosity of his master.

In short, during seventeen years that he continued in his service, he rendered himself so useful, that he was employed on confidential missions to every part of the empire and its dependencies; and sometimes also he travelled on his own private account, but always with the consent, and sanctioned by the authority, of the Great Khan. Under such circumstances it was that Marco Polo had the opportunity of acquiring a knowledge, either by his own observation, or what he collected from others, of so many things, until his time unknown, respecting the eastern parts of the World, and which he diligently and regularly committed to writing, as in the sequel will appear. And by this means he obtained so much honour, that he provoked the jealousy of the other officers of the Court.

Chapter 5

HOW MESSER NICOLO ❧ MESSER MAFFEO ❧ AND MESSER MARCO ❧ ASKED LEAVE OF THE GREAT KHAN TO GO THEIR WAY

OUR Venetians having now resided many years at the imperial court, and in that time having realized considerable wealth, in jewels of value and in gold, felt a strong desire to revisit their native country, and, however honoured and caressed by the Sovereign, this sentiment was ever predominant in their minds. It became the more decidedly their object, when they reflected on the very advanced age of the Great Khan, whose death, if it should happen previously to their departure, might deprive them of that public assistance by which alone they could expect to surmount the innumerable difficulties of so long a journey, and reach their homes in safety; which on the contrary, in his lifetime, and through his favour, they might reasonably hope to accomplish.

Nicolo Polo accordingly took an opportunity one day, when he observed him to be more than usually cheerful, of throwing himself at his feet, and soliciting on behalf of himself and his family to be indulged with his Majesty's gracious permission for their departure. But far from showing himself disposed to comply with the request, he appeared hurt at the application, and asked what motive they could have for wishing to expose themselves to all the inconveniences and hazards of a journey in which they might probably lose their lives. If gain, he said, was their object, he was ready to give them the double of whatever they possessed, and to gratify them with honours to the

extent of their desires; but that, from the regard he bore
to them, he must positively refuse their petition.

It happened, about this period, that a queen named
Bolgana, the wife of Argon, Sovereign of India, died, and
as her last request—which she likewise left in a testamentary
writing—conjured her husband that no one might succeed
to her place on his throne and in his affections, who was not
a descendant of her own family, now settled under the
dominion of the Great Khan, in the country of Cathay.
Desirous of complying with this solemn entreaty, Argon
deputed three of his Barons, discreet men, whose names
were Ulatai, Apusca, and Goza, attended by a numerous
retinue, as his ambassadors to the Great Khan, with a
request that he might receive at his hands a maiden to wife,
from among the relatives of his deceased queen. The application was taken in good part, and under the directions of
his Majesty, choice was made of a damsel aged seventeen,
extremely handsome and accomplished, whose name was
Kogatin, and of whom the ambassadors, upon her being
shown to them, highly approved. When everything was
arranged for their departure, and a numerous suite of
attendants appointed, to do honour to the future consort of
King Argon, they received from the Great Khan a gracious
dismissal, and set out on their return by the way they came.
Having travelled for eight months, their further progress
was obstructed and the roads shut up against them, by fresh
wars that had broken out amongst the Tartar Princes.
Much against their inclinations, therefore, they were constrained to adopt the measure of returning to the court of
the Great Khan, to whom they stated the interruption they
had met with.

About the time of their reappearance, Marco Polo happened to arrive from a voyage he had made, with a few

vessels under his orders, to some parts of the East Indies, and reported to the Great Khan the intelligence he brought respecting the countries he had visited, with the circumstances of his own navigation, which, he said, was performed in those seas with the utmost safety. This latter observation having reached the ears of the three Barons, who were extremely anxious to return to their own country, from whence they had now been absent three years, they presently sought a conference with our Venetians, whom they found equally desirous of revisiting their home; and it was settled between them that the former, accompanied by their young Queen, should obtain an audience of the Great Khan, and represent to him with what convenience and security they might effect their return by sea, to the dominions of their master; whilst the voyage would be attended with less expense than the journey by land, and be performed in a shorter time; according to the experience of Marco Polo, who had lately sailed in those parts.

Should his Majesty incline to give his consent to their adopting that mode of conveyance, they were then to urge him to suffer the three Europeans, as being persons well skilled in the practice of navigation, to accompany them until they should reach the territory of King Argon. The Great Khan upon receiving this application showed by his countenance that it was exceedingly displeasing to him, averse as he was to parting with the Venetians. Feeling nevertheless that he could not with propriety do otherwise than consent, he yielded to their entreaty. Had it not been that he found himself constrained by the importance and urgency of this peculiar case, they would never otherwise have obtained permission to withdraw themselves from his service.

He sent for them, however, and addressed them with

much kindness and condescension, assuring them of his regard, and requiring from them a promise that when they should have resided some time in Europe and with their own family, they would return to him once more. With this object in view he caused them to be furnished with two golden tablets which contained his orders for their having free and safe conduct through every part of his dominions, with the needful supplies for themselves and their attendants. He likewise gave them authority to act in the capacity of his ambassadors to the Pope, the Kings of France and Spain, and the other Christian Princes.*

Chapter 6

HOW THE TWO BROTHERS AND MESSER MARCO TOOK LEAVE OF THE GREAT KHAN ◆ AND RETURNED TO THEIR OWN COUNTRY

At the same time preparations were made for the equipment of fourteen ships, each having four masts, and capable of being navigated with nine sails, the construction and rigging of which would admit of ample description; but it is for the present omitted. Among these vessels there were at least four or five that had crews of two hundred and fifty or two hundred and sixty men. On them were embarked the Barons, having the Queen under their protection, together with Nicolo, Maffeo, and Marco Polo, when they had first taken their leave of the Great Khan, who presented them with many rubies and other handsome jewels of great value. He also gave directions that the ships should be furnished with stores and provisions for two years.

After a navigation of about three months, they arrived at an island which lay in a southerly direction, named Java,

---

* The French manuscript translated by Yule also mentions the King of England.

PRINCESS KOGATIN

where they saw various objects worthy of attention, of which notice shall be taken in the sequel of the work. Taking their departure from thence, they employed eighteen months in the Indian seas before they were enabled to reach the place of their destination in the territory of King Argon; and during this part of their voyage also they had an opportunity of observing many things, which shall, in like manner, be related hereafter. But here it may be proper to mention, that between the day of their sailing and that of their arrival, they lost by deaths, of the crews of the vessels and others who were embarked, about 600 persons; and of the three Barons, only one, whose name was Goza, survived the voyage; whilst of all the ladies and female attendants one only died.

Upon landing they were informed that King Argon had died some time before, and that the government of the country was then administered, on behalf of his son, who was still a youth, by a person of the name of Kiacatu. From him they desired to receive instructions as to the manner in which they were to dispose of the Princess, whom, by the orders of the late King, they had conducted thither. His answer was, that they ought to present the lady to Kasan, the son of Argon, who was then at a place on the borders of Persia, which has its denomination from the Arbor Secco, where an army of sixty thousand men was assembled for the purpose of guarding certain passes against the irruption of the enemy.

This they proceeded to carry into execution, and having effected it, they returned to the residence of Kiacatu, because the road they were afterwards to take lay in that direction. Here, however, they reposed themselves for the space of nine months. When they took their leave he furnished them with four golden tablets, each of them a cubit in length, five inches wide, and weighing three or four marks of gold. Their inscription began with invoking the blessing of the Almighty upon the Great Khan, that his name might be held in reverence for many years, and denouncing the punishment of death and confiscation of goods to all who should refuse obedience to the mandate.

It then proceeded to direct that the three ambassadors, as his representatives, should be treated throughout his dominions with due honour, that their expenses should be defrayed, and that they should be provided with the necessary escorts. All this was fully complied with and from many places they were protected by bodies of two hundred horse; nor could this have been dispensed with as the government of Kiacatu was unpopular, and the people were disposed to commit insults and proceed to outrages, which they would not have dared to attempt under the rule of their proper sovereign. In the course of their journey our travellers received intelligence of the Great Khan Kublai having departed this life; which entirely put an end to all prospect of their revisiting those regions. Pursuing, therefore, their intended route, they at length reached the city of Trebizond, from whence they proceeded to Constantinople, then to Negropont, and finally to Venice, at which place, in the enjoyment of health and abundant riches, they safely arrived in the year 1295.

On this occasion they offered up their thanks to God, who had now been pleased to relieve them from such great fatigues, after having preserved them from innumerable perils. The foregoing narrative may be considered as a preliminary chapter, the object of which is to make the reader acquainted with the opportunities Marco Polo had of acquiring a knowledge of things he describes, during a residence of so many years in the eastern parts of the world.

BOOK I

ACCOUNT OF REGIONS VISITED OR HEARD OF ON THE JOURNEY FROM THE LESSER ARMENIA TO THE COURT OF THE GREAT KHAN AT SHANGTU

Chapter 1

ARMENIA MINOR ❧ THE PORT OF LAIASSUS ❧ AND OF THE BOUNDARIES OF THE PROVINCE

IN COMMENCING THE DE-scription of the countries which Marco Polo visited in Asia, and of things worthy of notice which he observed therein, it is proper to mention that we are to distinguish two Armenias, the Lesser and the Greater. The king of the Lesser Armenia dwells in a city called Sebastoz, and rules his dominions with strict re-gard to justice. The towns, fortified places, and castles are numerous. There is abundance of all necessaries of life, as well as of those things which contribute to its comfort. Game, both of beasts and birds, is in plenty. It must be said, however, that the air of the country is not remarkably healthy. In former times its gentry were esteemed expert and brave soldiers; but at the present day they are great drinkers, mean-spirited, and worthless.

On the sea-coast there is a city named Laiassus, a place of considerable traffic. Its port is frequented by merchants from Venice, Genoa, and many other places, who trade in spices and drugs of different sorts, manufactures of silk and of wool, and other rich commodities. Those persons who design to travel into the interior of the Levant, usually proceed in the first instance to this port of Laiassus. The boundaries of the Lesser Armenia are, on the south, the Land of Promise, now occupied by the Saracens; on the north, Karamania, inhabited by Turkomans; towards the north-east lie the cities of Kaisariah, Sevasta, and many others subject to the Tartars; and on the western side it is bounded by the sea, which extends to the shores of Christendom.

Chapter 2

OF THE PROVINCE CALLED TURKOMANIA ❦ WHERE ARE THE CITIES OF KOGNI ❦ KAISARIAH ❦ AND SEVASTA ❦ AND OF ITS COMMERCE

THE inhabitants of Turkomania may be distinguished into three classes. The Turkomans, who reverence Mahomet and follow his law, are a rude people, and dull of intellect. They dwell amongst the mountains and in places difficult of access, where their object is to find good pasture for their cattle, as they live entirely upon animal food. There is here an excellent breed of horses which has the appellation of Turki, and fine mules which are sold at high prices. The other classes are Greeks and Armenians, who reside in the cities and fortified places, and gain their living by commerce and manufacture. The best and handsomest carpets in the world are wrought here, and also silks of crimson and other rich colours. Amongst its cities are those of Kogni, Kaisariah, and Sevasta, in which last Saint Blaise obtained the glorious crown of martyrdom. They are all subject to the Great Khan, Emperor of the Oriental Tartars, who appoints governors to them. We shall now speak of the Greater Armenia.

ARMENIA

Chapter 3

OF ARMENIA MAJOR ❧ IN WHICH ARE THE CITIES OF
ARZINGAN ❧ ARGIRON ❧ AND DARZIZ ❧ OF THE
MOUNTAIN WHERE THE ARK OF NOAH
RESTED ❧ AND OF A REMARKABLE
FOUNTAIN OF OIL

ARMENIA Major is an extensive province, at the entrance of which is a city named Arzingan, where there is a manufacture of very fine cotton cloth called bombazines, as well as of many other curious fabrics, which it would be tedious to enumerate. It possesses the handsomest and most excellent baths of warm water, issuing from the earth, that are anywhere to be found. Its inhabitants are for the most part native Armenians, but under the dominion of the Tartars. In this province there are many cities, but Arzingan is the principal, and the seat of an archbishop; and the next in consequence are Argiron and Darziz. It is very extensive, and, in the Summer season, the station of a part of the army of the Eastern Tartars, on account of the good pasture it affords for their cattle; but on the approach of Winter they are obliged to change their quarters, the fall of snow being so very deep that the horses could not find subsistence, and for the sake of warmth and fodder they proceed to the southward. Within a castle named Paipurth, which you meet with in going from Trebizond to Tauris, there is a rich mine of silver.

In the central part of Armenia stands an exceedingly large and high mountain, upon which, it is said, the Ark of Noah rested, and for this reason it is termed the Mountain of the Ark.* The circuit of its base cannot be compassed in less than two days. The ascent is impracticable

---

* Ararat has an altitude of 16,953 feet and was first ascended in 1829.

on account of the snow towards the summit, which never melts, but goes on increasing by each successive fall. In the lower region, however, near the plain, the melting of the snow fertilizes the ground, and occasions such an abundant vegetation, that all the cattle which collect there in summer from the neighbouring country, meet with a never-failing supply.

Bordering upon Armenia, to the southwest, are the districts of Mosul and Maredin, which shall be described hereafter, and many others too numerous to particularize. To the north lies Georgiania, near the confines of which there is a fountain of oil which discharges so great a quantity as to furnish loading for many camels. The use made of it is not for the purpose of food, but as an unguent for the cure of cutaneous distempers in men and cattle, as well as other complaints; and it is also good for burning. In the neighbouring country no other is used in their lamps, and people come from distant parts to procure it.

Chapter 4

OF THE PROVINCE OF GEORGIANIA AND ITS BOUNDARIES OF THE PASS WHERE ALEXANDER THE GREAT CONSTRUCTED THE GATE OF IRON ❧ AND OF THE MIRACULOUS CIRCUMSTANCES ATTENDING A FOUNTAIN AT TEFLIS

In Georgiania the king is usually styled David Melik, which in our language signifies David the King.* One part of the country is subject to the Tartars, and the other part, in consequence of the strength of its fortresses, has remained in the possession of its native princes. It is situated between two seas, of which that on the northern [western] side is called the Greater Sea [Euxine], and

---

* Georgia was annexed by Russia in 1801 but until then had nine reigning princes all named David.

the other on the eastern side, is called the Sea of Abakù
[Caspian]. This latter is in circuit two thousand eight
hundred miles, and partakes of the nature of a lake, not
communicating with any other sea. It has several islands,
with handsome towns and castles, some of which are inhabited by people who fled before the Grand Tartar, when he
laid waste the kingdom or province of Persia, and took
shelter in these islands or in the fastnesses of the mountains,
where they hoped to find security. Some of the islands are
uncultivated. This sea produces abundance of fish, particularly sturgeon and salmon at the mouths of the rivers, as
well as others of a large sort. The general wood of the
country is the box-tree. I was told that in ancient times
the kings of the country were born with the mark of an
eagle on the right shoulder. The people are well made,
bold sailors, expert archers, and fair combatants in battle.
They are Christians, observing the ritual of the Greek
Church, and wear their hair short, in the manner of the
Western clergy.

This is the province into which, when Alexander the
Great attempted to advance northwards, he was unable
to penetrate, by reason of the narrowness and difficulty
of a certain pass, which on one side is washed by the sea,
and is confined on the other by high mountains and woods,
for the length of four miles; so that a very few men were
capable of defending it against the whole world. Disappointed in this attempt, Alexander caused a great wall to
be constructed at the entrance of the pass, and fortified it
with towers, in order to restrain those who dwelt beyond
it from giving him molestation. From its uncommon
strength the pass obtained the name of the Gate of Iron,
and Alexander is commonly said to have enclosed the Tartars between two mountains. It is not correct, however, to

call the people Tartars, which in those days they were not, but of a race named Cumani, with a mixture of other nations. In this province there are many towns and castles; the necessaries of life are in abundance; the country produces a great quantity of silk, and a manufacture is carried on of silk interwoven with gold. Here are found vultures of a large size, of a species named *avigi*. The inhabitants in general gain their livelihood by trade and manual labour. The mountainous nature of the country, with its narrow and strong defiles, has prevented the Tartars from effecting the entire conquest of it.

At a convent of monks dedicated to Saint Lunardo, the following miraculous circumstances are said to take place. In a salt-water lake, four days' journey in circuit, upon the border of which the Church is situated, the fish never make their appearance until the first day of Lent, and from that time to Easter-eve they are found in vast abundance; but on Easter-day they are no longer to be seen, nor during the remainder of the year. It is called the Lake of Geluchalat. Into the before-mentioned Sea of Abakù, which is encompassed with mountains, the great rivers Herdil, Geihon, Kur, and Araz, with many others, disembogue. The Genoese merchants have recently begun to navigate it, and they bring from thence the kind of silk called *ghellie*. In this province there is a handsome city named Teflis, around which are suburbs and many fortified posts. It is inhabited by Armenian and Georgian Christians, as well as by some Mahometans and Jews; but these last are in no great numbers. Manufactures of silks and of many other articles are carried on there. Its inhabitants are subjects of the great king of the Tartars. Although we speak only of a few of the principal cities in each province, it is to be understood that there are many others, which it is unnecessary to particularize, unless they happened to contain something remarkable; but should the occasion present itself, these will be hereafter described. Having spoken of the countries bordering on Armenia to the north, we shall now mention those which lie to the south and to the east.

Chapter 5

OF THE PROVINCE OF MOSUL AND ITS DIFFERENT INHABIT-ANTS ◕ OF THE PEOPLE NAMED KURDS ◕ AND OF THE TRADE OF THIS COUNTRY

MOSUL is a large province inhabited by various descriptions of people, one class of whom pay reverence to Mahomet, and are called Arabians. The others profess the Christian faith, but not according to the Canons of the Church, which they depart from in many instances, and are denominated Nestorians, Jacobites, and Armenians. They have a patriarch whom they call Jacolit, and by him Archbishops, Bishops, and Abbots are consecrated and sent to all parts of India, to Baudas, or to Cathay, just as the Pope of Rome does in the Latin countries.

All those cloths of gold and of silk which we call muslins are of the manufacture of Mosul, and all the great merchants termed Mossulini, who convey spices and drugs, in large quantities, from one country to another, are from this province.

In the mountainous parts there is a race of people named Kurds, some of whom are Christians and others Mahometans. They are all an unprincipled people, whose occupation it is to rob the merchants. In the vicinity of this province there are places named Mus and Maredin, where cotton is produced in great abundance, of which they prepare the cloths called boccasini, and many other fabrics. The inhabitants are manufacturers and traders, and are all subjects of the king of the Tartars. We shall now speak of the city of Baudas.

Chapter 6

OF THE GREAT CITY OF BAUDAS ❧ ANCIENTLY CALLED BABYLON ❧ AND OF THE VARIOUS SCIENCES STUDIED IN THAT CITY AND HOW IT WAS TAKEN

BAUDAS (Baghdad) is a large city, heretofore the residence of the Calif or Pontiff of all the Saracens, as the Pope is of all Christians. A great river flows through the midst of it, by means of which the merchants transport their goods to and from the Sea of India; the distance being computed at seventeen days' navigation, in consequence of the windings of its course. Those who undertake the voyage, after leaving the river, touch at a place named Kisi, from whence they proceed to sea: but previously to their reaching this anchorage they pass a city named Balsara, in the vicinity of which are groves of palm-trees producing the best dates in the world.

In Baudas there is a manufacture of silks wrought with gold, and also of damasks, as well as of velvets ornamented with the figures of birds and beasts. Almost all the pearls brought to Europe from India have undergone the process of boring, at this place. The Mahometan law is here regularly studied, as are also magic, physics, astronomy, geomancy, and physiognomy. It is the noblest and most extensive city to be found in this part of the world.

The Calif, who is understood to have amassed greater treasures than had ever been possessed by any other sovereign, perished miserably under the following circumstances. At the period when the Tartar princes began to extend their dominion, there were amongst them four brothers, of whom the eldest, named Mangu, reigned in the royal seat of the

B A G D A D

family. Having subdued the country of Cathay, and other districts in that quarter, they were not satisfied, but coveting further territory, they conceived the idea of Universal Empire, and proposed that they should divide the world amongst them. With this object in view, it was agreed that one of them should proceed to the east, that another should make conquests in the south, and that the other two should direct their operations against the remaining quarters.

The Southern portion fell to the lot of Alaù, who assembled a vast army, and having subdued the provinces through which his route lay, proceeded in the year 1255 to the attack of this city of Baudas. Being aware, however, of its great strength and the prodigious number of its inhabitants, he trusted rather to stratagem than to force for its reduction, and in order to deceive the enemy with regard to the number of his troops, which consisted of a hundred thousand horse, besides foot soldiers, he posted one division of his army on the one side, another division on the other side of the approach to the city, in such a manner as to be concealed by a wood. Then placing himself at the head of a third, advanced boldly to within a short distance of the gate. The Calif made light of a force apparently so inconsiderable, and confident in the efficacy of the usual Mahometan ejaculation, thought of nothing less than its entire destruction, and for that purpose marched out of the city with his guards. But as soon as Alaù perceived his approach, he feigned retreat before him, until by this means he had drawn him beyond the wood where the other divisions were posted. By the closing of these from both sides, the army of the Calif was surrounded and broken, and he was made prisoner, and the city surrendered to the conqueror. Upon entering it, Alaù discovered, to his great astonishment, a tower filled with gold. He called the Calif before him, and after reproaching him with his greediness, that prevented him from employing his treasures in the formation of an army for the defence of his capital against the powerful invasion with which it had long been threatened, gave orders for his being shut up in this same tower, without sustenance; and there, in the midst of his wealth, he soon finished a miserable existence.

Chapter 7

HOW THE CALIF OF THE BUDAS TOOK COUNSEL TO SLAY ALL THE CHRISTIANS IN HIS LAND

I JUDGE that our Lord Jesus Christ herein thought proper to avenge the wrongs of his faithful Christians, so abhorred by this Calif. From the time of his accession in 1225, his daily thoughts were employed on the means of converting to his religion those who resided within his dominions, or, upon their refusal, in forming pretences for putting them to death. Consulting with his learned men for this purpose, they discovered a passage in the Gospel where it is said: "If ye have faith as a grain of mustard seed, ye shall say unto this mountain,—Remove hence to yonder place, and it shall remove," and being rejoiced at the discovery, persuaded as he was that the thing was utterly impossible, he gave orders for assembling all the Nestorian and Jacobite Christians who dwelt in Baghdad, and who were very numerous.

To these the question was propounded, whether they believed all that is asserted in the text of their Gospel to be true, or not. They made answer that it was true. "Then," said the Calif, "if it be true, let us see which of you will give the proof of his faith; for certainly if there is not to be found one amongst you who possesses even so small a portion of faith in his Lord, as to be equal to a grain of mustard, I shall be justified in regarding you, henceforth, as a wicked, reprobate, and faithless people. I allow you therefore ten days, before the expiration of which you must either, through the power of Him whom you worship, remove the mountain now before you, or embrace the law of our prophet. In either of which cases you will be safe; but otherwise you must all expect to suffer the most cruel deaths."

Chapter 8

HOW THE CHRISTIANS WERE IN GREAT DISMAY BECAUSE OF WHAT THE CALIF HAD SAID

THE Christians, acquainted as they were with his merciless disposition, as well as his eagerness to despoil them of their property, upon hearing these words, trembled for their lives; but nevertheless, having confidence in their Redeemer, that He would deliver them from their peril, they held an assembly and deliberated on the course they ought to take. None other presented itself than that of imploring the Divine Being to grant them the aid of his mercy.

To obtain this, every individual, great and small, prostrated himself night and day upon the earth, shedding tears profusely, and attending to no other occupation than that of prayer to the Lord. When they had thus persevered during eight days, a divine revelation came at length, in a dream, to a Bishop of exemplary life, directing him to proceed in search of a certain cobbler—whose name is not known —having only one eye, whom he should summon to the mountain, as a person capable of effecting its removal, through Divine Grace.

Chapter 9

HOW THE ONE-EYED COBBLER PRAYED FOR THE CHRISTIANS

HAVING found the cobbler and made him acquainted with the revelation, he replied that he did not feel himself worthy of the undertaking, his merits not being such as to entitle him to the reward of such abundant Grace. Importuned, however, by the poor terrified Christians, he at length assented. It should be understood that he was a man of strict morals and pious conversation, having his mind pure and faithful to his God, regularly attending the celebration of the Mass and other divine offices, fervent in works of charity, and rigid in the observance of fasts.

It once happened to him, that a handsome young woman who came to his shop in order to be fitted with a pair of slippers, in presenting her foot, accidentally exposed a part of her leg, the beauty of which excited in him momentary sinful thoughts. Calling to mind the words of the Gospel, where it is said, "If thine eye offend thee, pluck it out and cast it from thee; for it is better to enter the kingdom of God with one eye, than having two eyes, to be cast into Hell Fire," he immediately, with an instrument of his trade, scooped out his right eye. By this act you can judge the excellence of his Faith.

The appointed day being arrived, Divine service was performed at an early hour, and a solemn procession was made to the plain where the mountain stood, the Holy Cross being borne in front. The Calif likewise, in the conviction of its proving a vain ceremony on the part of the Christians, chose to be present, accompanied by a number of his guards, for the purposing of destroying them in the event of failure.

Chapter 10

HOW THE PRAYER OF THE ONE-EYED COBBLER CAUSED THE MOUNTAIN TO MOVE

HERE the pious artisan, kneeling before the Cross, and lifting up his hands to heaven, humbly besought his Creator that he would compassionately look down upon earth, and for the glory and excellence of his name, as well as for the support and confirmation of the Christian faith, would lend assistance to his people in the accomplishment of the task imposed upon them, and thus manifest his power to the revilers of his law. Having concluded his prayer, he cried with a loud voice: "In the name of the Father, Son, and Holy Ghost, I command thee, O mountain, to remove thyself!"

Upon these words being uttered, the mountain moved, and the earth at the same time trembled in a wonderful and alarming manner. The Calif and all those by whom he was surrounded, were struck with terror, and remained in a state of stupefaction. Many of the latter became Christians, and even the Calif secretly embraced Christianity, always wearing a cross concealed under his garment, which after his death was found upon him; and on this account it was that they did not entomb him in the shrine of his predecessors. In commemoration of this singular grace bestowed upon them by God, all the Christians, Nestorians, and Jacobites, from that time forth have continued to celebrate in a solemn manner the return of the day on which the miracle took place; keeping a fast also on the vigil.

Chapter 11

OF THE NOBLE CITY OF TAURIS ❧ IN IRAK ❧ AND OF ITS COMMERCIAL AND OTHER INHABITANTS

Tauris is a large and very noble city belonging to the province of Irak, which contains many other cities and fortified places, but this is the most eminent and most populous. The inhabitants support themselves principally by commerce and manufactures, which latter consist of various kinds of silk, some of them interwoven with gold, and of high price. It is so advantageously situated for trade, that merchants from India, from Baudas, Mosul, Cremessor, as well as from different parts of Europe, resort thither to purchase and to sell a number of articles. Precious stones and pearls in abundance may be procured at this place.

The merchants concerned in foreign commerce acquire considerable wealth, but the inhabitants in general are poor. They consist of a mixture of various nations and sects, Nestorians, Armenians, Jacobites, Georgians, Persians, and the followers of Mahomet, who form the bulk of the population, and are those properly called Taurisians. Each description of people have their peculiar language. The city is surrounded with delightful gardens, producing the finest fruits.

The Mahometan inhabitants are treacherous and unprincipled. According to their doctrine, whatever is stolen or plundered from others of a different faith, is properly taken, and the theft is no crime; whilst those who suffer death or injury by the hands of Christians, are considered as martyrs. If, therefore, they were not prohibited and restrained by the powers who now govern them, they would commit many outrages. These principles are common to all the Saracens. When they are at the point of death, their priest attends upon them, and asks whether they believe that Mahomet was the true apostle of God. If their answer be that they do believe, their salvation is assured to them; and in consequence of this facility of absolution, they have succeeded in converting to their faith a great proportion of the Tartars.

From Tauris to Persia is twelve days' journey.

Chapter 12

OF THE MONASTERY OF SAINT BARSAMO ❧ IN THE NEIGHBOURHOOD OF TAURIS

NOT far from Tauris is a monastery that takes its name from the holy Saint Barsamo, and is eminent for devotion. There is here an Abbot and many Monks, who resemble the Order of Carmelites in the fashion of their dress. That they may not lead a life of idleness, they employ themselves continually in the weaving of woollen girdles, which they place upon the altar of their Saint during the celebration of divine service, and when they make the circuit of the provinces, soliciting alms—in the same manner as do the brethren of the Order of the Holy Ghost—they present these girdles to their friends and to persons of distinction; being esteemed good for rheumatic pains, on which account they are devoutly sought for by all ranks.

Chapter 13

OF THE PROVINCE OF PERSIA

PERSIA was anciently a large and noble province, but it is now a great part destroyed by the Tartars.

In Persia there is a city which is called Saba, from whence were the three Magi who came to adore Christ in Bethlehem; and the three are buried in that city in a fair sepulchre, and they are all three entire with their beards and hair. One was called Balthasar, the second Jaspar, and the third Melchior. Marco inquired often in that city concerning the three Magi, and nobody could tell him anything about them, except that the three Magi were buried there in ancient times. After three days' journey you come to a castle which is called Cala Ataperistan, which means the Castle of the Fire-Worshippers; and it is true that the inhabitants of that castle worship fire, and the following is given as the reason.

The men of that castle say, that anciently three kings of that country went to worship a certain Prophet who was newly born, and carried with them three offerings, namely, Gold, Frankincense, and Myrrh; in order to ascertain whether that Prophet were God, or an earthly King or a Physician. For, said they, if he take the Gold, then he is an earthly King; if he take the Incense he is God; if he take the Myrrh, he is a Physician.

When these Magi were presented to Christ, the youngest of the three adored him first, and it appeared to him that Christ was of his stature and age. The middle one came next, and then the eldest, and to each he seemed to be of their own stature and age. Having compared their observations together, they agreed to go all to worship at once, and then he appeared to them all of his true age.

Chapter 14

WHAT BEFELL WHEN THE THREE MAGI RETURNED TO THEIR OWN COUNTRY

WHEN they went away, the infant gave them a closed box, which they carried with them for several days, and then becoming curious to see what he had given them, they opened the box and found in it a stone. This was intended for a sign that they should remain as firm as a stone in the faith they had received from him. When, however, they saw the stone, they marvelled, and thinking themselves deluded, they threw the stone into a certain pit, and instantly fire burst forth in the pit.

When they saw this, they repented bitterly of what they had done, and taking some of the fire with them they carried it home. And having placed it in one of their churches, they keep it continually burning, and adore that fire as a god, and make all their sacrifices with it. And if ever it happen to be extinguished, they go for more to the original fire in the pit where they threw the stone, which is never extinguished, and they take of none other fire. And therefore the people of that country worship fire.

Marco was told all this by the people of the country; and it is true that one of those kings was of Saba [Savah], and the second was of Dyava [Avah], and the third was of the castle where they still worshipped fire.* Now we will treat of the people of Persia and of their customs.

Chapter 15

OF THE NAMES OF THE EIGHT KINGDOMS THAT CONSTITUTE THE PROVINCE OF PERSIA ❦ AND OF THE BREED OF HORSES AND ASSES FOUND THEREIN

In Persia, which is a large province, there are eight kingdoms, the names of which are as follows:—The first which you meet with upon entering the country is Kasibin; the second, lying towards the south is Kurdistan; the third is Lor; towards the north, the fourth is Suolistan; the fifth,

---

* The ruins of this castle are said to exist in a place about twenty miles from Kashan in which city fire is still worshipped by a small sect. See monograph on *The Magi in Marco Polo* by Prof. A. V. Williams Jackson. *Journal of the Am. Oriental Soc.,* 1905.

Spaan; the sixth, Siras; the seventh, Soncara; the eighth, Timochain, which is at the extremity of Persia. All these kingdoms lie to the south, excepting Timochain, and this is to the north, near the place called Arbor Secco.

The country is distinguished for its excellent breed of horses, many of which are carried for sale to India, and bring high prices, not less in general than two hundred livres tournois.* It produces also the largest and handsomest breed of asses in the world, which sell—on the spot—at higher prices than the horses, because they are more easily fed, are capable of carrying heavier burthens, and travel further in the day than either horses or mules, which cannot support an equal degree of fatigue. The merchants, therefore, who in travelling from one province to another are obliged to pass extensive deserts and tracts of sand, where no kind of herbage is to be met with, and where, on account of the distance between wells or other watering places, it is necessary to make long journeys in the course of the day, are desirous of providing themselves with asses in preference, as they get sooner over the ground and require a smaller allowance of food. Camels also are employed here, and these in like manner carry great weights and are maintained at little cost, but they are not so swift as the asses. The traders of these parts convey the horses to Kisi, to Ormus, and to other places on the coast of the Indian Sea, where they are purchased by those who carry them to India. In consequence, however, of the greater heat of that country, they do not last many years, being natives of a temperate climate.

In some of these districts, the people are savage and bloodthirsty, making a common practice of wounding and

---

* A trifle less than £200 sterling!

murdering each other. They would not refrain from doing injury to the merchants and travellers, were they not in terror of the Eastern Tartars, who cause them to be severely punished. A regulation is also established, that in all roads where danger is apprehended, the inhabitants shall be obliged, upon the requisition of the merchants, to provide active and trusty conductors for their guidance and security, between one district and another; who are to be paid at the rate of two or three groats for each loaded beast, according to the distance. They are all followers of the Mahometan religion.

In the cities, however, there are merchants and numerous artisans, who manufacture a variety of stuffs of silk and gold. Cotton grows abundantly in this country, as do wheat, barley, millet, and several other sorts of grain; together with grapes and every species of fruit.

Should any one assert that the Saracens do not drink wine, being forbidden by their law, it may be answered that they quiet their consciences on this point by persuading themselves that if they take the precaution of boiling it over the fire, by which it is partly consumed and becomes sweet, they may drink it without infringing the commandment; for having changed its taste, they change its name, and no longer call it wine, although it is such in fact.

Chapter 16

OF THE CITY OF YASDI AND ITS MANUFACTURES ❦ AND OF THE ANIMALS FOUND IN THE COUNTRY BETWEEN THAT PLACE AND KIERMAN

YASDI is a considerable city on the confines of Persia, where there is much traffic. A species of cloth of silk and gold manufactured there is known by the appellation of Yasdi, and is carried from thence by the merchants to all

parts of the world. Its inhabitants are of the Mahometan
religion.

Those who travel from that city, employ eight days in
passing over a plain, in the course of which they meet with
only three places that afford accommodation. The road lies
through extensive groves of the date-bearing palm, in which
there is abundance of game, as well beasts as partridges and
quails; and those travellers who are fond of the amusements
of the chase, may here enjoy excellent sport. Wild asses
are likewise to be met with, very numerous and handsome.
At the end of eight days you arrive at a kingdom named
Kierman.

Chapter 17

*OF THE KINGDOM OF KIERMAN ✎ BY THE ANCIENTS NAMED
KARMANIA ✎ OF ITS FOSSIL AND MINERAL PRODUC-
TIONS ✎ ITS MANUFACTURES ✎ ITS FALCONS ✎
AND OF A GREAT DESCENT OBSERVED UPON
PASSING OUT OF THAT COUNTRY*

KIERMAN [Kirman] is a kingdom on the eastern confines of Persia, which was formerly governed by its own
monarchs, in hereditary succession; but since the Tartars
have brought it under their dominion, they appoint governors to it at their pleasure. In the mountains of this country
are found the precious stones that we call turquoises. There
are also veins of steel and of antimony in large quantities.
They manufacture here in great perfection all the articles
necessary for warlike equipment, such as saddles, bridles,
spurs, swords, bows, quivers, and every kind of arms in use
amongst these people. The women and young persons
work with the needle, in embroideries of silk and gold, in a
variety of colours and patterns, representing birds and beasts,
with other ornamental devices. These are designed for the

curtains, coverlets, and cushions of the sleeping places of the rich; and the work is executed with so much taste and skill as to be an object of admiration.

In the mountainous parts are bred the best falcons that anywhere take wing. They are smaller than the Peregrine falcon; reddish about the breast, belly, and under the tail; and their flight is so swift that no bird can escape them.

Upon leaving Kierman, you travel for seven days along a plain, by a pleasant road, and rendered still more delightful by the abundance of partridges and other game. You also meet frequently with towns and castles, as well as scattered habitations; until at length you arrive at a mountain whence there is a considerable descent, which occupies two days. Fruit trees are found there in great numbers; the district having formerly been peopled, though at present without inhabitants, except herdsmen alone, who are seen attending the pasturing of their cattle. In that part of the country which you pass before you reach the descent, the cold is so severe that a man can with difficulty defend himself against it by wearing many garments and pelisses.

Chapter 18

OF THE CITY OF KAMANDU ❧ AND THE DISTRICT OF REOBARLE ❧ OF CERTAIN BIRDS FOUND THERE ❧ OF A PECULIAR KIND OF OXEN ❧ AND OF THE KARAUNAS ❧ A TRIBE OF ROBBERS

AT the end of the descent of this mountain, you arrive at a plain that extends, in a southern direction, to the distance of five days' journey; at the commencement of which there is a town named Kamandu, formerly a very large place and of much consequence, but not so at this day, having been repeatedly laid waste by the Tartars. The neighbouring district is called Reobarle. The temperature of the plain is very warm. It produces wheat, rice, and other grains.

On that part of it which lies nearest to the hills, dates, pomegranates, quinces, and a variety of other fruits, grow, amongst which is one called Adam's apple, not known in our cool climate. Turtle-doves are found here in vast numbers, attracted by the plenty of small fruits which supply them with food, but they are not eaten by the Mahometans, who hold them in abomination. There are likewise many pheasants and francolins, which latter do not resemble those of other countries, their colour being a mixture of white and black with red legs and beak.

Among the cattle also there are some of an uncommon kind, particularly a species of large white oxen, with short, smooth coats—the effect of a hot climate—horns short, thick, and obtuse, and having between the shoulders a gibbous rising or hump, about the height of two palms. They are beautiful animals, and being very strong are made to carry great weights. Whilst loading, they are accustomed to kneel down like the camel, and then to rise up with the burthen. We find here also sheep that are equal to the ass in size, with long thick tails, weighing thirty pounds and upwards, which are fat and excellent to eat.*

In this province there are many towns encompassed with lofty and thick walls of earth, for the purpose of defending the inhabitants against the incursions of the Karaunas, who scour the country and plunder every thing within their reach. In order that the reader may understand what people these are, it is necessary to mention that there was a prince named Nugodar, the nephew of Zagataï, who was

---

* Yule quotes many explorers who say this is no exaggeration. See also evidence in the additional volume of *Notes and Addenda to Ser Marco Polo* by the distinguished French scholar Henri Cordier.

brother of the Great Khan Oktaï, and reigned in Turkestan. This Nugodar, whilst living at Zagataï's court, became ambitious of being himself a sovereign, and having heard that in India there was a province called Malabar, governed at that time by a king named As-idin Sultan, which had not yet been brought under the dominion of the Tartars, he secretly collected a body of about ten thousand men, the most profligate and desperate he could find, and separating himself from his uncle without giving him any intimation of his designs, proceeded through Balashan to the kingdom of Kesmur, where he lost many of his people and cattle, from the difficulty and badness of the roads, and at length entered the province of Malabar. Coming thus upon As-idin by surprise, he took from him by force a city called Dely, as well as many others in its vicinity, and there began to reign. The Tartars whom he carried thither, and who were men of light complexion, mixing with the dark Indian women, produced the race to whom the appellation of Karaunas is given, signifying, in the language of the country, a mixed breed; and these are the people who have since been in the practice of committing depredations, not only in the country of Reobarle, but in every other to which they have access.

In India they acquired the knowledge of magical and diabolical arts, by means of which they are enabled to produce darkness, obscuring the light of day to such a degree, that persons are invisible to each other, unless within a very small distance. Whenever they go on their predatory excursions, they put this art in practice, and their approach is consequently not perceived.* Most frequently this dis-

---

* Travellers in upper India have observed this phenomenon and call it Dry Fog which often is combined with the Dust Storm. See Yule's quotations from Major Sykes and other explorers.

trict is the scene of their operations; because when the merchants from various parts assemble at Ormus, and wait for those who are on their way from India, they send, in the winter season, their horses and mules, which are out of condition from the length of their journey, to the plain of Reobarle, where they find abundance of pasture and become fat. The Karaunas, aware that this will take place, seize the opportunity of effecting a general pillage, and make slaves of the people who attend the cattle, if they have not the means of ransom.

Marco Polo himself was once enveloped in a factitious obscurity of this kind, but escaped from it to the castle of Konsalmi. Many of his companions, however, were taken and sold, and others were put to death. These people have a king named Corobar.

Chapter 19

OF THE CITY OF ORMUS ❧ OF ITS COMMERCIAL IMPORTANCE ❧ AND OF THE HOT WIND THAT BLOWS THERE

At the extremity of the plain before mentioned as extending in a southern direction to the distance of five days' journey, there is a descent for about twenty miles, by a road that is extremely dangerous, from the multitude of robbers by whom travellers are continually assaulted and plundered. This downward path conducts you to another plain, very beautiful in its appearance, two days' journey in extent, which is called the plain of Ormus. Here you cross a number of fine streams, and see a country covered with date-palms, amongst which are found the francoline partridge, birds of the parrot kind, and a variety of others unknown to our climate. At length you reach the border of the ocean, where, upon an island, at no great distance from the shore, stands a city named Ormus, whose port is frequented by traders from all parts of India, who bring spices and drugs, precious stones, pearls, gold tissues, elephants' teeth, and various other articles of merchandise. These they dispose of to a different set of traders, by whom they are dispersed throughout the world. This city, indeed, is eminently commercial, has towns and castles dependent upon it, and is esteemed the principal place in the kingdom of Kierman. Its ruler is named Rukmedin Achomak, who governs with absolute authority, but at the same time acknowledges the king of Kierman as his liege lord. When any foreign merchant happens to die within his jurisdiction, he confiscates the property, and deposits the amount in his treasury.

During the summer season, the inhabitants do not remain in the city, on account of the excessive heat, which renders the air unwholesome, but retire to their gardens along the shore or on the banks of the river, where with a kind of ozier-work they construct huts over the water. These they enclose with stakes, driven in the water on the one side, and on the other upon the shore, making a covering of leaves to shelter them from the sun. Here they reside during the period in which there blows, every day, from about the hour of nine until noon, a land-wind so intensely hot as to impede respiration, and to occasion death by suffocating the person exposed to it. None can escape from its effects who are overtaken by it on the sandy plain. As soon as the approach of this wind is perceived by the inhabitants, they immerge themselves to the chin in water, and continue in that situation until it ceases to blow.

In proof of the extraordinary degree of this heat, Marco Polo says that he happened to be in these parts when the following circumstance occurred. The ruler of Ormus having neglected to pay his tribute to the king of Kierman, the latter took the resolution of enforcing it at the season when the principal inhabitants reside out of the city, upon the main land, and for this purpose despatched a body of troops, consisting of sixteen hundred horse and five thousand foot, through the country of Reobarle, in order to seize them by surprise. In consequence, however, of their being misled by the guides, they failed to arrive at the place intended before the approach of night, and halted to take repose in a grove not far distant from Ormus; but upon recommencing their march in the morning, they were assailed by this hot wind, and were all suffocated; not one escaping to carry the fatal intelligence to his master. When the people of Ormus became acquainted with the event, and proceeded to bury the carcases, in order that their stench might not infect the air, they found them so baked by the intenseness of the heat, that the limbs, upon being handled, separated from the trunks,* and it became necessary to dig the graves close to the spot where the bodies lay.

The vessels built at Ormus are of the worst kind, and dangerous for navigation, exposing the merchants and others who make use of them to great hazards. Their defects proceed from the circumstance of nails not being employed in the construction; the wood being of too hard a quality, and liable to split or to crack like earthenware. When an attempt is made to drive a nail, it rebounds, and is frequently broken. The planks are bored, as carefully as possible, with an iron auger, near the extremities; and wooden pins or trenails being driven into them, they are in this manner fastened. After this they are bound, or rather sewed together, with a kind of rope-yarn stripped from the husk of the Indian nuts, which are of a large size,

---

* Many travellers, including Burton, have described similar conditions in this country due to this strange heat wind.

and covered with a fibrous stuff like horse-hair. This being steeped in water until the softer parts putrefy, the threads or strings remain clean, and of these they make twine for sewing the planks, which lasts long under water. Pitch is not used for preserving the bottoms of vessels, but they are smeared with an oil made from the fat of fish, and then caulked with oakum. The vessel has no more than one mast, one helm, and one deck. When she has taken in her lading it is covered over with hides, and upon these hides they place the horses which they carry to India. They have no iron anchors, but in their stead employ another kind of ground-tackle; the consequence of which is, that in bad weather,—and these seas are very tempestuous,—they are frequently driven on shore and lost.

The inhabitants of the place are of a dark colour, and are Mahometans. They sow their wheat, rice, and other grain in the month of November, and reap their harvest in March. The fruits also they gather in that month, with the exception of the dates, which are collected in May. Of these, with other ingredients, they make a good kind of wine. When it is drunk, however, by persons not accustomed to the beverage, it occasions an immediate flux; but upon their recovering from its first effects, it proves beneficial to them, and contributes to render them fat.

The food of the natives is different from ours; for were they to eat wheaten bread and flesh meat their health would be injured. They live chiefly upon dates and salted fish, such as the thunnus, cepole, and others which from experience they know to be wholesome. Excepting in marshy places, the soil of this country is not covered with grass, in consequence of the extreme heat, which burns up everything.

Upon the death of men of rank, their wives loudly be-

wail them, once in the course of each day, during four
successive weeks; and there are also people to be found here
who make such lamentations a profession, and are paid for
uttering them over the corpses of persons to whom they are
not related.*

Having spoken of Ormus, I shall for the present defer
treating of India, intending to make it the subject of a
separate Book, and now return to Kierman in a northerly
direction. Leaving Ormus, therefore, and taking a different road to that place, you enter upon a beautiful plain,
producing in abundance every article of food; and birds
are numerous, especially partridges. But the bread, which
is made from wheat grown in the country, cannot be eaten
by those who have not learned to accommodate their palates
to it, having a bitter taste derived from the quality of the
waters, which are all bitter and salsuginous. On every side
you perceive warm, healing streams, applicable to the cure
of cutaneous and other bodily complaints. Dates and other
fruits are in great plenty.

Chapter 20

OF THE GREAT DESERT COUNTRY BETWEEN KIERMAN AND
KOBIAM ❤ AND OF THE BITTER QUALITY OF THE WATER

UPON leaving Kierman and travelling three days, you
reach the borders of a desert extending to the distance of
seven days' journey, at the end of which you arrive at
Kobiam. The first three days but little water is to be met
with, and that little is impregnated with salt, green as grass,
and so nauseous that none can use it as drink. Should even
a drop of it be swallowed, frequent calls of nature will be
occasioned; and the effect is the same from eating a grain

---

* Professional mourners are still employed by many Eastern races including Jews in all
parts of the world.

of the salt made from this water. In consequence of this, persons who travel over the desert are obliged to carry a provision of water along with them. The cattle, however, are compelled by thirst to drink such as they find, and a flux immediately ensues. In the course of these three days not one habitation is to be seen. The whole is arid and desolate. Cattle are not found there, because there is no subsistence for them.

On the fourth day you come to a river of fresh water, but which has its channel for the most part under ground. In some parts however there are abrupt openings, caused by the force of the current, through which the stream becomes visible for a short space, and water is to be had in abundance. Here the wearied traveller stops to refresh himself and his cattle after the fatigues of the preceding journey. The circumstances of the latter three days resemble those of the former, and conduct him at length to the town of Kobiam.

Chapter 21

OF THE TOWN OF KOBIAM ❧ ITS MANUFACTURES

KOBIAM is a large town, the inhabitants of which observe the law of Mahomet. They have plenty of iron and other metals. Here they make mirrors of highly polished steel, of a large size and very handsome. Much antimony or zinc is found in the country, and they procure tutty which makes an excellent collyrium [eye-salve], together with spodium, by the following process. They take the crude ore from a vein that is known to yield such as is fit for the purpose, and put it into a heated furnace. Over the furnace they place an iron grating formed of small bars set close together. The smoke or vapour ascending from the ore in

burning attaches itself to the bars, and as it cools becomes
hard. This is the tutty; whilst the gross and heavy part,
which does not ascend, but remains as a cinder in the furnace, becomes the spodium.

Chapter 22

OF THE JOURNEY FROM KOBIAM TO THE PROVINCE OF TIMO-
CHAIN ON THE NORTHERN CONFINES OF PERSIA ◀ AND
OF A PARTICULAR SPECIES OF TREE

LEAVING Kobiam you proceed over a desert of eight days'
journey exposed to great drought; neither fruits nor any
kind of trees are met with, and what water is found has a
bitter taste. Travellers are therefore obliged to carry with
them so much as may be necessary for their sustenance.
Their cattle are constrained by thirst to drink such as the
desert affords, which their owners endeavour to render
palatable to them by mixing it with flour.

At the end of eight days you reach the province of Timochain, situated towards the north, on the borders of Persia,
in which are many towns and strong places.* There is here
an extensive plain remarkable for the production of a species
of tree called the tree of the sun, and by Christians *Arbre
Sec,* the dry or fruitless tree. Its nature and qualities are
these:—It is lofty, with a large stem, having its leaves green
on the upper surface, but white or bluish on the under.
It produces husks or capsules like those in which the chest-
nut is enclosed, but these contain no fruit. The wood is
solid and strong, and of a yellow colour resembling the
box. There is no other species of tree near it for the space
of a hundred miles, excepting in one quarter, where trees

* Timochain [*Tun-o-kain*]. Henri Cordier, Major Sykes, and Sven Hedin support Yule's
theory that Marco Polo traversed a portion of this perilous Salt Desert. In *Overland to
India,* Sven Hedin devotes a chapter to the probable route Marco Polo took through this
region.

are found within the distance of about ten miles. It is reported by the inhabitants of this district that a battle was
fought there between Alexander, king of Macedonia, and
Darius.

The towns are well supplied with every necessary and
convenience of life, the climate being temperate and not
subject to extremes either of heat or cold. The people are
of the Mahometan religion. They are in general a handsome race, especially the women, who, in my opinion, are
the most beautiful in the world.

Chapter 23

OF THE OLD MAN OF THE MOUNTAIN ❧ OF HIS PALACE AND GARDENS

HAVING spoken of this country, mention shall now be
made of the old man of the mountain. The district in
which his residence lay obtained the name of Mulehet,
signifying in the language of the Saracens, the place of
heretics, and his people that of Mulehetites, or holders of
heretical tenets; as we apply the term of Patharini to certain heretics amongst Christians. The following account
of this chief, Marco Polo testifies to having heard from
sundry persons.

He was named Aloadin, and his religion was that of Mahomet. In a beautiful valley enclosed between two lofty
mountains, he had formed a luxurious garden, stored with
every delicious fruit and every fragrant shrub that could
be procured. Palaces of various sizes and forms were
erected in different parts of the grounds, ornamented with
works in gold, with paintings, and with furniture of rich
silks. By means of small conduits contrived in these buildings, streams of wine, milk, honey, and some of pure water,
were seen to flow in every direction.

The inhabitants of these palaces were elegant and beautiful damsels, accomplished in the arts of singing, playing upon all sorts of musical instruments, dancing, and especially those of dalliance and amorous allurement. Clothed in rich dresses they were seen continually sporting and amusing themselves in the garden and pavilions, their female guardians being confined within doors and never suffered to appear. The object which the chief had in view in forming a garden of this fascinating kind, was this: that Mahomet having promised to those who should obey his will the enjoyments of Paradise, where every species of sensual gratification should be found, in the society of beautiful nymphs, he was desirous of its being understood by his followers that he also was a prophet and the compeer of Mahomet, and had the power of admitting to Paradise such as he should choose to favour.

In order that none without his licence might find their way into this delicious valley, he caused a strong and inexpugnable castle to be erected at the opening of it, through which the entry was by a secret passage. At his court, likewise, this chief entertained a number of youths, from the age of twelve to twenty years, selected from the inhabitants of the surrounding mountains, who showed a disposition for martial exercises, and appeared to possess the quality of daring courage. To them he was in the daily practice of discoursing on the subject of the paradise announced by the prophet, and of his own power of granting admission. And at certain times he caused opium to be administered to ten or a dozen of the youths; and when half dead with sleep he had them conveyed to the several apartments of the palaces in the garden.

THE OLD MAN OF THE MOUNTAIN

Chapter 24

HOW THE OLD MAN USED TO TRAIN HIS ASSASSINS

UPON awakening from the state of stupor, their senses were struck with all the delightful objects that have been described, and each perceived himself surrounded by lovely damsels, singing, playing, and attracting his regards by the most fascinating caresses, serving him also with delicate foods and exquisite wines; until intoxicated with excess of enjoyment amidst actual rivulets of milk and wine, he believed himself assuredly in Paradise, and felt an unwillingness to relinquish its delights.

When four or five days had thus been passed, they were thrown once more into a drugged state, and carried out of the garden. Upon their being introduced to his presence, and questioned by him as to where they had been, their answer was, "In Paradise, through the favour of your highness": and then before the whole court, who listened to them with eager curiosity and astonishment, they gave a circumstantial account of the scenes to which they had been witnesses.

The chief thereupon addressing them, said: "We have the assurances of our prophet that he who defends his lord shall inherit Paradise, and if you show yourselves devoted to the obedience of my orders, that happy lot awaits you." Animated to enthusiasm by words of this nature, all deemed themselves happy to receive the commands of their master, and were forward to die in his service.

The consequence of this system was, that when any of the neighbouring princes, or others, gave offence to this chief, they were put to death by these his disciplined assassins; none of whom felt terror at the risk of losing their own lives, which they held in little estimation, provided they could execute their master's will. On this account his tyranny became the subject of dread in all the surrounding countries.

He had also constituted two deputies or representatives of himself, of whom one had his residence in the vicinity of Damascus, and the other in Kurdistan; and these pursued the plan he had established for training their young dependents. Thus there was no person, however powerful, who, having become exposed to the enmity of the Old Man of the Mountain, could escape assassination.

Chapter 25
HOW THE OLD MAN CAME BY HIS END

His territory being situated within the dominions of Alaù, the brother of the Great Khan Mangu, that prince had information of his atrocious practices, as above related, as well as of his employing people to rob travellers in their passage through his country, and in the year 1252 sent one of his armies to besiege this chief in his castle. It proved, however, so capable of defence, that for three years no impression could be made upon it; until at length he was forced to surrender from the want of provisions, and being made prisoner was put to death. His castle was dismantled, and his garden of Paradise destroyed. And from that time there has been no Old Man of the Mountain.*

* The story is far from fiction. The fortress of Alamut in Persia was obtained by stratagem by Hassan, in 1090, who escaped from his many enemies in Egypt. He was the supreme ruler or *Sheik-al-Jabal,* or translated: Old Man of the Mountains, and the first of the sect of Assassins. The word assassin [*Hashishin*] comes from the drug *Hashish,* which was used to intoxicate the young men. The last Old Man of the Mountains was slain in 1255 and the fortress invaded in the year following when, "1,200 Assassins were massacred and their power in Persia was completely broken." Small bodies of this tribe "lingered about the mountains of Syria, and are believed still to exist there." See *Encyclopædia Britannica.*

Chapter 26

OF A FERTILE PLAIN OF SIX DAYS' JOURNEY ❦ SUCCEEDED BY A DESERT OF EIGHT ❦ TO BE PASSED IN THE WAY TO THE CITY OF SAPURGAN

LEAVING this castle, the road leads over a spacious plain, and then through a country diversified with hill and dale, where there is herbage and pasture, as well as fruits in great abundance, by which the army of Alaù was enabled to remain so long upon the ground. This country extends to the distance of full six days' journey. It contains many cities and fortified places, and the inhabitants are of the Mahometan religion. A desert then commences, extending forty or fifty miles, where there is no water; and it is necessary that the traveller should make provision of this article at his outset. As the cattle find no drink until this desert is passed, the greatest expedition is necessary, that they may reach a watering place.

At the end of the sixth day's journey, he arrives at a town named Sapurgan, which is plentifully supplied with every kind of provision, and is particularly celebrated for producing the best melons in the world. These are pre-served in the following manner. They are cut spirally, in thin slices, as the pumpkin with us, and after they have been dried in the sun, are sent in large quantities, for sale, to the neighbouring countries; where they are eagerly sought for, being sweet as honey. Game is also in plenty there, both of beasts and birds.

Leaving this place, we shall now speak of another named Balach; a large and magnificent city.

Chapter 27

OF THE CITY OF BALACH

BALACH was formerly still more considerable, but has sustained much injury from the Tartars, who in their frequent attacks have partly demolished its buildings. It contained many palaces constructed of marble, and spacious squares, still visible, although in a ruinous state. It was in this city, according to the report of the inhabitants, that Alexander took to wife the daughter of King Darius. The Mahometan religion prevails here also.

The dominion of the Lord of the Eastern Tartars extends to this place; and to it the limits of the Persian empire extend, in a north-eastern direction.

Upon leaving Balach and holding the same course for twelve days, you traverse a country that is destitute of every sign of habitation, the people having all fled to strong places in the mountains, in order to secure themselves against the predatory attacks of lawless marauders, by whom these districts are overrun. Here are extensive waters, and game of various kinds. Lions are also found in these parts, very large and numerous. Provisions, however, are scarce in the hilly tract passed during these twelve days, and the traveller must carry with him food sufficient both for himself and his cattle.

Chapter 28

OF THE CASTLE NAMED THAIKAN ❧ AND OF THE SALT-HILLS ❧ ALSO OF THE PROVINCE OF SCASSEM

AFTER those twelve days' journey you reach a castle named Thaikan, where a great market for corn is held, it being situated in a fine and fruitful country. The hills that lie to the south of it are large and lofty. They all consist of white salt, extremely hard, with which the people, to the distance of thirty days' journey round, come to provide themselves, for it is esteemed the purest that is found in the world; but it is at the same time so hard that it cannot be detached otherwise than with iron picks. The quantity is so great that all the countries of the earth might be supplied from thence. Other hills produce almonds and pistachio nuts, in which articles the natives carry on a considerable trade.

Leaving Thaikan and travelling three days, still in a north-east direction, you pass through a well-inhabited country, very beautiful, and abounding in fruit, corn, and vines. The people are Mahometans, and are blood-thirsty and treacherous. They are given also to debauchery, and to excess in drink, to which the excellence of their sweet wine encourages them. On their heads they wear nothing but a cord, about ten spans in length, with which they bind them round. They are keen sportsmen, and take many wild animals, wearing no other clothing than the skins of the beasts they kill, of which materials their shoes also are made. They are all taught to prepare the skins.

During a journey of three days there are cities and many castles, and at the end of that distance you reach a town named Scassem, governed by a chief whose title is equivalent to that of our barons or counts; and amongst the mountains he possesses other towns and strong places. Through the midst of this town runs a river of tolerable size. Here are found porcupines, which roll themselves up when the hunters set their dogs at them, and with great fury shoot out the quills or spines with which their skins are furnished, wounding both men and dogs.

The people of this country have their peculiar language. The herdsmen who attend the cattle have their habitations amongst the hills, in caverns they form for themselves; nor is this a difficult operation, the hills consisting, not of stone, but only of clay.

Upon departing from this place you travel for three days without seeing any kind of building, or meeting with any of the necessaries required by a traveller, excepting water; but for the horses there is sufficient pasture. You are therefore obliged to carry with you every article for which there may be occasion on the road. At the end of the third day you arrive at the province of Balashan.

Chapter 29

OF THE PROVINCE OF BALASHAN ❤ OF THE PRECIOUS STONES
FOUND THERE AND WHICH BECOME THE PROPERTY
OF THE KING ❤ AND OF THE DRESS WITH WHICH
THE WOMEN ADORN THEIR PERSONS

In the province of Balashan, the people are Mahometans, and have their peculiar language. It is an extensive kingdom, being in length full twelve days' journey, and is governed by princes in hereditary succession, who are all descended from Alexander, by the daughter of Darius, king of the Persians. All these have borne the title in the Saracenic tongue of Zulkarnen, being equivalent to Alexander; and this out of regard for Alexander the Great.

In this country are found the precious stones called Balass Rubies, of fine quality and great value, so called from the name of the province. They are imbedded in the high mountains, but are searched for only in one, named Sikinan. In this the king causes mines to be worked, in the same manner as for gold or silver; and through this channel alone they are obtained; no person daring under pain of death, to make an excavation for the purpose, unless as a special favour he obtains his majesty's licence.

THE PRECIOUS STONES OF BALASHAN

Occasionally the king gives them as presents to strangers who pass through his dominions, as they are not procurable by purchase from others, and cannot be exported without his permission. His object in these restrictions is, that the rubies of his country, with which he thinks his credit connected, should preserve their estimation and maintain their high price; for if they could be dug for indiscriminately, and every one could purchase and carry them out of the kingdom, so great is their abundance, that they would soon be of little value. Some he sends as complimentary gifts to other kings and princes; some he delivers as tribute to his superior Lord; and some also he exchanges for gold and silver. These he allows to be exported.

There are mountains likewise in which are found veins of lapis lazuli, the stone which yields the azure colour ultramarine, here the finest in the world. The mines of silver, copper, and lead, are likewise very productive. It is a cold country.

The horses bred here are of a superior quality, and have great speed. Their hoofs are so hard that they do not require shoeing. The natives are in the practice of galloping them on declines where other cattle could not or would not venture to run. They asserted that not long since there were still found in this province horses of the strain of Alexander's celebrated horse Bucephalus, which were all foaled with a particular mark in the forehead. The whole of the breed was in the possession of one of the king's uncles, who, upon his refusal to yield them to his nephew, was put to death. The widow then, exasperated at the murder, caused them all to be destroyed; and thus the race was lost to the world.

In the mountains there are falcons of the species called Saker, which are excellent birds, and of strong flight; as well as plenty of Lanners. There are also goshawks of a perfect kind, and sparrow hawks. The people of the country are expert at the chase both of beasts and birds. Good wheat is grown there, and a species of barley without the husk. There is no oil of olives, but they express it from certain nuts, and from the grain called sesame, which resembles the seed of flax, excepting that it is light-coloured; and the oil this yields is better, and has more flavour than any other. It is used by the Tartars and other inhabitants of these parts.

In this kingdom there are many narrow passes, and strong situations, which diminish the apprehension of any foreign power entering it with a hostile intention. The men are good archers and excellent sportsmen; generally clothing themselves with the skins of wild animals; other materials for the purpose being scarce. The mountains afford pasture for an innumerable quantity of sheep, which ramble about in flocks of four, five, and six hundred, all wild; and although many are taken and killed, there does not appear to be any diminution.

These mountains are exceedingly lofty, insomuch that it employs a man from morning till night to ascend to the top of them. Between them there are wide plains clothed with grass and with trees, and large streams of the purest water precipitating themselves through the fissures of the rocks. In these streams are trout and many other delicate sorts of fish. On the summits of the mountains the air is so pure and so salubrious, that when those who dwell in the towns, and in the plains and valleys below, find themselves attacked with fevers or other inflammatory complaints, they immediately remove to the hills, and remaining for three or four days in that situation, recover their health. Marco Polo affirms that he had experience in his own person of its excellent effects; for having been confined by sickness, in this country, for nearly a year, he was advised to change the air by ascending the hills; when he presently got well.

A peculiar fashion of dress prevails amongst the women of the superior class, who wear below their waists, in the manner of drawers, a kind of garment, in the making of which they employ, according to their means, eighty, or sixty ells of fine cotton cloth. This they gather or plait, in order to increase the apparent size of their hips; those being accounted the most handsome who are the most bulky in that part.

Chapter 30

OF THE PROVINCE OF BASCIA LYING TO THE SOUTH ❧ OF THE GOLDEN ORNAMENTS WORN BY THE INHABITANTS IN THEIR EARS ❧ AND OF THEIR MANNERS

LEAVING Balashan and travelling in a southerly direction for ten days, you reach the province of Bascia, the people of which have a peculiar language. They worship idols; are of a dark complexion, and of evil disposition; and are skilled in the art of magic, and the invocation of demons, a study to which they continually apply themselves. They wear in their ears pendent rings of gold and silver, adorned with pearls and precious stones. The climate of the province is in some parts extremely hot. The food of the inhabitants is meat and rice.

Chapter 31

OF THE PROVINCE OF KESMUR SITUATED TOWARDS THE SOUTH-EAST ❧ OF ITS INHABITANTS WHO ARE SKILLED IN MAGIC ❧ AND OF A CLASS OF HERMITS

KESMUR [Kashmir] is a province distant from Bascia seven days' journey. Its inhabitants also have their own peculiar language. They are adepts beyond all others in the art of magic; insomuch that they can compel their idols, although by nature dumb and deaf, to speak. They can likewise obscure the day, and perform many other miracles.* They are pre-eminent amongst the idolatrous nations, and from them the idols, worshipped in other parts, proceed.†

From this country there is a communication by water with the Indian Sea.

The natives are of a dark complexion, but by no means black; and the women, although dark, are very beautiful. Their food is flesh, with rice and other grains; yet they are in general of a spare habit. The climate is moderately warm. In this province, besides the capital, there are many other towns and strong places. There are also woods, desert tracts, and difficult passes in the mountains, which give security to the inhabitants against invasion. Their king is not tributary to any power.

They have amongst them a particular class of devotees, who live in communities, observe strict abstinence in regard to eating, drinking, and the intercourse of the sexes, and refrain from every kind of sensual indulgence, in order that they may not give offence to the idols whom they worship. These persons live to a considerable age.

They have several monasteries, in which certain superiors exercise the functions of our abbots, and by the mass of the people they are held in great reverence. The natives of this country do not deprive any creature of life, nor shed blood, and if they are inclined to eat flesh-meat, it is necessary that the Mahometans who reside amongst them should slay the animal. The article of coral brought from

---

* Conjurers from this province were employed in the Court of Kublai Khan.

† Tibetan Buddhism. Kesmur [*Kashmir*] was at one time a centre from which missionaries radiated and where many of the sacred books were translated.

Europe is sold at a higher price than in any other part of the world.

If I were to proceed in the same direction, it would lead me to India; but I have judged it proper to reserve the description of that country for a third book; and shall therefore return to Balashan, intending to pursue from there the straight road to Cathay [China], and to describe, as has been done from the commencement of the work, not only the countries through which the route immediately lies, but also those in its vicinity, to the right and left.

Chapter 32

OF THE PROVINCE OF VOKHAN ❦ OF AN ASCENT FOR THREE DAYS ❦ LEADING TO THE SUMMIT OF A HIGH MOUNTAIN ❦ OF THE EFFECT ON THE GREAT ELEVATION UPON FIRES

LEAVING the province of Balashan, and travelling in a direction between north-east and east, you pass many castles and habitations on the banks of the river, belonging to the brother of the king of that place, and after three days' journey, reach a province named Vokhan; which itself extends in length and width to the distance of three days' journey. The people are Mahometans, have a distinct language, are civilized in their manners, and accounted valiant in war. Their chief holds his territory as a fief dependent upon Balashan.

They practise various modes of taking wild animals. Upon leaving this country, and proceeding for three days, still in an east-north-east course, ascending mountain after mountain, you at length arrive at a point of the road, where you might suppose the surrounding summits to be the highest lands in the world. Here, between two ranges, you perceive a large lake, from which flows a handsome river, that pursues its course along an extensive plain, covered with the richest verdure. Such indeed is its quality that the leanest cattle turned upon it would become fat in the course of ten days.

In this plain there are wild animals in great numbers, particularly sheep of a large size, having horns, three, four, and even six palms in length. Of these the shepherds form ladles and vessels for holding their victuals; and with the same materials they construct fences for enclosing their cattle, and securing them against the wolves, with which, they say, the country is filled, and which, likewise destroy many of these wild sheep or goats. Their horns and bones being found in large quantities, heaps are made of them at the sides of the road, for the purpose of guiding travellers at the season when it is covered with snow.

For twelve days the course is along this elevated plain, which is named Pamer [Pamir Plateau], and as during all that time you do not meet with any habitations, it is necessary to make provision at the outset accordingly. So great is the height of the mountains, that no birds are to be seen near their summits; and however extraordinary it may be thought, it was affirmed, that from the keenness of the air, fires when lighted do not give the same heat as in lower situations, nor produce the same effect in cooking food.

After having performed this journey of twelve days, you have still forty days to travel in the same direction, over mountains, and through valleys, in perpetual succession, passing many rivers and desert tracts, without seeing any habitations or the appearance of verdure. Every article of provision must therefore be carried along with you. This region is called Beloro. Even amidst the highest of these

OVIS POLI

mountains, there live a tribe of savage, ill-disposed, and idolatrous people, who subsist upon the animals they can destroy, and clothe themselves with the skins.

Chapter 33

OF THE CITY OF KASHCAR ❦ AND OF THE COMMERCE OF ITS INHABITANTS

At length you reach a place called Kashcar [Kashgar], which, it is said, was formerly an independent kingdom, but it is now subject to the dominion of the Great Khan.* Its inhabitants are of the Mahometan religion. The province is extensive, and contains many towns and castles, of which Kashcar is the largest and most important. The language of the people is peculiar to themselves. They subsist by commerce and manufacture, particularly works of cotton.† They have handsome gardens, orchards, and vineyards. Abundance of cotton is produced there, as well as flax and hemp. Merchants from this country travel to all parts of the world; but in truth they are a wretched, sordid race, eating badly and drinking worse.‡ Besides the Mahometans there are amongst the inhabitants several Nestorian Christians, who are permitted to live under their own laws, and to have their churches. The extent of the province is five days' journey.

Chapter 34

OF THE CITY OF YARCAN ❦ AND OF THE MIRACULOUS COLUMN IN THE CHURCH OF ST. JOHN THE BAPTIST

Yarcan [Yarkand] is a noble city, adorned with beautiful gardens, and surrounded by a plain, in which are pro-

---

* Kashgar still remains the most westerly city of China. It was under Russian rule from 1865 to 1877.

† These industries continued until 1865 when the city fell under Russian rule.

‡ Their manners have not improved. See *Ancient Khotan*, Sir Aurel Stein.

duced all the fruits that man can desire. The inhabitants, who are partly Christians and partly Mahometans, are subject to the dominion of a nephew of the Great Khan, with whom, however, he is not upon amicable terms, but on the contrary there is perpetual strife and frequent wars between them. This city lies in the direction of north-east. A miracle is said to have taken place there, under the following circumstances. Not long ago, a prince named Zagataï, who was own brother to the then reigning Great Khan, became a convert to Christianity. This greatly delighted the Christian inhabitants of the place, who under the favour and protection of the prince, proceeded to build a church, and dedicated it to St. John the Baptist.

It was so constructed that all the weight of the roof, being circular, should rest upon upon a column in the centre, and beneath this, as a base, they fixed a square stone, which, with the permission of the prince, they had taken from a temple belonging to the Mahometans, who dared not to prevent them from so doing. But upon the death of Zagataï, his son who succeeded him showing no disposition to become a Christian, the Mussulmans had influence enough to obtain from him an order that their opponents should restore to them the stone they had appropriated; and although the latter offered to pay them a compensation in money, they refused to listen to the proposal, because they hoped that its removal would occasion the church to tumble down.

In this difficulty the afflicted Christians had no other resource than with tears and humility to recommend themselves to the protection of the glorious St. John the Baptist. When the day arrived on which they were to make restitution of the stone, it came to pass that through the intercession of the Saint, the pillar raised itself from its base to the height of three palms, in order to facilitate the removal of the stone; and in that situation, without any kind of support, it remains to the present day.

Enough being said of this, we shall now proceed to the province of Karkan.

Chapter 35

OF THE PROVINCE OF KARKAN ❧ THE INHABITANTS OF WHICH ARE TROUBLED WITH SWOLLEN LEGS AND WITH GOITRES

DEPARTING from thence you enter the province of Karkan [Yarkand], which continues to the distance of five days' journey. Its inhabitants, for the most part Mahometans, with some Nestorian Christians, are subjects of the Great Khan. Provisions are here in abundance, as is also cotton.

The people are expert artisans. They are in general afflicted with swellings in the legs, and tumours in the throat, occasioned by the quality of the water they drink.* In this country there is not anything further that is worthy of observation.

Chapter 36

OF THE CITY OF KOTAN ❧ WHICH IS ABUNDANTLY SUPPLIED WITH ALL THE NECESSARIES OF LIFE

FOLLOWING a course between north-east and east, you next come to the province of Kotan [Khotan], the extent of which is eight days' journey. It is under the dominion of the Great Khan, and the people are Mahometans. It contains many cities and fortified places, but the principal city, and which gives its name to the province, is Kotan.

---

* Sven Hedin, who was in Yarkand in 1895, says that three-fourths of the population of 150,000 are afflicted with goitre. *My Life as an Explorer.*

Everything necessary for human life is here in the greatest plenty. It yields likewise cotton, flax, hemp, grain, wine, and other articles. The inhabitants cultivate farms and vineyards, and have numerous gardens. They support themselves also by trade and manufactures, but they are not good soldiers. We shall now speak of a province named Peyn.

Chapter 37

OF THE PROVINCE OF PEYN ❦ OF THE CHALCEDONY AND JASPER FOUND IN ITS RIVER ❦ AND OF A PECULIAR CUSTOM WITH REGARD TO MARRIAGES

PEYN [Pein] is a province of five days' journey in extent, in the direction of east-north-east. It is under the dominion of the Great Khan, and contains many cities and strong places, the principal one of which is likewise named Peyn. Through this flows a river, and in its bed are found many of those stones called chalcedony and jasper.* All kinds of provision are obtained here. Cotton also is produced in the country.

The inhabitants live by manufacture and trade. They have this custom, that if a married man goes to a distance from home to be absent twenty days, his wife has a right, if she is inclined, to take another husband; and the men, on the same principle, marry wherever they happen to reside. All the before-mentioned provinces, that is to say, Kashcar, Kotan, Peyn, and as far as the desert of Lop, are within the limits of Turkistan. Next follows the province of Charchan.

---

* Chalcedony and jasper = varieties of jade.

Chapter 38

OF THE PROVINCE OF CHARCHAN ❧ AND OF THE NECESSITY THE INHABITANTS ARE UNDER OF FLYING TO THE DESERT ON THE APPROACH OF THE ARMIES OF THE TARTARS

CHARCHAN is also a province of Turkistan, lying in an east-north-east direction. In former times it was flourishing and productive, but has been laid waste by the Tartars. The people are Mahometans. Its chief city is likewise named Charchan. Through this province run several large streams, in which also are found chalcedony and jasper, which are carried for sale to Cathay, and such is their abundance that they form a considerable article of commerce. The country from Peyn to this district, as well as throughout its whole extent, is an entire sand, in which the water is for the most part bitter and unpalatable, although in particular places it is sweet and good. When an army of Tartars passes through these places, if they are enemies the inhabitants are plundered of their goods, and if friends their cattle are killed and devoured. For this reason, when they are aware of the approach of any body of troops, they flee, with their families and cattle, into the sandy desert, to the distance of two days' journey, towards some spot where they can find fresh water, and are by that means enabled to subsist. From the same apprehension, when they collect their harvest, they deposit the grain in caverns amongst the sands; taking monthly from the store so much as may be wanted for their consumption; nor can any persons besides themselves know the places to which they resort for this purpose, because the tracks of their feet are presently effaced by the wind.

Upon leaving Charchan the road lies for five days over

sands, where the water is generally, but not in all places, bad. Nothing else occurs here that is worthy of remark. At the end of these five days you arrive at the city of Lop, on the borders of the great desert.

Chapter 39

OF THE TOWN OF LOP ◗ OF THE VAST DESERT IN ITS VICINITY ◗ AND OF THE STRANGE NOISES HEARD BY THOSE WHO PASS OVER THE LATTER

THE town of Lop is situated towards the north-east, near the commencement of the great desert, which is called the Desert of Lop. It belongs to the dominions of the Great Khan, and its inhabitants are of the Mahometan religion. Travellers who intend to cross the desert usually halt for a considerable time at this place, as well to repose from their fatigues as to make the necessary preparations for their further journey. For this purpose they load a number of stout asses and camels with provisions and with their merchandise. Should the former be consumed before they have completed the passage, they kill and eat the cattle of both kinds; but camels are commonly here employed in preference to asses, because they carry heavy burdens and are fed with a small quantity of provisions.

The stock of provisions should be laid in for a month, that time being required for crossing the desert in the narrowest part. To travel it in the direction of its length would prove a vain attempt, as little less than a year must be consumed, and to convey stores for such a period would be found impracticable. During these thirty days the journey is invariably over either sandy plains or barren mountains; but at the end of each day's march you stop at a place where water is procurable; not indeed in sufficient quantity for large numbers, but enough to supply a hun-

THE DESERT OF LOP

dred persons, together with their beasts of burden. At
three or four of these halting-places the water is salt and
bitter, but at the others, amounting to about twenty, it is
sweet and good. In this tract neither beasts nor birds are
met with, because there is no kind of food for them.

It is asserted as a well-known fact that this desert is the
abode of many evil spirits, which amuse travellers to their
destruction with most extraordinary illusions. If, during
the day-time, any persons remain behind on the road, either
when overtaken by sleep or detained by their natural occasions, until the caravan has passed a hill and is no longer
in sight, they unexpectedly hear themselves called to by
their names, and in a tone of voice to which they are
accustomed. Supposing the call to proceed from their
companions, they are led away by it from the direct road,
and not knowing in what direction to advance, are left to
perish. In the night-time they are persuaded they hear
the march of a large cavalcade of people on one side or
the other of the road, and concluding the noise to be that
of the footsteps of their party, they direct theirs to the
quarter from whence it seems to proceed. But upon the
breaking of day, they find they have been misled and drawn
into a situation of danger. Sometimes likewise during the
day these spirits assume the appearance of their travelling
companions, who address them by name and endeavour to
conduct them out of the proper road. It is said also that
some persons, in their journey across the desert, have seen
what appeared to them to be a body of armed men advancing towards them, and apprehensive of being attacked
and plundered have taken to flight. Losing by this means
the right path, and ignorant of the direction they should
take to regain it, they have perished miserably of hunger.
Marvellous indeed and almost passing belief are the stories

related of these spirits of the desert, which are said at times to fill the air with the sounds of all kinds of musical instruments, and also of drums and the clash of arms; obliging the travellers to close their line of march and to proceed in more compact order. They find it necessary also to take the precaution before they repose for the night, to fix an advanced signal, pointing out the course they are afterwards to hold, as well as to attach a bell to each of the beasts of burden for the purpose of their being more easily kept from straggling. Such are the excessive troubles and dangers that must unavoidably be encountered in the passage of this desert.*

Chapter 40

OF THE PROVINCE OF TANGUTH ❦ THE CITY OF SACHION ❦ OF THE CUSTOMS OBSERVED THERE ❦ AND OF THE CEREMONY OF BURNING THE BODIES OF THE DEAD

WHEN the journey of thirty days across the desert has been completed, you arrive at a city called Sachion [Sachiu], which belongs to the Great Khan. The province is named Tanguth. The people are worshippers of idols. There are Turkomans among them, with a few Nestorian Christians and Mahometans. Those who are idolaters have a language distinct from the others. This city lies towards the east-north-east. They are not a commercial, but an agricultural people, having much wheat.

There are in this country a number of monasteries and abbeys, which are filled with idols of various descriptions. To these, which they regard with the profoundest rever-

---

* This bone strewn and barren waste has since been crossed by very few travellers and it is natural that natives along its borders should believe in evil spirits. The sound of musical instruments and drums, however, is a phenomenon produced among sandhills when the sand is disturbed. See note recorded by Yule and *Notes and Addenda* by Cordier.

ence, they also offer sacrifices; and upon the birth of a son, they recommend him to the protection of some one of their idols. In honour of this deity the father rears a sheep in his house until the expiration of a year, when, upon the day of the idol's peculiar festival, they conduct their son, together with the sheep, into its presence, and there sacrifice the animal. The flesh they boil, and then they carry it and lay it before the idol, and stand there until they have finished a long prayer, the subject of which is to entreat the idol to preserve the health of their child; and they believe that during this interval it has sucked in all the savoury juices of the meat. The remaining substance they then carry home, and, assembling all their relations and friends, eat it with much devout festivity. They collect the bones, and preserve them in handsome urns. The priests of the idol have for their portion the head, the feet, the intestines, and the skin, together with some parts of the flesh.

In respect to the dead, likewise, these idolaters have particular ceremonies. Upon the decease of a person of rank, whose body it is intended to burn, the relations call together the astrologers, and make them acquainted with the year, the day, and the hour in which he was born; whereupon these proceed to examine the horoscope, and having ascertained the constellation or sign, and the planet therein presiding, declare the day on which the funeral ceremony shall take place. If it should happen that the same planet be not then in the ascendant, they order the body to be kept a week or more, and sometimes even for the space of six months, before they allow the ceremony to be performed. In the hope of a propitious aspect, and dreading the effects of a contrary influence, the relations do not presume to burn the corpse until the astrologers have fixed the proper time.

It being necessary on this account that, in many cases, the body should remain long in the house, in order to guard against the consequences of putrefaction, they prepare a coffin made of boards a palm in thickness, well fitted together and painted, in which they deposit the corpse, and along with it a quantity of sweet-scented gums, camphor, and other drugs. The joints or seams they smear with a mixture of pitch and lime, and the whole is then covered with silk. During this period the table is spread every day with bread, wine, and other provisions, which remain so long as is necessary for a convenient meal, as well as for the spirit of the deceased, which they suppose to be present on the occasion, to satisfy itself with the fumes of the victuals. Sometimes the astrologers signify to the relations that the body must not be conveyed from the house through the principal door, in consequence of their having discovered from the aspect of the heavens, or otherwise, that such a course would be unlucky, and it must therefore be taken out from a different side of the house. In some instances, indeed, they oblige them to break through the wall, and to convey the corpse through that aperture; persuading them that if they should refuse to do so, the spirit of the defunct would be incensed against the family and cause them some injury.

Accordingly, when any misfortune befalls a house, or any person belonging to it meets with an accident or loss, or with an untimely death, the astrologers do not fail to attribute the event to a funeral not having taken place during the ascendency of the planet under which the deceased relative was born, but, on the contrary, when it was

exposed to an evil influence, or to its not having been conducted through the proper door.

As the ceremony of burning the body must be performed
without the city, they erect from space to space in the
road by which the procession is to pass, small wooden buildings, with a portico which they cover with silk; and under
these, as it arrives at each, the body is set down. They
place before it meats and liquors, and this is repeated until
they reach the appointed spot, believing, as they do, that
the spirit is thereby refreshed and acquires energy to attend the funeral pile. Another ceremony also is practised
on these occasions. They provide a number of pieces of
paper, made of the bark of a certain tree, upon which are
painted the figures of men, women, horses, camels, pieces
of money, and dresses, and these they burn along with the
corpse, in the belief that in the next world the deceased
will enjoy the services and use of the domestics, cattle, and
all the articles depicted on the paper. During the whole
of these proceedings, all the musical instruments belonging
to the place are sounded with an incessant din.

Having now spoken of this city, others lying towards
the north-west, near the head of the desert, shall next be
mentioned.

Chapter 41

OF THE DISTRICT OF KAMUL ❦ AND OF SOME PECULIAR CUSTOMS RESPECTING THE ENTERTAINMENT OF STRANGERS

KAMUL is a district situated within the great province
of Tanguth, subject to the Great Khan, and contains many
towns and castles, of which the principal city is also named
Kamul. This district lies in the intermediate space between two deserts; that is to say, the great desert already

described, and another of smaller extent, being only about three days' journey across. The inhabitants are worshippers of idols, and have their peculiar language. They subsist on the fruits of the earth, which they possess in abundance, and are enabled to supply the wants of travellers. The men are addicted to pleasure, and attend to little else than playing upon instruments, singing, dancing, reading, writing, according to the practice of the country, and the pursuit, in short, of every kind of amusement.

When strangers arrive, and desire to have lodging and accommodation at their houses, it affords them the highest gratification. They give positive orders to their wives, daughters, sisters, and other female relations, to indulge their guests in every wish, whilst they themselves leave their homes, and retire into the city, and the stranger lives in the house with the females as if they were his own wives, and they send whatever necessaries may be wanted; but for which, it is to be understood, they expect payment: nor do they return to their houses so long as the strangers remain in them. This abandonment of the females of their family to accidental guests, who assume the same privileges and meet with the same indulgences as if they were their own wives, is regarded by these people as doing them honour and adding to their reputation; considering the hospitable reception of strangers, who after the perils and fatigues of a long journey, stand in need of relaxation, as an action agreeable to their deities, calculated to draw down the blessing of increase upon their families, to augment their substance, and to procure them safety from all dangers, as well as a successful issue to all their undertakings. The women are in truth very handsome, very sensual, and fully disposed to conform in this respect to the injunction of their husbands.

It happened at the time when Mangu Kaan held his court in this province, that the above scandalous custom coming to his knowledge, he issued an edict strictly commanding the people of Kamul to relinquish a practice so disgraceful to them, and forbidding individuals to furnish lodging to strangers, but to provide hostelries for travellers. In grief and sadness the inhabitants obeyed for about three years the command of their master; but finding at length that the earth ceased to yield the accustomed fruits, and that many unfortunate events occurred in their families, they resolved to despatch a deputation to the Mangu Kaan, in their names, to beseech him that he should be pleased to suffer them to resume the observance of a custom that had been solemnly handed down to them by their fathers, from their ancestors in the remotest times. And especially as since they had failed in the exercise of these offices of hospitality and gratification to strangers, the interest of their families had gone progressively to ruin. The Kaan, having listened to this application, replied: "Since you appear so anxious to persist in your own shame, let it be granted as you desire. Go, live according to your base customs and manners, and let your wives continue to receive the beggarly wages of their prostitution." With this answer the deputies returned home, to the great delight of all the people, who, to the present day, observe their ancient practice.

Chapter 42

OF THE CITY OF CHINCHITALAS

NEXT to the district of Kamul follows that of Chinchitalas, which in its northern part borders on the desert, and is in length sixteen days' journey. It is subject to the Great Khan and contains cities and several strong places. Its inhabitants consist of three religious sects. A few of them confess Christ, according to the Nestorian doctrine; others are followers of Mahomet; and a third class worship idols. There is in this district a mountain where the mines produce steel, and also zinc or antimony.

A substance is likewise found of the nature of the salamander, for when woven into cloth, and thrown into the fire, it remains incombustible. The following mode of preparing it I learned from one of my travelling companions, named Curficar, a very intelligent Turkoman, who had the direction of the mining operations of the province for three years. The fossil substance procured from the mountain consists of fibres not unlike those of wool. This, after being exposed to the sun to dry, is pounded in a brass mortar, and is then washed until all the earthly particles are separated. The fibres thus cleansed and detached from each other, they then spin into thread and weave into cloth. In order to render the texture white, they put it into the fire, and suffer it to remain there about an hour, when they draw it out uninjured by the flame, and become white as snow. And so again whenever they become dirty they are bleached by being put in the fire.

Of the salamander under the form of a serpent, supposed to exist in fire, I could never discover any traces in the eastern regions. It is said that they preserve at Rome a napkin woven from this material, sent as a gift from the Great Khan to the Pope to make a wrapper for the Holy Sudarium of Jesus Christ.

Chapter 43

OF THE DISTRICT OF SUCCUIR ◄ WHERE THE RHUBARB IS PRODUCED ◄ AND FROM WHENCE IT IS CARRIED TO ALL PARTS OF THE WORLD

Upon leaving the district last mentioned, and proceeding for ten days in the direction of east-north-east, through a country where there are few habitations, and little of any kind worthy of remark, you arrive at a district named Succuir [Sukchu], in which are many towns and castles, the principal one being likewise named Succuir. The inhabitants are in general idolaters, with some Christians. They are subject to the dominion of the Great Khan.

The General Province, which contains all these three provinces is called Tanguth.

Throughout all the mountainous parts of it the most excellent kind of rhubarb is produced, in large quantities, and the merchants who come to buy it convey it to all parts of the world. It is a fact that when they take that road, they cannot venture amongst the mountains with any beasts of burden excepting those accustomed to the country, on account of a poisonous plant growing there, which, if eaten by them, has the effect of causing the hoofs of the animal to drop off. Those of the country, however, being aware of its dangerous quality, take care to avoid it.* The people of Succuir depend for subsistence upon the fruits of the earth and the flesh of their cattle, and do not engage in trade. The district is perfectly healthy, and the complexion of the natives is brown.

---

* Sir Aurel Stein, in *Ruins of Desert Cathay*, speaks of this wild rhubarb and also tells of the difficulties with his ponies and the poisonous grass in this region.

Chapter 44

OF THE CITY OF CAMPICHU ❧ OF THE NATURE OF THEIR IDOLS ❧ OF THE ALMANAC THEY MAKE USE OF ❧ AND THE CUSTOMS OF MARRIAGE

CAMPICHU, the chief city of the province of Tanguth, is large and magnificent, and has jurisdiction over all the province. The bulk of the people worship idols, but there are some who follow the religion of Mahomet, and some Christians. The latter have three large and handsome churches in the city. The idolaters have many religious houses, or monasteries and abbeys, built after the manner of the country, and in these a multitude of idols, some of which are of wood, some of stone, and some of clay. They are all highly polished and covered with gilding. They are carved in a masterly style. Among these are some of very large size, and others are small. The former are full ten paces in length, and lie in a recumbent posture; the small figures stand behind them, and have the appearance of disciples in the act of reverential salutation. Both great and small are held in extreme veneration. Those persons amongst the idolaters who are devoted to the services of religion lead more virtuous lives, according to their ideas of morality, than the other classes. They abstain from the indulgence of carnal and sensual appetites. The unlicensed intercourse of the sexes is not in general considered by these people as a serious offence; and their maxim is, that if the advances are made by the female, the connexion does not constitute an offence, but it is held to be such when the proposal comes from the man.

They employ an almanac, in many respects like our own, according to the rules of which, during five, four, or three days in the month, they do not shed blood, nor eat flesh or fowl; as is our usage in regard to Friday, the Sabbath, and the vigils of the saints.*

The laity take to themselves as many as thirty wives, some more, some fewer, according to their ability to maintain them; for they do not receive any dowry with them, but, on the contrary, settle dowers upon their wives, in cattle, slaves, and money. The wife who is first married always maintains the superior rank in the family and if the husband observes that any one amongst them does not conduct herself well to the rest, or if she becomes otherwise disagreeable to him, he can send her away. They take to their beds those who are cousins by blood, and even espouse their mothers-in-law. Many other mortal sins are regarded by them with indifference, and they live in this respect like the beasts of the field.

In this city Marco Polo remained, along with his father and uncle, about the space of one year, which the state of their concerns rendered necessary.

Chapter 45

OF THE CITY OF EZINA ❦ OF THE KINDS OF CATTLE AND VARIOUS BIRDS FOUND THERE ❦ AND OF A DESERT EXTENDING FORTY DAYS' JOURNEY TOWARDS THE NORTH

Leaving this city of Campichu, and travelling for twelve days in a northerly direction, you come to a city named Ezina, at the commencement of the sandy desert [Gobi], and within the province of Tanguth. The inhabitants are idolaters. They have camels, and much cattle of various sorts. Here you find Lanners and many excellent Sakers.†

---

* Tibetan Buddhism.

† Since these early observations regarding birds of China many books and articles have been written on this subject. A valuable list of over 140 important works and papers on the ornithology of China may be found in the *Encyclopædia Sinica*.

The fruits of the soil and the flesh of the cattle supply the wants of the people, and they do not concern themselves with trade.

Travellers passing through this city lay in a store of provisions for forty days, because, upon their leaving it to proceed northwards, that space of time is employed in traversing a desert, where there is not any appearance of dwelling, nor are there any inhabitants excepting a few during the summer, among the mountains and in some of the valleys. In these situations, frequented by wild asses and other animals equally wild, they find water and woods of pine-trees.

Having passed this desert, you arrive at a city on the northern side of it, named Karakoran.

Chapter 46

OF THE CITY OF KARAKORAN ❦ THE FIRST IN WHICH THE TARTARS FIXED THEIR RESIDENCE ❦ AND THE ORIGIN OF THEIR KINGDOM

THE city of Karakoran is about three miles in circuit, and is the first place in which the Tartars established their residence in remote times. It is surrounded with a strong rampart of earth, there not being any good supply of stone in that part of the country. On the outside of the rampart, but near to it, stands a castle of great size, in which is a handsome palace occupied by the Governor of the place.

The circumstances under which these Tartars first began to exercise dominion shall now be related. They dwelt in the north on the borders of Chorche, but without fixed habitations, that is, without towns or fortified places; where there were extensive plains, good pasture, large rivers, and plenty of water. They had no sovereign of their own, and were tributary to a powerful prince, who, as I have been informed, was named in their language, Unc Can, by some thought to have the same signification as Prester John in ours. To him these Tartars paid tribute the tenth part of their cattle.

In process of time the tribe multiplied so exceedingly that Unc Can, that is to say, Prester John, becoming apprehensive of their strength, conceived the plan of separating them into different bodies, who should take up their abode in distinct tracts of country. With this view also, whenever the occasion presented itself, such as a rebellion in any of the provinces subject to him, he drafted three or four in the hundred of these people, to be employed on the service of quelling it; and thus their power was gradually diminished. He in like manner despatched them upon other expeditions, and sent among them some of his principal officers to see that his intentions were carried into effect.

At length the Tartars, becoming sensible of the slavery to which he attempted to reduce them, resolved to maintain a strict union amongst themselves, and seeing that nothing short of their final ruin was in contemplation, they adopted the measure of removing from the places which they then inhabited. They proceeded in a northerly direction across a wide desert, until they felt assured that the distance afforded them security, when they refused any longer to pay to Unc Can the accustomed tribute.

Chapter 47

CONCERNING CHINGHIS ❦ THE FIRST KAAN OF THE TARTARS ❦ AND HIS WARFARE WITH UNC CAN ❦ WHOM HE OVERTHREW ❦ AND OF WHOSE KINGDOM HE POSSESSED HIMSELF

SOME time after the migration of the Tartars to this place, and about the year of our Lord 1187, they proceeded

to elect for their King a man who was named Chinghis
Kaan, one of approved integrity, great wisdom, commanding
eloquence, and eminent for his valour. He began his reign
with so much justice and moderation, that he was beloved
and revered as their Lord rather than their Sovereign. The
fame of his great and good qualities spreading over that part
of the world, all the Tartars, however dispersed, placed
themselves under his command.

Finding himself thus at the head of so many brave men,
he became ambitious of emerging from the deserts and
wildernesses by which he was surrounded, and gave them
orders to equip themselves with bows and such other
weapons as they were expert at using. He then proceeded
to render himself master of cities and provinces; and such
was the effect produced by his character for justice and
other virtues, that wherever he went, he found the people
disposed to submit to him, and to esteem themselves happy
when admitted to his protection and favour. In this manner
he acquired the possession of about nine provinces. Nor is
his success surprising, when we consider that at this period
each town and district was either governed by the people
themselves, or had its petty King or Lord; and as there
existed amongst them no general confederacy, it was impossible for them to resist, separately, so formidable a power.
Upon the subjugation of these places, he appointed governors to them, who were so worthy in their conduct that the
inhabitants did not suffer, either in their persons or their
properties.

Seeing how prosperously his enterprises succeeded, he
resolved upon attempting still greater things. With this
view he sent ambassadors to Prester John, charged with a
message, which he knew would not be listened to by that
Prince, demanding his daughter in marriage. Upon receiv-

ing the application, the monarch indignantly exclaimed: "Whence arises this presumption in Chinghis Kaan, who, knowing himself to be my servant, dares to ask for the hand of my child? Depart instantly," he said, "and let him know from me, that upon the repetition of such a demand, I shall put him to an ignominious death." The ambassadors, on receiving this reply, departed straightway, and made haste to their master, and related all that Prester John had ordered them to say, keeping nothing back.

Chapter 48

HOW CHINGHIS MUSTERED HIS PEOPLE TO MARCH AGAINST PRESTER JOHN

ENRAGED at this reply, Chinghis Kaan collected a very large army, at the head of which he entered the territory of Prester John, and encamping on a great plain called Tenduk, sent a message desiring him to defend himself.

Chapter 49

HOW PRESTER JOHN MARCHED TO MEET CHINGHIS

PRESTER JOHN advanced likewise to the plain with a vast army, and took his position at the distance of about ten miles from the other. In this conjuncture Chinghis Kaan commanded his astrologers and magicians to declare to him which of the two armies, in the approaching conflict, should obtain the victory. Upon this they took a green reed, and dividing it lengthways into two parts, they wrote upon one the name of their master, and upon the other the name of Prester John. They then placed them on the ground, at some distance from each other, and gave notice to the king that during the time of their pronouncing their incantations, the two pieces of reed, through the power of their idols, would advance towards each other, and that the victory would fall to the lot of that monarch whose piece should be seen to mount upon the other.

The whole army was assembled to be spectators of this ceremony, and whilst the astrologers were employed in reading their books, they perceived the two pieces begin to move and to approach, and after some small interval of time, that inscribed with the name of Chinghis Kaan to place itself upon the top of its adversary.

Chapter 50

THE BATTLE BETWEEN CHINGHIS KAAN AND PRESTER JOHN

Upon witnessing this, the king and his band of Tartars marched with exultation to the attack of the army of Prester John, broke through its ranks and entirely routed it. Prester John himself was killed, his kingdom fell to the conqueror, and Chinghis Kaan espoused his daughter. After this battle he continued during six years to render himself master of additional kingdoms and cities; until at length, in the siege of a castle named Thaigin, he was struck by an arrow in the knee, and dying of the wound, was buried in the mountain of Altaï.

Chapter 51

OF SIX SUCCESSIVE EMPERORS OF THE TARTARS ◆ AND OF THE CEREMONIES THAT TAKE PLACE WHEN THEY ARE CARRIED FOR INTERMENT TO THE MOUNTAIN OF ALTAI

To Chinghis Kaan succeeded Cuy Kaan; the third was Batuy Kaan, the fourth Alacou Kaan, the fifth Mongou Kaan, the sixth Kublai Kaan, who became greater and more powerful than all the others who went before him: in fact,

if you were to take all those five together, they would not
be so powerful as he.   Nay, I will say yet more; for if you
put together all the Christians in the world, with their
Emperors and their Kings, the whole of these Christians,—
aye, and throw in the Saracens to boot,—would not have
such power, or be able to do so much as this Kublai, who is
the Lord of all the Tartars in the world, those of the
Levant and of the Ponent included.   For these are all his
liegmen and subjects.*

The title of Khan or Kaan, is equivalent to emperor in
our language.   It has been an invariable custom, that all the
Great Khans, and chiefs of the race of Chinghis, their first
Lord, should be carried for interment to a certain lofty
mountain named Altaï, and in whatever place they may
happen to die, although it should be at the distance of a
hundred days' journey, they are nevertheless conveyed
thither.

It is likewise the custom, during the progress of removing the bodies of these Princes, for those who form the
escort to sacrifice such persons as they chance to meet on the
road, saying to them, "Depart for the next world, and there
attend upon your deceased Lord," being impressed with the
belief that all whom they thus slay do actually become his
servants in the next life.   They do the same also with
respect to horses, killing the best of the stud, in order that
he may have the use of them.   When the corpse of Mongou
Kaan was transported to this mountain, the horsemen who
accompanied it, slew upwards of twenty thousand persons
who fell in their way.

* This important paragraph not contained in the Italian manuscript but is incorporated
from the Yule version.

Chapter 52

OF THE WANDERING LIFE OF THE TARTARS ☙ OF THEIR DOMESTIC MANNERS ☙ THEIR FOOD ☙ AND THE VIRTUE AND USEFUL QUALITIES OF THEIR WOMEN

Now that I have begun speaking of the Tartars, I will tell you more about them. The Tartars never remain fixed, but as the winter approaches remove to the plains of a warmer region, in order to find sufficient pasture for their cattle; and in summer they frequent cold situations in the mountains, where there is water and vegetation, and their cattle are free from the annoyance of horse-flies and other biting insects. During two or three months they progressively ascend higher ground, and seek fresh pasture, the grass not being adequate in any one place to feed the multitudes of which their herds and flocks consist.

Their huts or tents are formed of rods covered with felt, and being exactly round, and nicely put together, they can gather them into one bundle, and make them up as packages, which they carry along with them in their migrations, upon a sort of car with four wheels. When they have occasion to set them up again, they always make the entrance front to the south. Besides these cars they have a superior kind of vehicle upon two wheels, covered likewise with black felt, and so effectually as to protect those within it from wet, during a whole day of rain. These are drawn by oxen and camels, and serve to convey their wives and children, their utensils, and such provisions as they require. It is the women who attend to their trading concerns, who buy and sell, and provide everything necessary for their husbands and their families; the time of the men being entirely devoted to hunting, hawking, and matters that relate to the

THE TARTARS

military life. They have the best falcons in the world, and also the best dogs.

They subsist entirely upon flesh and milk, eating the produce of their sport, and a certain small animal, not unlike a rabbit, which, during the summer season are found in great abundance in the plains. But they likewise eat flesh of every description, horses, camels, and even dogs, provided they are fat. They drink mares' milk, which they prepare in such a manner that it has the qualities and flavour of white wine.

Their women are not excelled in the world for chastity and decency of conduct, nor for love and duty to their husbands. Infidelity to the marriage bed is regarded by them as a vice not merely dishonourable, but of the most infamous nature. It is also admirable to observe the loyalty of the husbands towards their wives, amongst whom, although there are perhaps ten or twenty, there prevails a degree of quiet and union that is highly laudable. No offensive language is ever heard, their attention being fully occupied with their own affairs and their several domestic employments, such as the provision of necessary food for the family, the management of the servants, and the care of the children, which are amongst them a common concern.

The men are allowed the indulgence of taking as many wives as they choose. Their expense to the husband is not great, and on the other hand the benefit he derives from their training and from the occupations in which they are constantly engaged, is considerable. On this account he makes payment to the mother. The wife who is the first espoused has the privilege of superior attention, and is held to be the most legitimate, which extends also to the children borne by her. In consequence of this unlimited number of wives, the offspring is more numerous than amongst any other people. Upon the death of the father, the son may take to himself the wives he leaves behind, with the exception of his own mother. They cannot take their sisters to wife, but upon the death of their brothers they can marry their sisters-in-law. Every marriage is solemnized with great ceremony.

Chapter 53

OF THE GOD OF THE TARTARS ◀ AND OF THEIR MODES OF WORSHIP ◀ OF THEIR DRESS

THE doctrine and faith of the Tartars are these: They believe in a deity whose nature is Sublime and Heavenly. To him they burn incense, and offer up prayers only for the enjoyment of intellectual and bodily health.

They worship another likewise, named Natigay, whose image, covered with felt or other cloth, every individual preserves in his house. To this deity they associate a wife and children, placing the former on his left side, and the latter before him. Him they consider as the divinity who presides over the Earth, protects their children, and guards their cattle and their grain. They show him great respect, and at their meals they never omit to take a fat morsel of the flesh, and with it to grease the mouth of the idol, and at the same time the mouths of its wife and children. They then throw out of the door some of the liquor in which the meat has been dressed, as an offering to the other spirits. This being done, they consider that their deity and his family have had their proper share, and proceed to eat and drink without further ceremony.

The wealthy Tartars dress in cloth of gold and silks, with skins of the sable, the ermine, and other animals, all in the richest fashion.

Chapter 54

CONCERNING THE TARTAR CUSTOMS OF WAR & OF THEIR ARMS AND OBEDIENCE TO THEIR LEADERS

THEIR arms are bows, iron maces, and in some instances, spears; but the first is the weapon at which they are the most expert, being accustomed, from children, to employ it in their sports. They wear defensive armour made from buffalo and hides of other beasts, dried by the fire, and thus rendered extremely hard and strong. They are brave in battle, almost to desperation, setting little value upon their lives, and exposing themselves without hesitation to all manner of danger. Their disposition is cruel.

They are capable of supporting every kind of privation, and when there is a necessity for it, can live for a month on the milk of their mares, and upon such wild animals as they may chance to catch. Their horses are fed upon grass alone, and do not require barley or other grain. The men are trained to remain on horseback during two days and two nights, without dismounting; sleeping in that situation whilst their horses graze. No people upon earth can surpass them in fortitude under difficulties, nor show greater patience under wants of every kind. They are most obedient to their chiefs, and are maintained at small expense. From these qualities, so essential to the formation of soldiers, it is, that they are fitted to subdue the world, as in fact they have done in regard to a considerable portion of it.

When one of the great Tartar chiefs proceeds on an expedition, he puts himself at the head of an army of an hundred thousand horse, and organizes them in the following manner. He appoints an officer to the command of every ten men, and others to command an hundred, a thousand, and ten thousand men, respectively. Thus ten of the officers commanding ten men take their orders from him who commands a hundred; of these, each ten, from him who commands a thousand; and each ten of these latter, from him who commands ten thousand.

By this arrangement each officer has only to attend to the management of ten men or ten bodies of men. Every company of a hundred men is denominated a *Tuc*, and ten of these constitute a *Toman*. When the army proceeds on service, a body of two hundred men is sent two days' march in advance, and parties are stationed upon each flank and in the rear, in order to prevent its being attacked by surprise.

When the service is distant they carry but little with them, and that, chiefly what is requisite for their encampment, and utensils for cooking. They subsist for the most part upon milk, as has been said. They are provided with small tents made of felt, under which they shelter themselves against rain. Should circumstances render it necessary, in the execution of a duty that requires despatch, they can march for ten days without lighting a fire or taking a meal. During this time they subsist upon the blood drawn from their horses, each man opening a vein, and drinking from his own cattle.

They make provision also of milk, thickened and dried to the state of a paste, which is prepared in the following manner. They boil the milk, and skimming off the rich or creamy part as it rises to the top, put it into a separate vessel as butter; for so long as that remains in the milk, it will not become hard. The latter is then exposed to the sun until it dries. Upon going on service they carry with them about ten pounds for each man, and of this, half a pound is put, every morning, into a leathern bottle, with as much water as is thought necessary. By their motion in riding the contents are violently shaken, and a thin porridge is produced, upon which they make their dinner.

When these Tartars come to engage in battle, they never mix with the enemy, but keep hovering about him, discharging their arrows first from one side and then from the other, occasionally pretending to fly, and during their flight shooting arrows backwards at their pursuers, killing men and horses, as if they were combating face to face. In this sort of warfare the adversary imagines he has gained a victory, when in fact he has lost the battle; for the Tartars, observing the mischief they have done him, wheel about, and renewing the fight, overpower his remaining troops, and make them prisoners in spite of their utmost exertions. Their horses are so well broken-in to quick changes of movement, that upon the signal given, they instantly turn in any direction; and by these rapid manœuvres many victories have been obtained.

All that has been here related is spoken of the original manners of the Tartar chiefs; but at the present day they are much degenerated. Those who dwell in Cathay, forsaking their own laws, have adopted the customs of the people who worship idols, and those who inhabit the eastern provinces have adopted the manners of the Saracens.

Chapter 55

OF THE RULES OF JUSTICE ◄ AND OF AN IMAGINARY KIND OF MARRIAGE BETWEEN THE DECEASED CHILDREN OF DIFFERENT FAMILIES

Justice is administered by them in the following manner. When a person is convicted of a robbery not meriting the punishment of death, he is condemned to receive a certain number of strokes with a cane,—seven, seventeen, twenty-seven, thirty-seven, forty-seven, or as far as one hundred and seven, according to the value of the article stolen and circumstances of the theft. Many die under this chastisement. When for stealing a horse or other article that subjects the offender to capital punishment, he is condemned to suffer death, the sentence is executed by cutting his body in two with a sword. But if the thief has the means of paying nine times the value of the property stolen, he escapes all further punishment.*

It is usual for every Chief of a tribe or other person possessing cattle, such as horses, mares, camels, oxen, or cows, to distinguish them by his mark, and then to suffer them to graze at large, in any part of the plains or mountains, without employing herdsmen to look after them. If any of them should happen to mix with the cattle of other proprietors, they are restored to the person whose mark they bear. Sheep and goats, on the contrary, have people to attend them. Their cattle of every kind are well-sized, fat, and exceedingly handsome.

When one man has had a son, and another man a daughter, although both may have been dead for some years, they have a practice of contracting a marriage between their deceased children, and of bestowing the girl upon the youth. They at the same time paint upon pieces of paper human figures to represent attendants with horses and other animals, dresses of all kinds, money, and every article of furniture; and all these, together with the marriage contract, which is regularly drawn up, they commit to the flames, in order that these things may be conveyed to their children in the other world, and that they may become husband and wife in due form. After this ceremony, the

---

* This method of escaping punishment is said by Chinese to be practised today in Europe and America on a lavish scale. In America groups of people banded together have been required to pay as high as twenty-nine million dollars for practising a kind of profitable lawlessness.

fathers and mothers consider themselves as mutually related, in the same manner as if a real connexion had taken
place between their living children.

Having thus given an account of the manners and customs
of the Tartars, although not yet of the brilliant acts and
enterprises of their Great Khan, who is Lord of all the
Tartars, we shall now return to our former subject, that is,
to the extensive plain which we were traversing when we
stopped to relate the history of this people.

Chapter 56

OF THE PLAIN OF BARGU NEAR KARAKORAN ◀ OF THE CUSTOMS OF ITS INHABITANTS ◀ OF THE OCEAN ◀ AND OF THE FALCONS PRODUCED IN THE COUNTRY

UPON leaving Karakoran and the mountains of Altaï,
the burial-place, as has been said, of the imperial Tartar
family, you proceed, in a northern direction, through a
country termed the plain of Bargu, extending to the distance
of about forty days' journey. The people who dwell there
are calleu Mescript, a rude tribe, who live upon the flesh
of animals, the largest of which are of the nature of stags;
and these they also make use of for the purposes of travelling. They feed likewise upon the birds that frequent their
numerous lakes and marshes, as well as upon fish. It is at
the moulting season, or during summer, that the birds seek
these waters, and being then, from want of feathers, incapable of flight, they are taken by the natives without difficulty.
This plain borders on the ocean at its northern extremity.
The customs and manners of the people resemble those of
the Tartars that have been described, and they are subjects
of the Great Khan. They have neither corn nor wine; and
although in summer they derive subsistence from the chase,
yet in winter the cold is so excessive that neither birds nor

beasts can remain there. Upon travelling forty days, as it is said, you reach the ocean. Near to this is a mountain, in which, as well as in the neighbouring plain, vultures and peregrine falcons have their nests. Neither men nor cattle are found there, and of birds there is only a species called bargelak, and the falcons to which they serve for food. The former are about the size of a partridge, with tails like the swallow, claws like those of the parrot kind, and are swift of flight. When the Great Khan is desirous of having a brood of peregrine falcons, he sends to procure them at this place. In an island lying off the coast, gerfalcons are found in such numbers that his Majesty may be supplied with as many of them as he pleases. It must not be supposed that the gerfalcons sent from Europe for the use of the Tartars are conveyed to the court of the Great Khan. They go only to some of the Tartar or other chiefs of the Levant, bordering on the countries of the Comanians and Armenians. This island is situated so far to the north that the North Star appears to be behind you, and to have in part a southerly bearing.

Having thus spoken of the regions in the vicinity of the Northern Ocean, we shall now describe the provinces lying nearer to the residence of the Great Khan, and shall return to that of Campichu, of which mention has already been made.

Chapter 57

OF THE KINGDOM OF ERGINUL ❧ ADJOINING TO THAT OF CAMPICHU ❧ AND OF THE PROVINCE OF SINJU ❧ AND OF THE CUSTOMS OF THAT COUNTRY ❧ AND THE BEAUTY OF THE WOMEN

UPON leaving Campichu, and proceeding five days' journey towards the east, in the course of which travellers are frequently terrified in the night-time by the voices of spirits, they reach a kingdom named Erginul, subject to the Great Khan, and included in the province of Tanguth. Within the limits of this kingdom are several principalities, the inhabitants of which are, in general, idolaters, with some few Nestorian Christians and worshippers of Mahomet.

Amongst many cities and strong places the principal one is Erginul. Proceeding from thence in a south-eastern direction, the road takes you to Cathay, and in that route you find a city called Sinju, in a district of the same name, where are many towns and castles, in like manner belonging to Tanguth, and under the dominion of the Great Khan. The population of this country consists chiefly of idolaters; but there are also some Mahometans and Christians. Here are found many wild cattle that, in point of size, may be compared to elephants.* Their colour is a mixture of white and black, and they are very beautiful to the sight. The hair upon every part of their bodies lies down smooth, excepting upon the shoulder, where it stands up to the height of about three palms. This hair, or rather wool, is white, and more soft and delicate than silk. Marco Polo carried some of it to Venice, as a singular curiosity, and such it was esteemed by all who saw it. Many of these cattle taken wild have become domesticated, and the breed produced between them and the common cow are noble animals, and better qualified to resist fatigue than any other kind. They are accustomed to carry heavier burthens and to perform twice the labour in husbandry that could be derived from the ordinary sort, being both active and powerful.

In this country it is that the finest and most valuable musk is procured. The animal which yields it is a kind of gazelle. Its coat is like that of the larger kind of deer:

* Wild Yak.

its feet and tail are those of the antelope, but it has not the horns. It is provided with four projecting teeth or tusks, three inches in length, two in the upper jaw pointing down-wards, and two in the lower jaw pointing upwards; small in proportion to their length, and white as ivory. Upon the whole it is a handsome creature. The musk is obtained in the following manner. At the time when the moon is at the full, a bag or skin of coagulated blood forms itself about the umbilical region, and those whose occupation it is to take the animal avail themselves of the moonlight for that pur-pose, when they cut off the membrane, and afterwards dry it, with its contents, in the sun. It proves the finest musk that produces that powerful perfume. Great numbers are caught, and the flesh is esteemed good to eat. Marco Polo brought with him to Venice the head and the feet of one of them dried.

The inhabitants of this country employ themselves in trade and manufactures. They have grain in abundance. The extent of the province is twenty-five days' journey. Pheasants are found in it that are twice the size of ours, but something smaller than the peacock. The tail feathers are eight or ten palms in length.* There are other pheasants also, in size and appearance like our own, as well as a great variety of other birds, some of which have beauti-ful plumage.

The inhabitants are idolaters. In person they are inclined to be fat, and their noses are small. Their hair is black, and they have scarcely any beard, or only a few scattered hairs on the chin. The women of the superior class are in like manner free from superfluous hairs; their skins are fair, and they are well formed. The men are much devoted

---

* These tail feathers, over six feet in length, are often worn in the cap of the hero of a Chinese drama.

to female society; and, according to their laws and customs, they may have as many wives as they please, provided they are able to maintain them. If a young woman, although poor, be handsome, the rich are induced to take her to wife, and in order to obtain her, make valuable presents to her parents and relations, beauty alone being the quality held in estimation. We shall now take our leave of this district, and proceed to speak of another, situated further to the eastward.

Chapter 58

OF THE PROVINCE OF EGRIGAIA ❧ AND OF THE CITY OF KALACHA ❧ OF THE MANNERS OF ITS PEOPLE ❧ AND OF THE CAMLETS MANUFACTURED THERE

DEPARTING from Erginul, and proceeding easterly for eight days, you come to a country named Egrigaia, still belonging to the great province of Tanguth, and subject to the Great Khan, in which there are many cities and castles, the principal one of which is called Calachan. The inhabitants are in general idolaters; but there are three churches of Nestorian Christians. In this city they manufacture beautiful camlets, the finest known in the world, of the hair of camels and likewise of white wool. These are of a beautiful white, for they also have white camels. They are purchased by the merchants in considerable quantities, and carried to many other countries, especially to Cathay.

Leaving this province, we shall now speak of another situated towards the east, and shall thus enter upon the territory of Prester John.

Chapter 59

OF THE PROVINCE OF TENDUK ❧ GOVERNED BY PRINCES OF THE RACE OF PRESTER JOHN

TENDUK, belonging to the territory of Prester John, is an eastern province, in which there are many cities and castles, subject to the rule of the Great Khan; all the princes of that family having remained dependent, since Chinghis, the first emperor, subdued the country. The capital is likewise named Tenduk. The greater part of the inhabitants are Christians. This king holds his country as a fief of the Great Khan; not, indeed, the entire possessions of the original Prester John, but a certain portion of them; and the Khan always bestows upon him, as well as upon the other princes of his house, his daughters, and other females of the royal family, in marriage.

In this province, the stone of which the azure colour is made is found in abundance, and of fine quality. Here likewise they manufacture stuffs of camels' hair. The people gain their subsistence by agriculture, trade, and mechanical labours. Amongst the inhabitants, however, there are both worshippers of idols and followers of the law of Mahomet as well as Christians. The rule of the province is in the hands of the Christians. There is likewise a class of people known by the appellation of Argon, because they are produced from a mixture of two races, namely, those natives of Tenduk who are idolaters, and the Mahometans. The men of this country are fairer complexioned and better looking than those in the other countries of which we have been speaking, and also better instructed, and more skilful traders.

In this province of Tenduk, was the principal seat of government of the sovereigns styled Prester John, when they ruled over the Tartars of this and the neighbouring countries, and which their successors occupy to the present hour. George, the present King, is the fourth in descent from Prester John, of whose family he is regarded as the head. There are two regions in which they exercise dominion.

These in our part of the world are named Gog and Magog,* but by the natives Ung and Mongul; in each of which there is a distinct race of people. In Ung they are Gog, and in Mongul they are Tartars.

Travelling seven days through this province, in an easterly direction, towards Cathay, you pass many towns inhabited by idolaters, as well as by Mahometans and Nestorian Christians. They gain their living by trade and manufactures, weaving, fine-gold tissues, ornamented with mother-of-pearl, and silks of different textures and colours, not unlike those of Europe; together with a variety of woollen cloths.

These people are all subjects of the Great Khan. One of the towns, named Sindichu, is celebrated for the manufacture of all kinds of arms, and every article necessary for the equipment of troops. In the mountainous part of the province there is a place called Ydifu, in which is a rich mine of silver, from whence large quantities of that metal are obtained. There are also plenty of birds and beasts.

---

* It is curious that Marco Polo makes no mention of the Great Wall of China. His route has crossed the wall several times and in this province crosses it again. Sir Henry Yule seems to feel that the Great Wall was in Marco Polo's mind when he referred to the people of this province as "Gog and Magog." Certainly his many references to the habits of the Mohammedans would lead us to suppose an acquaintanceship with the Koran, where the following passage occurs: "They said 'O Dhu'l Qarnain! verily, Yagug and Magug [Gog and Magog] are doing evil in the land. Shall we pay thee tribute, on condition that thou set between us and them a rampart?' He said, 'What my Lord hath established me in is better; so help me with strength, and I will set between you and them a barrier'."

Chapter 60

OF THE CITY OF CHANGANOR ❧ OF DIFFERENT SPECIES OF CRANES ❧ AND OF PARTRIDGES AND QUAILS BRED IN THAT PART BY THE ORDERS OF THE GREAT KHAN

LEAVING the city and province last mentioned, and travelling three days, you arrive at a city named Changanor, which signifies, the White Pool. At this place the Khan has a great Palace, which he is fond of visiting, because it is surrounded with pieces of water and streams, which are the haunt of many swans. There is also a fine plain, where are found in great numbers, cranes, pheasants, partridges, and other birds. He derives the highest degree of amusement from sporting with gerfalcons and hawks, the game being here in vast abundance.

Of the cranes they reckon five species. The first sort are entirely black as coals, and have long wings. The second sort have wings still longer than the first, but are white, and the feathers of the wings are full of eyes, round like those of the peacock, but of a gold colour and very bright; the head is red and black, and well formed; the neck is black and white, and the general appearance of the bird is extremely handsome. The third sort are of the size of ours. The fourth are small cranes, having the feathers prettily streaked with red and azure. The fifth are of a grey colour, with the head red and black, and are of a large size.

Near to this city is a valley frequented by great numbers of partridges and quails, for whose food the Great Khan causes millet and other grains suitable to such birds, to be sown along the sides of it every season, and gives strict command that no person shall dare to reap the seed; in order that the birds may not be in want of nourishment.

Many keepers, likewise, are stationed there for the preservation of the game, that it may not be taken or destroyed, as well as for the purpose of throwing the millet to the birds during the winter. So accustomed are they to this feeding, that upon the grain being scattered and the man's whistling, they immediately assemble from every quarter. The Great Khan also directs that a number of small buildings be prepared for their shelter during the night; and, in consequence of these attentions, he always finds abundant sport when he visits this country; and even in the winter, at which season, on account of the severity of the cold, he does not reside there, he has camel-loads of the birds sent to him, wherever his court may happen to be at the time. Leaving this place, we shall now direct our course three days' journey towards the north-east.

Chapter 61

OF THE GREAT KHAN'S BEAUTIFUL PALACE IN THE CITY OF SHANDU ❦ AND OF THE CEREMONIES PRACTICED IN THE HALL OF THE ROYAL PALACE

DEPARTING from the city last mentioned, and proceeding three days' journey in a north-easterly direction, you arrive at a city called Shandu [Shangtu], built by the Great Khan Kublai, now reigning. In this he caused a palace to be erected, of marble and other handsome stones, admirable as well for the elegance of its design as for the skill displayed in its execution.

The halls and chambers are all gilt, and very handsome. It presents one front towards the interior of the city, and the other towards the wall; and from each extremity of the building runs another wall to such an extent as to enclose sixteen miles in circuit of the adjoining plain, to which there is no access but through the palace. Within the bounds of this royal Park there are rich and beautiful meadows, watered by many rivulets, where a variety of animals of the deer and goat kind are pastured, to serve as food for the hawks and other birds employed in the chase, whose pens are also in the grounds. The number of these birds is upwards of two hundred, without counting the hawks; and the Great Khan goes in person, once every week, to inspect them. Frequently, when he rides about this enclosed forest, he has one or more small leopards carried on horseback, behind their keepers; and when he pleases to give direction for their being slipped, they instantly seize a stag, goat, or fallow deer, which he gives to his hawks, and in this manner he amuses himself.

In the centre of these grounds, where there is a beautiful grove of trees, he has built a Royal Pavilion, supported upon a colonnade of handsome pillars, gilt and varnished. Round each pillar a dragon, likewise gilt, entwines its tail, whilst its head sustains the projection of the roof, and its talons or claws are extended to the right and left. The roof, like the rest, is of bamboo cane, and so well varnished that no wet can injure it. The bamboos used for this purpose are three palms in circumference and ten fathoms in length, and being cut at the joints, are split into two equal parts, so as to form gutters, and with these, laid concave and convex, the pavilion is covered. But to secure the roof against the effect of wind, each of the bamboos is tied at the ends to the frame. The building is supported on every side like a tent by more than two hundred very strong silken cords, and otherwise, from the lightness of the materials, it would be liable to oversetting by the force of high winds. The whole is constructed with so much ingenuity of contrivance that all the parts may be taken apart, removed, and again set up, at his Majesty's pleasure. This spot he has selected for his recreation on account of the mild temperature and salubrity of the air, and he accordingly makes it his residence during the three months of the year, namely, June, July, and August. Every year, on the twenty-eighth day of the moon, in the last of these months, it is his established custom to depart and proceed to an appointed place, in order to perform certain sacrifices, in the following manner.

It is to be understood that the Khan keeps up a stud of about ten thousand horses and mares, which are white as snow. Of the milk of these mares no person can presume to drink who is not of the family descended from Chinghis Khan, with the exception only of one other family, named Horiad, to whom that monarch gave the honourable privilege, in reward of valorous achievements in battle, performed in his own presence.

So great, indeed, is the respect shown to these horses that, even when they are at pasture in the royal meadows or forests, no one dares to place himself before them, or otherwise to check their movements. The astrologers whom he entertains in his service, and who are deeply versed in the art of magic have pronounced it to be his duty, annually, on the twenty-eighth day of the moon in August, to scatter in the wind the milk taken from these mares, as an honour to all the spirits and idols whom they adore. On such occasion these astrologers, or magicians as they may be termed, sometimes display their skill in a wonderful manner; for if it should happen that the sky becomes cloudy and threatens rain, they ascend the roof of the Palace where the Great Khan resides at the time, and by the force of their magic they prevent the rain from falling and stay the tempest. In the surrounding country, storms of rain, wind, and thunder may be experienced but the Palace itself remains unaffected by the elements. The sorcerers who do this are persons called Tebeth and Kesmir, which are the names of two nations of Idolaters. They persuaded the vulgar that these works are effected through the help of God. They exhibit themselves in a filthy and indecent state, and are devoid of respect for themselves, or for those who see them. They suffer their faces to continue always unwashed and their hair uncombed, living altogether in a squalid style.

They are addicted, moreover, to this beastly and horrible practice, that when any culprit is condemned to death, they carry off the body, dress it on the fire and devour it. But of persons who die a natural death they do not eat the bodies.

Besides the marvels before mentioned, by which they are distinguished from each other, they are likewise termed Bacsi, which applies to their religious sect or order. So expert are they in their infernal art, they may be said to perform whatever they will; and one instance shall be given, although it may be thought to exceed the bounds of credibility. When the Great Khan sits at meals, in his hall of state—as shall be more particularly described in the following book—the table which is placed in the centre is elevated to the height of about eight cubits, and at a distance from it stands a large buffet, where all the drinking vessels are arranged. Now, by means of their supernatural art, they cause the flagons of wine, milk, or any other beverage, to fill the cups spontaneously, without being touched by the attendants, and the cups to move through the air the distance of ten paces until they reach the hand of the Great Khan! As he empties them, they return to the place from whence they came; and this is done in the presence of such persons as are invited by his Majesty to witness the performance.*

These Bacsi, when the festival days of their idols draw near, go to the Palace of the Great Khan, and thus address him:—"Sire, be it known to your Majesty, that if the honours and offering are not paid to our deities, they will in their anger afflict us with bad seasons, with blight to our grain, pestilence to our cattle, and with other plagues. On this account we beg your Majesty to grant us a certain number of sheep with black heads, together with so many pounds of incense and of lignaloes, in order that we may be enabled to perform the customary rites with due solemnity."

Their words, however, are not spoken directly to the Great Khan, but to certain great officers, by whom the communication is made to him. Upon receiving it he never fails to comply with the whole of their request. Accordingly, when the day arrives, they sacrifice the sheep, and by pouring out the liquor in which the meat has been seethed, in the presence of their idols, perform the ceremony of worship.

In this country there are great Monasteries and Abbeys, so extensive indeed that they might pass for small cities, some of them containing as many as two thousand monks, who are devoted to the service of their divinities, according to the established religious customs of the people. These are clad in a better style of dress than the other inhabitants; they shave their heads and their beards, and celebrate the festivals of their idols with the utmost possible solemnity,

---

* This feat of magic as well as many others are still practised by the Red Lamas but repudiated and despised by the orthodox Yellow Lamas who are opposed to these "grosser exhibitions of common magic and charlatanism; . . . but as the vulgar will not dispense with these marvels, every great orthodox monastery in Tibet keeps a conjuror, who is a member of the unreformed and does not belong to the brotherhood of the convent." According to Yule, who quotes many references, the "practitioners possess no literature, and hand down their mysteries only by tradition."

having bands of vocal music and burning tapers. Some of this class are allowed to take wives.

There is likewise another religious order, the members of which are named Sensin, who observe strict abstinence and lead very austere lives, having no other food than bran, which they mix in warm water. That is their food: bran, and nothing but bran; and water for their drink. This sect sometimes pay adoration to fire, and are considered by the others as heretics, not worshipping idols as they do. There is a material difference between them in regard to the rules of their orders, and these last described never marry in any instance. They shave their heads and beards like the others, and wear hempen garments of a black and blue colour; but even if the material were silk, the colour would be the same. They sleep upon coarse mats, and suffer greater hardships in their mode of living than any people in the world.

We shall now quit this subject, and proceed to speak of the wonderful magnificence of the Great Lord of Lords; the Sovereign of the Tartars, Kublai Khan.

BOOK II

ACCOUNT OF THE GREAT
KUBLAI KHAN, HIS CAPITAL,
COURT AND GOVERNMENT.
ALSO OF CITIES AND PROV-
INCES VISITED ON JOURNEYS
WESTWARD AND SOUTHWARD

Chapter 1

OF THE ADMIRABLE DEEDS OF KUBLAI KHAN ❦ THE EMPEROR NOW REIGNING ❦ AND HIS GREAT POWER

IN THIS BOOK IT IS OUR DEsign to treat all of the great and admirable achievements of the Great Khan now reigning, who is styled Kublai Kaan; the latter word implying in our language Lord of Lords, and of a surety he hath good right to such a title, for in respect to number of subjects, extent of territory, and amount of revenue, he surpasses every sovereign that has heretofore been or that now is in the world; nor has any other been served with such implicit obedience by those whom he governs. This will so evidently appear in the course of our work, as to satisfy every one of the truth of our assertion.

Chapter 2

CONCERNING THE REVOLT OF NAYAN THE UNCLE OF THE GREAT KHAN

KUBLAI KHAN, it is to be understood, is the lineal and legitimate descendant of Chinghis Khan the first emperor, and the rightful sovereign of the Tartars. He is the sixth Great Khan, and began his reign in the year 1256. He obtained the sovereignty by his consummate valour, his virtues, and his prudence, in opposition to the designs of his brothers, who were supported by many of the great officers and members of his own family. But the succession was his in law and right.

It is forty-two years since he began to reign to the present year, 1298, and he is fully eighty-five years of age.* Previously to his ascending the throne he had served as a volunteer in the army, and endeavoured to take a share in every enterprise. Not only was he brave and daring in action, but in point of judgment and military skill he was considered to be the most able and successful commander that ever led the Tartars to battle. From that period, however, he ceased to take the field in person, and entrusted the expeditions to his sons and his captains; excepting in one instance, the occasion of which was as follows.

A certain chief named Nayan, who, although only thirty years of age, was kinsman to Kublai, had succeeded to the dominion of many cities and provinces, which enabled him to bring into the field an army of three hundred thousand horse. His predecessors, however, had been vassals of the Great Khan. Actuated by youthful vanity upon finding himself at the head of so great a force, he formed the design of throwing off his allegiance, and seizing the sovereignty. With this view he privately dispatched messengers to Kaidu, another powerful chief, whose territories lay towards the greater Turkey, and who, although a nephew of the Great Khan, was in rebellion against him, and bore him determined ill-will, proceeding from the apprehension of punishment for former offences.

To Kaidu, therefore, the propositions made by Nayan were highly satisfactory, and he accordingly promised to bring to his assistance an army of a hundred thousand horse.

---

* The Polos sailed from China in 1292, and therefore Marco did not know that Kublai died in 1294 at the age of 78.

KUBLAI KHAN

Both princes immediately began to assemble their forces, but it could not be effected so secretly as not to come to the knowledge of Kublai.

Chapter 3

HOW THE GREAT KHAN MARCHED AGAINST NAYAN

THE Great Khan upon hearing of their preparations lost no time in occupying all the passes leading to the countries of Nayan and of Kaidu, in order to prevent them from having any information respecting the measures he was himself taking. He then gave orders for collecting, with the utmost speed, the whole of the troops stationed within ten days' march of the city of Kanbalu [Peking]. These amounted to three hundred and sixty thousand horse, to which was added a body of a hundred thousand foot, consisting of those who were usually about his person, and principally his falconers and domestic servants.

In the course of twenty days they were all in readiness. Had he assembled the armies kept up for the constant protection of the different provinces of Cathay, it must necessarily have required thirty or forty days. During this time the enemy would have gained information of his arrangements, and would have united and occupied such strong positions as would best suit with their designs.

His object was, by promptitude, which is ever the companion of victory, to anticipate the preparations of Nayan, and by falling upon him whilst single, destroy his power with more certainty and effect than after he should have been joined by Kaidu.

It may be proper here to observe, whilst on the subject of the armies of the Great Khan, that in every province of Cathay and of Manji, as well as in other parts of his dominions, there were many disloyal and seditious persons, who at all times were disposed to break out in rebellion against their sovereign. On this account it became necessary to keep armies in such of the provinces as contained large cities and an extensive population, which are stationed at the distance of four or five miles from those cities, and can enter them at their pleasure. These armies the Great Khan makes it a practice to change every second year, and the same with respect to the officers who command them. By means of such precautions the people are kept in quiet subjection, and no movement nor innovation of any kind can be attempted. The troops are maintained not only from the pay they receive out of the imperial revenues of the province, but also from the cattle and their milk, which belong to them individually, and which they send into the cities for sale. In this manner they are distributed over the country, in various places, to the distance of thirty, forty, and even sixty days' journey. If even the half of these corps were to be collected in one place, the statement of their number would appear marvellous and scarcely entitled to belief.

Having formed his army in the manner above described, the Great Khan proceeded towards the territory of Nayan, and by forced marches, continued day and night, he reached it at the expiration of twenty-five days. So prudently, at the same time, was the expedition managed, that neither that prince himself nor any of his dependents were aware of it, all the roads being guarded in such a manner that no persons who attempted to pass could escape being made prisoners.

Chapter 4

OF THE BATTLE THAT THE GREAT KHAN FOUGHT WITH NAYAN

UPON arriving at a certain range of hills, on the other side of which was the plain where Nayan's army lay encamped, Kublai halted his troops, and allowed them two days of rest. Confident of success, they ascended the hill with cheerful willingness the next morning, and presented themselves before the army of Nayan, which they found poorly posted, without advanced parties or scouts, whilst the chief himself was asleep in his tent, accompanied by one of his favourite wives. Upon awaking, he hastened to form his troops in the best manner that circumstances would allow, lamenting that his junction with Kaidu had not been sooner effected.

Kublai took his station in a large wooden castle, borne on the backs of four elephants, whose bodies were protected with coverings of thick leather hardened by fire, over which were housings of cloth of gold. The castle contained many cross-bow-men and archers, and on the top of it was hoisted the imperial standard, adorned with representations of the sun and moon.

His army, which consisted of thirty battalions of horse, each battalion containing ten thousand men, armed with bows, he disposed in three grand divisions. Those which formed the left and right wings he extended in such a manner as to out-flank the army of Nayan. In front of each battalion of horse were placed five hundred infantry, armed with short lances and swords, who, whenever the cavalry made a show of flight, were practised to mount behind the riders and accompany them, alighting again when they returned to the charge, and killing with their lances the horses of the enemy.

As soon as the order of battle was arranged, an infinite number of wind instruments of various kinds were sounded, and these were succeeded by songs, according to the custom of the Tartars before they engage in fight, which commences upon the signal given by the cymbals and drums, and there was such a beating of the cymbals and drums, and such singing, that it was wonderful to hear.

This signal, by the orders of the Great Khan, was first given to the right and left wings, and the great drums of Kublai Khan began to sound. Then a fierce and bloody conflict began. The air was instantly filled with a cloud of arrows that poured down on every side, and vast numbers of men and horses were seen to fall to the ground. The loud cries and shouts of the men, together with the noise of the horses and the weapons, were such as to inspire terror into those who heard them. When their arrows had been discharged, the hostile parties engaged in close combat with their lances, swords, and maces shod with iron; and such was the slaughter, and so large were the heaps of the carcases of men, and more especially of horses, on the field, that it became impossible for the one party to advance upon the other.

The fortune of the day remained for a long time undecided, and victory wavered between the contending parties from morning until noon; for so zealous was the devotion of Nayan's people to the cause of their master, who was most liberal and indulgent towards them, that they were all ready to meet death rather than turn their backs to the enemy.

At length, however, Nayan, perceiving that he was nearly surrounded, attempted to save himself by flight, but was

THE DRUMS OF KUBLAI KHAN

presently made prisoner, and conducted to the presence of Kublai, who gave orders for his being put to death.

Chapter 5

HOW THE GREAT KHAN CAUSED NAYAN TO BE PUT TO DEATH

THIS was carried into execution by enclosing Nayan between two carpets, which were violently shaken until the spirit had departed from the body,* the motive for this peculiar sentence being, that the sun and the air should not witness the shedding of the blood of one who belonged to the imperial family. Those of his troops which survived the battle came to make their submission, and swear allegiance to Kublai. They were inhabitants of the four noble provinces of Chorza, Karli, Barskol, and Sitingui.

Nayan, who had privately undergone the ceremony of baptism, but never made open profession of Christianity, thought proper, on this occasion, to bear the sign of the cross in his banners, and he had in his army a vast number of Christians, who were left amongst the slain. When the Jews † and the Saracens perceived that the banner of the cross was overthrown, they taunted the Christian inhabitants with it, saying, "Behold the state to which your banners, and those who followed them, are reduced!"

On account of these derisions the Christians were compelled to lay their complaints before the Great Khan, who

---

* In 1688 the King of Siam was put to death by being placed in a large iron mortar and pounded with wooden pestles. Royal criminals of Siam are treated in this manner because of the belief that royal blood must not be spilt on the ground. This is to prevent divine blood being contaminated by mixing it with earth. In the ceremonies of certain Australian tribes blood is not allowed to fall on the ground and in West Sussex, England, there are people who hold that ground upon which human blood has been shed will remain barren for ever. See chapters on *Tabooed Things* in Frazer's *The Golden Bough*.

† Persian Jews settled in China in 1163. In 1279 their old synagogue in K'ai-feng was rebuilt and in 1386 the first Emperor of the Ming dynasty presented the Jewish community with a piece of ground on which they might live in peace. See *Les Juifs en Chine* by Henri Cordier, *Jewish Encyclopedia* and Perlman's *History of the Jews in China*.

ordered the former to appear before him, and sharply re-
buked them. "If the Cross of Christ," he said, "has not
proved advantageous to the party of Nayan, the effect has
been consistent with reason and justice, inasmuch as he was
a Rebel against his Lord, and to such wretches it could
not afford its protection. Let none therefore presume to
charge with injustice the God of the Christians, who is
Himself the perfection of goodness and of justice."

Chapter 6

OF THE RETURN OF THE GREAT KHAN TO THE CITY OF KANBALU AFTER HIS VICTORY ❧ AND OF THE HONOUR HE CONFERS ON THE CHRISTIANS AND THE JEWS ❧ AND OTHER SUBJECTS

THE Great Khan, having obtained this signal victory,
returned with great pomp and triumph to the capital city
of Kanbalu [Peking]. This took place in the month of
November, and he continued to reside there during the
months of February and March, in which latter was our
festival of Easter. Being aware that this was one of our
principal solemnities, he commanded all the Christians to
attend him, and to bring with them their Book, which contains the four Gospels of the Evangelists.

After causing it to be repeatedly perfumed with incense,
in a ceremonious manner, he devoutly kissed it, and directed that the same should be done by all his nobles who
were present. This was his usual practice upon each of
the principal Christian festivals, such as Easter and Christ-
mas; and he observed the same at the festivals of the Saracens, Jews, and idolaters.

Upon being asked his motive for this conduct, he said:
"There are four great Prophets who are reverenced and
worshipped by the different classes of mankind. The

Christians regard Jesus Christ as their divinity; the Saracens, Mahomet; the Jews, Moses; and the idolaters, Sogomombar-kan, the most eminent amongst their idols. I do honour and show respect to all the four, and invoke to my aid whichever amongst them is in truth Supreme in Heaven." But from the manner in which his majesty acted towards them, it is evident that he regarded the faith of the Christians as the truest and the best; nothing, as he observed, being enjoined to its professors that was not filled with virtue and holiness.

By no means, however, would he permit them to bear the cross before them in their processions, because upon it so exalted a personage as Christ had been scourged and put to death. It may perhaps be asked by some, why, if he showed such a preference to the faith of Christ, he did not conform to it, and become a Christian?

His reason for not so doing, he assigned to Nicolo and Mafeo Polo, when, upon the occasion of his sending them as his ambassadors to the Pope, they ventured to address a few words to him on the subject of Christianity. "Wherefore," he said, "should I become a Christian? You yourselves must perceive that the Christians of these countries are ignorant, inefficient persons, who do not possess the faculty of performing anything miraculous; whereas you see that the idolaters can do whatever they will. When I sit at table the cups that were in the middle of the hall come to me filled with wine and other beverage, spontaneously and without being touched by human hand, and I drink from them. They have the power of controlling bad weather and obliging it to retire to any quarter of the heavens, with many other wonderful gifts of that nature. You are witnesses that their idols have the faculty of speech, and predict whatever is required.

"Should I become a convert to the faith of Christ, and profess myself a Christian, the nobles of my court and other persons who do not incline to that religion will ask me what sufficient motives have caused me to receive baptism, and to embrace Christianity.* 'What extraordinary powers,' they will say, 'what miracles have been displayed by its ministers? Whereas the idolaters declare that what they exhibit is performed through their own sanctity, and the influence of their idols.'

"To this I shall not know what answer to make, and I shall be considered by them as labouring under a grievous error, whilst the idolaters, who by means of their profound art can effect such wonders, may without difficulty compass my death. But return you to your pontiff, and request of him, in my name, to send hither a hundred persons well skilled in your law, who being confronted with the idolaters shall have power to restrain them, and showing that they themselves are endowed with similar art, but which they refrain from exercising, because it is derived from the agency of evil spirits, shall compel them to desist from practices of such a nature in their presence. When I am witness of this, I shall place them and their religion under a ban, and shall allow myself to be baptized. Following my example, all my nobility will then in like manner receive baptism, and this will be imitated by my subjects in general. In the end the Christians of these parts

* A good part of this chapter is not contained in the French manuscript used by Yule for his translation. It is true that Kublai Khan honoured Christians as well as other men of learning but it was his policy always to deal with religion as a political matter and he regarded the worship of God as a byproduct of civilization. It seemed a ready means of civilizing his people. The Lamas had learning and the Christians, too, had learning. But they failed to send the hundred men; and the civilization is now different but not to be despised. "When I went to China," says Bertrand Russell in *The Problem of China,* "I went to teach; but every day that I stayed I thought less of what I had to teach them and more of what I had to learn from them."

will exceed in number those who inhabit your own country."

From this discourse it must be evident that if the Pope had sent out persons duly qualified to preach the gospel, the Great Khan would have embraced Christianity, for which, it is certainly known, he had a strong predilection.

To return to our subject, we shall now speak of the rewards and honours he bestows on such as distinguish themselves by their valour in battle.

Chapter 7

OF THE KIND OF REWARDS GRANTED TO THOSE WHO CONDUCT THEMSELVES WELL IN FIGHT ❦ AND OF THE GOLDEN TABLETS WHICH THEY RECEIVE

THE Great Khan appoints twelve of the most intelligent amongst his nobles, whose duty it is to make themselves acquainted with the conduct of the officers and men of his army, particularly upon expeditions and in battles, and to present their reports to him. Upon their respective merits he advances them in his service, raising those who commanded a hundred men to the command of a thousand, and presenting many with vessels of silver, as well as the customary Tablets or warrants of Authority.

The tablets given to those commanding a hundred men are of silver; to those commanding a thousand, of gold or of silver gilt; and those who command ten thousand receive tablets of gold, bearing the head of a lion; the former being of the weight of a hundred and twenty *saggi*, and these with the lion's head, two hundred and twenty.* On the tablet is an inscription to this effect: "*By the strength of the great God, and of the great grace which He hath*

---

* These tablets were oblong sheets of metal, with rounded corners, about three-and-a-half inches by twelve. They are reported to have weighed between 18 and 40 or more ounces and had a hole drilled at the upper end through which a cord was passed and suspended the plate.

accorded to our Emperor, be the name of the Kaan blessed;
and let all such as disobey him be slain and destroyed." The
officers who hold these tablets have privileges attached to
them, and in the inscription is specified what are the duties
and the powers of their respective commands.

He who is at the head of a hundred thousand men, or
the commander in chief of a grand army, has a golden
tablet weighing three hundred *saggi*, with the sentence
above mentioned, and at the bottom is engraved the figure
of a lion, together with the sun and moon. He exercises
also the privileges of his high command, as set forth in this
magnificent tablet. Whenever he rides in public, an um-
brella is carried over his head, denoting the rank and authority he holds; and when he is seated, it is always upon a
silver chair.

The Great Khan confers likewise upon certain of his
nobles tablets on which are represented figures of the gerfalcon, in virtue of which they have the power to take with
them as their guard of honour the whole army of any great
prince. They can also make use of the horses of the imperial stud at their pleasure, and can appropriate the horses
of any officers inferior to themselves in rank.

Chapter 8

OF THE FIGURE AND STATURE OF THE GREAT KHAN ❦ OF HIS FOUR PRINCIPAL WIVES ❦ AND OF THE ANNUAL SELECTION OF YOUNG WOMEN FOR HIM IN THE PROVINCE OF UNGUT

KUBLAI, who is styled the Great Khan, or Lord of Lords,
is of middle stature, that is, neither tall nor short. His
limbs are well formed, and in his whole figure there is a
just proportion. His complexion is fair, and occasionally
suffused with red, like the bright tint of the rose, which

adds much grace to his countenance.   His eyes are black and handsome, his nose is well shaped and prominent.

He has four wives of the first rank, who are esteemed legitimate, and the eldest born son of any one of these succeeds to the empire, upon the decease of the Great Khan. They bear equally the title of empress, and have their separate courts.   None of them have fewer than three hundred young female attendants of great beauty, together with a multitude of youths as pages, and other eunuchs, as well as ladies of the bedchamber; so that the number of persons belonging to each of their respective courts amounts to ten thousand.

When his majesty is desirous of the company of one of his empresses, he either sends for her, or goes himself to her palace.   Besides these, he has many concubines provided for his use, from a province of Tartary named Ungut, the inhabitants of which are distinguished for beauty of features and fairness of complexion.   Every second year, or oftener, as it may happen to be his pleasure, the Great Khan sends thither his officers, who collect for him, one hundred or more, of the handsomest of the young women, according to the estimation of beauty communicated to them in their instructions.

The mode of their appreciation is as follows.   Upon the arrival of these commissioners, they give orders for assembling all the young women of the province, and appoint qualified persons to examine them, who, upon careful inspection of each of them separately, that is to say, of the hair, the countenance, the eyebrows, the mouth, the lips, and other features, as well as the symmetry of these with each other, estimate their value at sixteen, seventeen, eighten, or twenty, or more carats, according to the greater or less degree of beauty.   The number required by the Great

Khan, at the rates, perhaps, of twenty or twenty-one carats, to which their commission was limited, is then selected from the rest, and they are conveyed to his court.

Upon their arrival in his presence, he causes a new examination to be made by a different set of inspectors, and from amongst them a further selection takes place, when thirty or forty are retained for his own chamber at a higher valuation. These are committed separately to the care of certain elderly ladies of the palace, whose duty it is to observe them attentively during the course of the night, in order to ascertain that they have not any concealed imperfections, that they sleep tranquilly, do not snore, have sweet breath, and are free from unpleasant scent in any part of the body. Having undergone this rigorous scrutiny, they are divided into parties of five, each taking turn for three days and three nights, in his majesty's interior apartment, where they are to perform every service that is required of them, and he does with them as he likes.

When this term is completed, they are relieved by another party, and in this manner successively, until the whole number have taken their turn; when the first five recommence their attendance. But while one party officiates in the inner chamber, another is stationed in the outer apartment adjoining. If his majesty should have occasion for anything, such as drink or victuals, the former may signify his commands to the latter, by whom the article required is immediately procured. In this way the duty of waiting upon his majesty's person is exclusively performed by these young females. The remainder of them, whose value had been estimated at an inferior rate, are assigned to the different lords of the household; under whom they are instructed in cookery, in dressmaking, and other suitable

THE WIVES OF KUBLAI KHAN

works; and upon any person belonging to the court expressing an inclination to take a wife, the Great Khan bestows upon him one of these damsels, with a handsome portion. In this manner he provides for them all amongst his nobility.

It may be asked whether the people of the province do not feel themselves aggrieved in having their daughters thus forcibly taken from them by the sovereign? Certainly not; but, on the contrary, they regard it as a favour and an honour done to them; and those who are the fathers of handsome children feel highly gratified by his condescending to make choice of their daughters. "If," say they, "my daughter is born under an auspicious planet and to good fortune, his majesty can best fulfill her destinies, by matching her nobly; which it would not be in my power to do." If, on the other hand, the daughter misconducts herself, or any mischance befalls her, by which she becomes disqualified, the father attributes the disappointment to the evil influence of her stars.

Chapter 9

OF THE NUMBER OF THE GREAT KHAN'S SONS BY HIS FOUR WIVES ❧ WHOM HE MAKES KINGS OF DIFFERENT PROVINCES ❧ AND OF CHINGHIS HIS FIRST-BORN

THE Great Khan has had twenty-two sons by his four legitimate wives, the eldest of whom, named Chinghis, was designed to inherit the government of the empire; and this nomination was confirmed to him during the life-time of his father. But, as it came to pass he died and left a son, whose name is Themur. He, as the representative of his father, is to succeed to the dominion. The disposition of this prince is good, and he is endowed with wisdon and valour; of the latter he has given proofs in several successful battles.

Besides these, his majesty has twenty-five sons by his concubines, all of them brave soldiers, having been continually employed in the military profession. These he has placed in the rank of nobles. Of his legitimate sons, seven are at the head of extensive provinces and kingdoms, which they govern with wisdom and prudence, as might be expected of the children of one whose great qualities have not been surpassed, in the general estimation, by any person of the Tartar race.

Chapter 10

OF THE GREAT AND ADMIRABLE PALACE OF THE GREAT KHAN • NEAR TO THE CITY OF KANBALU

THE Great Khan usually resides during three months of the year, namely December, January, and February, in the great city of Kanbalu [Peking], situated towards the north-eastern extremity of the province of Cathay. Here, on the southern side of the new city, is the site of his vast palace, the form and dimensions of which are as follows.

In the first place is a square enclosed with a wall and deep ditch; each side of the square being eight miles in length, and having at an equal distance from each extremity an entrance-gate, for the concourse of people resorting thither from all quarters. Within this enclosure there is, on the four sides, an open space one mile in breadth, where the troops are stationed. This is bounded by a second wall, enclosing a square of six miles, having three gates on the south side, and three on the north, the middle portal of each being larger than the other two, and always kept shut, excepting on the occasions of the emperor's entrance or de-

THE PALACE OF KUBLAI KHAN

parture. Those on each side always remain open for the use of common passengers.

In the middle of each division of these walls is a handsome and spacious building, and consequently within the enclosure there are eight such buildings, in which are deposited the royal military stores; one building being appropriated to the reception of each class of stores. Thus, for instance, the bridles, saddles, stirrups, and other furniture serving for the equipment of cavalry, occupy one storehouse; the bows, strings, quivers, arrows, and other articles belonging to archery, occupy another; cuirasses, corselets, and other armour formed of leather, a third storehouse; and so of the rest.

Within this walled enclosure there is still another, of great thickness, and its height is full twenty-five feet. The battlements or notched parapets are all white. This also forms a square four miles in extent, each side being one mile, and it has six gates, disposed like those of the former enclosure. It contains in like manner eight large buildings, similarly arranged, which are appropriated to the wardrobe of the emperor. The spaces between the one wall and the other are ornamented with many handsome trees, and contain meadows in which are kept various kinds of beasts, such as stags, the animals that yield the musk, roe-bucks, fallow-deer, and others of the same class. Every interval between the walls, not occupied by buildings, is stocked in this manner. The pastures have abundant herbage. The roads across them being raised three feet above their level, and paved, no mud collects upon them, nor rain-water settles, but on the contrary runs off, and contributes to improve the vegetation.

Within these walls, which constitute the boundary of four miles, stands the palace of the Great Khan, the most

extensive that has ever yet been known. It reaches from
the northern to the southern wall, leaving only a vacant
court, where persons of rank and the military guards pass
and repass. It has no upper floor, but the roof is very
lofty. The paved foundation or platform on which it
stands is raised ten spans above the level of the ground, and
a wall of marble, two paces wide, is built on all sides. This
wall serves as a terrace, where those who walk on it are
visible from without. Along the exterior edge of the wall
is a handsome balustrade, with pillars, which the people
are allowed to approach. The sides of the great halls and
the apartments are ornamented with dragons in carved work
and gilt, figures of warriors, of birds, and of beasts, with
representations of battles. The inside of the roof is contrived in such a manner that nothing besides gilding and
painting presents itself to the eye.

On each of the four sides of the palace there is a grand
flight of marble steps, by which you ascend from the level
of the ground to the wall of marble which surrounds the
building, and which constitute the approach to the palace
itself.

The grand hall is extremely long and wide, and admits
of dinners being there served to great multitudes of people.
The palace contains a number of separate chambers, all
highly beautiful, and so admirably disposed that it seems
impossible to suggest any improvement to the system of
their arrangement. The exterior of the roof is adorned
with a variety of colours, red, green, azure, and violet, and
the sort of covering is so strong as to last for many years.
The glazing of the windows is so well wrought and so
delicate as to have the transparency of crystal.

In the rear of the body of the palace there are large
buildings containing several apartments, where is deposited

the private property of the monarch, or his treasure in gold and silver bullion, precious stones, and pearls, and also his vessels of gold and silver plate. Here are likewise the apartments of his wives and concubines; and in this retired situation he dispatches business with convenience, being free from every kind of interruption.

On the other side of the grand palace, and opposite to that in which the emperor resides, is another palace, in every respect similar, appropriated to the residence of Chinghis, his eldest son, at whose court are observed all the ceremonials belonging to that of his father, as the prince who is to succeed to the government of the empire. Not far from the palace, on the northern side, and about a bow-shot distance from the surrounding wall, is an artificial mount of earth, the height of which is full a hundred paces, and the circuit at the base about a mile. It is covered with the most beautiful evergreen trees; for whenever his Majesty receives information of a handsome tree growing in any place, he causes it to be dug up, with all its roots and the earth about them, and however large and heavy it may be, he has it transported by means of elephants to this mount, and adds it to the verdant collection. Because the trees on this hill are always green it has acquired the name of the Green Mount.

On its summit is erected an ornamental pavilion, which is likewise entirely green. The view of this altogether,— the mount itself, the trees, and the building, form a delightful and at the same time a wonderful scene. In the northern quarter also, and equally within the precincts of the city, there is a large and deep excavation, judiciously formed, the earth from which supplied the material for raising the mount. It is furnished with water by a small rivulet, and has the appearance of a fish-pond, but its use is for watering

the cattle. The stream passing from thence along an aque-
duct, at the foot of the Green Mount, proceeds to fill another great and very deep excavation formed between the
private palace of the emperor and that of his son Chingis;
and the earth from hence equally served to increase the
elevation of the mount. In this latter basin there is great
store and variety of fish, from which the table of his
Majesty is supplied with any quantity that may be wanted.

The stream discharges itself at the opposite extremity of
the piece of water, and precautions are taken to prevent
the escape of the fish by placing gratings of copper or iron
at the places of its entrance and exit. It is stocked also
with swans and other water birds. From the one palace to
the other there is a communication by means of a bridge
thrown across the water. Such is the description of this
great palace. We shall now speak of the situation and
circumstances of the city of Taidu.

Chapter 11

OF THE NEW CITY OF TAIDU ❧ BUILT NEAR TO THAT OF KANBALU ❧ OF A RULE OBSERVED RESPECTING THE ENTERTAINMENT OF AMBASSADORS ❧ AND OF THE NIGHTLY CITY POLICE

THE city of Kanbalu is situated near a large river in the
province of Cathay, and was in ancient times eminently
magnificent and royal. The name itself implies "the city
of the Emperor"; but his Majesty was informed by the
astrologers, that it was destined to become rebellious to
his authority and resolved upon the measure of building
another capital, upon the opposite side of the river, where
stand the palaces just described. The new and the old cities
are separated from each other only by the stream that runs
between them. The new-built city received the name of

Taidu, and all the Cathaians, that is, all those of the inhabitants who were natives of the province of Cathay, were compelled to evacuate the ancient city, and to take up their abode in the new. Some of the inhabitants, however, of whose loyalty he did not entertain suspicion, were suffered to remain, especially because the new one, although of the dimensions that shall presently be described, was not capable of containing the same number as the former, which was of vast extent.

This new city is of a form perfectly square, and twenty-four miles in extent, each of its sides being six miles. It is enclosed with walls of earth, that at the base are about ten paces thick, but gradually diminish to the top, where the thickness is not more than three paces. In all parts the battlements are white. The whole plan of the city was regularly laid out by line, and the streets in general are consequently so straight, that when a person ascends the wall over one of the gates, and looks right forward, he can see the gate opposite to him on the other side of the city. In the public streets there are, on each side, booths and shops of every description. All the allotments of ground upon which the habitations throughout the city were constructed are square, and exactly on a line with each other; each allotment being sufficiently spacious for handsome buildings, with corresponding courts and gardens. One of these was assigned to each head of a family. Afterwards the property passed from hand to hand. In this manner the whole interior of the city is disposed in squares, so as to resemble a chess-board, and planned out with a degree of precision and beauty impossible to describe. The wall of the city has twelve gates, three on each side of the square, and over each gate and compartment of the wall there is a handsome building; so that on each side of the square there are five such buildings, containing large rooms, in which are disposed the arms of those who form the garrison of the city, every gate being guarded by a thousand men. It is not to be understood that such a force is stationed there in consequence of the apprehension of danger from any hostile power whatever, but as a guard suitable to the honour and dignity of the sovereign. Yet it must be allowed that the declaration of the astrologers has excited in his mind a degree of suspicion with regard to the Cathaians.

In the centre of the city there is a great bell suspended in a lofty building, which is sounded every night, and after the third stroke no person dares to be found in the streets, unless upon some urgent occasion, such as to call assistance to a woman in labour, or a man attacked with sickness. In such necessary cases the person is required to carry a light.

Outside of each of the gates is a suburb so wide that it reaches to and unites with those of the other nearest gates on both sides, and in length extends to the distance of three or four miles, so that the number of inhabitants in these suburbs exceeds that of the city itself. Within each suburb there are, at intervals, as far perhaps as a mile from the city, many hotels, or caravanserais, in which the merchants arriving from various parts take up their abode; and to each description of people a separate building is assigned, as we should say, one to the Lombards, another to the Germans, and a third to the French.

The number of public women who prostitute themselves for money, reckoning those in the new city as well as those in the suburbs of the old, is twenty-five thousand. To each hundred and to each thousand of these there are superintending officers appointed, who are under the orders of a captain-general. The motive for placing them under such command is this: when ambassadors arrive charged with any business in which the interests of the Great Khan are concerned, it is customary to maintain them at his Majesty's expense, and in order that they may be treated in the most honourable manner, the captain is ordered to furnish nightly to each individual of the embassy one of these courtezans, who is likewise to be changed every night. As this service is considered in the light of a tribute they owe to the sovereign, they do not receive any remuneration.

Guards, in parties of thirty or forty, continually patrol the streets during the course of the night, and make diligent search for persons who may be from their homes at an unseasonable hour, that is, after the third stroke of the great bell. When any are met with under such circumstances, they immediately apprehend and confine them, and take them in the morning for examination before officers appointed for that purpose. Upon proof of any delinquency, they are sentenced according to the nature of the offence, to a severer or lighter infliction of the bastinade, which sometimes, however, occasions their death. It is in this manner that crimes are usually punished amongst these people, from a disinclination to the shedding of blood, which their learned astrologers instruct them to avoid.

Having thus described the interior of the city of Taidu, we shall now speak of the disposition to rebellion shown by its Cathaian inhabitants.

Chapter 12

OF THE PERSONAL GUARD OF THE GREAT KHAN

THE body-guard of the Great Khan consists, as is well known to every one, of twelve thousand horsemen, who

are termed Kasitan, which signifies "Knights devoted to
their Lord." It is not, however, from any apprehensions
entertained by him that he is surrounded by this guard, but
as matter of state.

These twelve thousand men are commanded by four
superior officers, each of whom is at the head of three
thousand; and each three thousand does constant duty in
the palace during three successive days and nights, at the
expiration of which they are relieved by another division.
When all the four have completed their period of duty, it
comes again to the turn of the first.

During the day-time, the nine thousand who are off
guard do not, however, quit the palace, unless when employed upon the service of his Majesty, or when the individuals are called away for their domestic concerns, in
which case they must obtain leave of absence through their
commanding officer.

Chapter 13

OF THE STYLE IN WHICH THE GREAT KHAN HOLDS HIS PUBLIC COURTS ❤ AND SITS AT TABLE WITH ALL HIS NOBLES

WHEN his Majesty holds a grand and public court, those
who attend it are seated in the following order. The table
of the sovereign is placed on an elevation, and he takes his
seat on the northern side, with his face turned towards the
south; and next to him, on his left hand, sits the Empress.
On his right hand are placed his sons, grandsons, and other
persons connected with him by blood, upon seats somewhat
lower, so that their heads are on a level with the Emperor's
feet. The other princes and the nobility have their places
at still lower tables; and the same rules are observed with
respect to the females, the wives of the sons, grandsons,

and other relatives of the Great Khan being seated on the left hand, at tables in like manner gradually lower; then follow the wives of the nobility and military officers: so that all are seated according to their respective ranks and dignities, in the places assigned to them, and to which they are entitled.

The tables are arranged in such a manner that the Great Khan, sitting on his elevated throne, can overlook the whole. It is not, however, to be understood that all who assemble on such occasions can be accommodated at tables. The greater part of the officers, and even of the nobles, on the contrary, eat, sitting upon carpets, in the halls; and on the outside stand a great multitude of persons who come from different countries, and bring with them many rare curiosities.

In the middle of the hall, where the Great Khan sits at table, there is a magnificent piece of furniture, made in the form of a square coffer, each side of which is three paces in length, exquisitely carved in figures of animals, and gilt. It is hollow within, for the purpose of receiving a capacious vase, of pure gold, calculated to hold many gallons. On each of its four sides stands a smaller vessel, containing about a hogshead, one of which is filled with mare's milk, another with that of the camel, and so of the others, according to the kinds of beverage in use. Within this buffet are also the cups or flagons belonging to his Majesty, for serving the liquors. Some of them are of beautiful gilt plate. Their size is such that, when filled with wine or other liquor, the quantity would be sufficient for eight or ten men.

Before every two persons who have seats at the tables, one of these flagons is placed, together with a kind of ladle, in the form of a cup with a handle, also of plate;

to be used not only for taking the wine out of the flagon, but for lifting it to the head. This is observed as well with respect to the women as the men. The quantity and richness of the plate belonging to his Majesty is quite incredible.

Officers of rank are likewise appointed, whose duty it is to see that all strangers who happen to arrive at the time of the festival, and are unacquainted with the etiquette of the court, are suitably accommodated with places; and these stewards are continually visiting every part of the hall, inquiring of the guests if there is anything with which they are unprovided, or whether any of them wish for wine, milk, meat, or other articles, in which case it is immediately brought to them by the attendants.

At each door of the grand hall, or of whatever part the Great Khan happens to be in, stand two officers, of a gigantic figure, one on each side, with staves in their hands, for the purpose of preventing persons from touching the threshold with their feet, and obliging them to step beyond it. If by chance any one is guilty of this offence, these janitors take from him his garment, which he must redeem for money; or, when they do not take the garment, they inflict on him such number of blows as they have authority for doing. But, as strangers may be unacquainted with the prohibition, officers are appointed to introduce and warn them. This precaution is used because touching the threshold is regarded as a bad omen. In departing from the hall, as some of the company may be affected by the liquor, it is impossible to guard against the accident, and the order is not then strictly enforced.

The numerous persons who attend at the sideboard of his Majesty, and who serve him with victuals and drink, are all obliged to cover their noses and mouths with hand-

some veils or cloths of worked silk, in order that his victuals
or his wine may not be affected by their breath.   When
drink is called for by him, and the page in waiting has
presented it, he retires three paces and kneels down, upon
which the courtiers, and all who are present, in like manner make their prostration.   At the same moment all the
musical instruments, of which there is a numerous band,
begin to play, and continue to do so until he has ceased
drinking, when all the company recover their posture.   This
reverential salutation is made as often as his Majesty drinks.
It is unnecessary to say anything of the victuals, because it
may well be imagined that their abundance is excessive.

When the repast is finished, and the tables have been removed, persons of various descriptions enter the hall, and
amongst these a troop of comedians and performers on different instruments.   Also tumblers and jugglers, who exhibit their skill in the presence of the Great Khan, to the
high amusement and gratification of all the spectators.
When these sports are concluded, the people separate, and
each returns to his own house.

Chapter 14

OF THE FESTIVAL THAT IS KEPT THROUGHOUT THE DOMINIONS OF THE GREAT KHAN EVERY YEAR ON HIS BIRTHDAY

ALL the Tartar and other subjects of the Great Khan
celebrate as a festival the day of his Majesty's birth, which
took place on the twenty-eighth day of the month of
September.   This is their greatest festival, excepting the one
kept on the first day of the year, which shall be hereafter
described.   Upon this anniversary the Great Khan appears
in a superb dress of cloth of gold, and on the same occasion
full twenty thousand nobles and military officers are clad

by him in dresses similar to his own in point of colour and form; but the materials are not equally rich. They are, however, of silk, and of the colour of gold; and along with the vest they likewise receive a girdle of chamois leather, curiously worked with gold and silver thread, and also a pair of boots. Some of the dresses are ornamented with precious stones and pearls to the value of ten thousand bezants of gold, and are given to those nobles who, from their confidential employments, are nearest to his Majesty's person. These dresses are appointed to be worn on the thirteen solemn festivals celebrated in the year, when those who are clad in them make an appearance that is truly royal. When his Majesty assumes any particular dress, the nobles of his court wear corresponding, but less costly, dresses, which are always in readiness. They are not annually renewed, but on the contrary are made to last about ten years. From this parade an idea may be formed of the magnificence of the Great Khan, which is unequalled by that of any monarch in the world.

On the occasion of this festival of the Great Khan's birthday, all his Tartar subjects, and likewise the people of every kingdom and province throughout his dominions, send him valuable presents, according to established usage. Many persons who repair to court in order to solicit principalities to which they have pretensions, also bring presents, and his Majesty accordingly gives direction to the tribunal of twelve, who have charge of such matters, to assign to them such territories and governments as may be proper.

Upon this day likewise all the Christians, Idolaters, and Saracens, together with every other description of people, offer up devout prayers to their respective Gods and Idols, that they may bless and preserve the sovereign, and bestow upon him long life, health, and prosperity. Such, and so extensive, are the rejoicings on the return of his Majesty's birthday.

We shall now speak of another festival, termed the White Feast, celebrated at the New Year.

Chapter 15

OF THE WHITE FEAST HELD ON NEW YEAR'S DAY ❦ AND OF THE NUMBER OF PRESENTS THEN BROUGHT

It is well ascertained that the Tartars date the commencement of their year from the month of February, and on that occasion it is customary for the Great Khan, as well as all who are subject to him, in their several countries, to clothe themselves in white garments, which, according to their ideas, are the emblem of good fortune. This is done in the hope that, during the whole course of the year nothing but what is fortunate may happen to them, and that they may enjoy pleasure and comfort.

Upon this day the inhabitants of all the provinces and kingdoms who hold lands or rights of jurisdiction under the Great Khan, send him valuable presents of gold, silver, and precious stones, together with many pieces of white cloth, which they add, with the intent that his Majesty may experience throughout the year uninterrupted enjoyment, and possess treasures adequate to all his expenses. With the same view the nobles, princes, and all ranks of the community, make reciprocal presents, at their respective houses, of white articles; embracing each other with demonstrations of joy and festivity, and saying "May good fortune attend you through the coming year, and may everything you undertake succeed to your wish." On this occasion great numbers of beautiful white horses are presented to the Great Khan; or if not perfectly white, it is at least the prevailing colour. In this country white horses are not uncommon.

It is moreover the custom in making presents to the Great Khan, for those who have it in their power to furnish nine times nine of the article of which the present consists. Thus, for instance, if a province sends a present of horses, there are nine times nine, or eighty-one head in the drove. And so also of gold, or of cloth, nine times nine pieces. His Majesty receives at this festival no fewer than a hundred thousand horses.

On this day it is that all his elephants, amounting to five thousand, are exhibited in procession, covered with housings of cloth, fancifully and richly worked with gold and silk, in figures of birds and beasts. Each of these supports upon its shoulders two coffers filled with vessels of plate and other apparatus for the use of the court. Then follows a train of camels, in like manner laden with various necessary articles of furniture. When the whole are properly arranged, they pass in review before his Majesty, and form a pleasing spectacle.

On the morning of the festival, before the tables are spread, all the Princes, the nobility of various ranks, the cavaliers, astrologers, physicians, and falconers, with many others holding public offices, the prefects of the people and of the lands, together with the officers of the army, make their entry into the grand hall, in front of the Emperor. Those who cannot find room within, stand on the outside of the building, in such a situation as to be within sight of their sovereign.

The assemblage is marshalled in the following order. The first places are assigned to the sons and grandsons of his Majesty and all the imperial family. Next to these are the provincial Kings and the nobility of the empire, accord-

THE WHITE FEAST

ing to their several degrees, in regular succession. When all have been disposed in the places appointed for them, a person of high dignity, or as we should express it, a great prelate, rises and says with a loud voice: "Bow down and do reverence"; when instantly all bend their bodies until their foreheads touch the floor. And this adoration they repeat four times. This being done, the prelate advances to an altar, richly adorned, upon which is placed a red tablet inscribed with the name of the Great Khan. Near to this stands a censer of burning incense, with which the prelate, on the behalf of all who are assembled, perfumes the tablet and the altar, with great reverence; when every one present humbly prostrates himself before the tablet.

This ceremony being concluded, they return to their places, and then make the presentation of their respective gifts; such as have been mentioned. When a display has been made of these, and the Great Khan has cast his eyes upon them, the tables are prepared for the feast, and the company, including women as well as men, arrange themselves there in the manner and order described in a former chapter. After dinner the musicians and theatrical performers exhibit for the amusement of the court, as has been already related. But on this occasion a lion is conducted into the presence of his Majesty, so tame, that it is taught to lay itself down at his feet. The sports being finished, every one returns to his own home.

Chapter 16

CONCERNING THE TWELVE THOUSAND BARONS WHO RECEIVE ROBES OF CLOTH OF GOLD FROM THE EMPEROR ON THE GREAT FESTIVALS

Now you must know that the Great Khan hath set apart twelve thousand of his men who are distinguished by the name of Keshican; and on these twelve thousand Barons he bestows thirteen changes of raiment, which are all different from one another. In one set twelve thousand are all of one colour and there are thirteen different sets of colours. These robes are garnished with gems and pearls and other precious things in a very rich and costly manner.

The Emperor himself has thirteen suits corresponding to those of his Barons; in colour, though his are grander, richer and costlier. And you may see that all this costs an amount which it is scarcely possible to calculate.

Chapter 17

OF THE QUANTITY OF GAME TAKEN AND SENT TO THE COURT DURING THE WINTER MONTHS

AT the season when the Great Khan resides in the capital of Cathay, which is during the three months of December, January, and February, at which time the cold is excessive, he gives orders for general hunting parties to take place in all the countries within forty days' journey of the court.

The governors of districts are required to send all sorts of game of the larger kind, such as wild boars, stags, fallow deer, roebucks, and bears, which are taken in the following manner:—All persons possessed of land in the province repair to the places where these animals are to be found, and proceed to enclose them within a circle, when they are killed, partly with dogs, but chiefly by shooting them with arrows. Such of them as are intended for his Majesty's use are first gutted and then forwarded on carriages, in large quantities, by those who reside within thirty stages of the capital. Those, in fact, who are at the distance of forty stages, do not, on account of the length of the journey, send the carcases, but only the skins, some dressed and others raw, to be made use of for the service of the army as his Majesty may judge proper.

Chapter 18

OF LEOPARDS AND LYNXES USED FOR HUNTING DEER ◀ OF LIONS HABITUATED TO THE CHASE OF VARIOUS ANIMALS ◀ AND OF EAGLES TAUGHT TO SEIZE WOLVES

THE Great Khan has many leopards and lynxes kept for the purpose of chasing deer, and also many lions which are larger than the Babylonian lions, have good skins and of a handsome colour—being streaked on the sides, with white, black, and red stripes. They are active in seizing boars, wild oxen and asses, bears, stags, roebucks, and other beasts that are the objects of sport. It is an admirable sight, when the lion is let loose in pursuit of the animal, to observe the savage eagerness and speed with which he overtakes it. His Majesty has them conveyed for this purpose, in cages placed upon cars, and along with them is confined a little dog, with which they become familiarized. The reason for thus shutting them up is, that they would otherwise be so keen and furious at the sight of the game that it would be impossible to keep them under the necessary constraint. It is proper that they should be led in a direction opposite to the wind, in order that they may not be scented by the game, which would immediately run off, and offer no chance of sport.

His Majesty has eagles also, which are trained to catch wolves, and such is their size and strength that none, however large, can escape from their talons.*

---

* To this day eagles are trained and thus employed in Eastern Turkestan.

Chapter 19

OF TWO BROTHERS WHO ARE PRINCIPAL OFFICERS OF THE CHASE OF THE GREAT KHAN

His Majesty has in his service two Barons, brothers, one of them named Bayan and the other Mingan, who are, what in the language of the Tartars are called Chinuchi, that is to say, "keepers of the mastiffs." They have charge of the hounds, fleet and slow, and of the mastiffs. Each of these has under his orders a body of ten thousand men; those under the one brother wearing a red uniform, and those under the other, a blue, whenever they accompany the Lord to the chase.

The dogs of different descriptions which accompany them to the field are not fewer than five thousand. The one brother, with his division, takes the ground to the right hand of the Emperor, and the other to the left, with his division, and each advances in regular order, until they have enclosed a tract of country to the extent of a day's march. By this means no beast can escape them. It is a beautiful and glorious sight to watch the exertions of the huntsmen and the working of the dogs, when the Emperor is within the circle, engaged in the sport, and they are seen pursuing the stags, bears, and other animals, in every direction.

The two brothers are under an engagement to furnish the court daily, from the commencement of October to the end of March, with a thousand pieces of game, quails being excepted; and also with fish, of which as large a quantity as possible is to be supplied, estimating the fish that three men can eat at a meal as equivalent to one piece of game.

Chapter 20

OF THE GREAT KHAN'S PROCEEDING TO THE CHASE ❧ WITH HIS GERFALCONS AND HAWKS ❧ OF HIS TWELVE FALCONERS ❧ AND OF HIS TENTS

WHEN his Majesty has resided the usual time in the metropolis, and leaves it in the month of March, he proceeds in a north-easterly direction, to within two days' journey of the ocean, attended by full ten thousand falconers, who carry with them a vast number of gerfalcons, peregrine falcons, and sakers, as well as many vultures, in order to pursue the game along the banks of the river. It must be understood that he does not keep all this body of men together in one place, but divides them into several parties of one or two hundred or more, who follow the sport in various directions. The greater part of the quarry is brought to his Majesty. He has likewise with him ten thousand men of those who are termed Tascaol, implying that their business is to be upon the watch, and, who, for this purpose, are detached in small parties of two or three to stations not far distant from each other, in such a manner as to encompass a considerable tract of country. Each of them is provided with a whistle and a hood, by which they are enabled, when necessary, to call in and to secure the hawk. Upon the command being given for flying the hawks, those who let them loose are not under the necessity of following them, because the others, whose duty it is, look out so attentively that the birds cannot direct their flight to any quarter where they are not secured, or promptly assisted if there should be occasion.

Every bird belonging to his Majesty, or to any of his nobles, has a small silver label fastened to its leg, on which is engraved the name of the owner and also the name of *t*he keeper. In consequence of this precaution, as soon as the hawk is secured, it is immediately known to whom it belongs, and restored accordingly. If it happens that, although the name appears, the owner, not being personally known to the finder, cannot be ascertained in the first instance, the bird is, in that case, carried to an officer termed Bularguchi, whose title means that he is the "guardian of unclaimed property." If a horse, therefore, a sword, a bird, or any other article is found, and it does not appear to whom it belongs, the finder carries it directly to this officer, by whom it is received in charge and carefully preserved. If, on the other hand, a person finds any article that has been lost, and fails to carry it to the proper depositary, he is punished as a thief. Those by whom any property has been lost make their application to this officer, by whom it is restored to them. His situation is always in the most elevated part of the camp, and distinguished by a particular flag, in order that he may be the more readily found by such as have occasion to apply to him. The effect of this regulation is, that no articles are ultimately lost.

When his Majesty makes his progress in this manner, towards the shores of the ocean, many interesting occurrences attend the sport, and it may truly be said that it is unrivalled by any other amusement in the world. On account of the narrowness of the passes in some parts of the country where the Great Khan follows the chase, he is borne upon two elephants only, or sometimes a single one, being more convenient than a greater number. Under other circumstances he makes use of four, upon the backs of which is placed a pavilion of wood, handsomely carved, the inside being lined with cloth of gold, and the outside covered with the skins of lions, a mode of conveyance which is

THE HUNT

rendered necessary to him during his hunting excursions, in consequence of the gout, with which he is troubled.

In the pavilion he always carries with him twelve of his best gerfalcons, with twelve officers, from amongst his favourites, to bear him company and amuse him. Those who are on horseback by his side give him notice of the approach of cranes or other birds, upon which he raises the curtain of the pavilion, and when he espies the game, gives direction for letting fly the gerfalcons, which seize the cranes and overpower them after a long struggle. The view of this sport, as he lies upon his couch, affords extreme satisfaction to his Majesty, as well as to the officers who attend him, and to the horsemen by whom he is surrounded. After having thus enjoyed the amusement for some hours, he repairs to a place named Cachar Modun, where are pitched the pavilions and tents of his Sons, and also of his Barons, his Ladies and the falconers; exceeding ten thousand in number, and making a handsome appearance. The tent of his Majesty, in which he gives his audiences, is so long and wide that under it ten thousand soldiers might be drawn up, leaving room for the superior officers and other persons of rank. Its entrance faces the south, and on the eastern side it has another tent connected with it, forming a capacious saloon. This tent the Emperor usually occupies, with a few of his nobility, and when he thinks proper to speak to any other persons, they are introduced to him in this apartment. In the rear of this there is a large and handsome chamber, where he sleeps; and there are many other tents and apartments, for the different branches of the household, but which are not immediately connected with the great tent.

These halls and chambers are all constructed and fitted up in the following manner. Each of them is supported by three pillars of wood, richly carved and gilt. The tents are covered on the outside with the skins of lions, streaked white, black, and red, and so well joined together that neither wind nor rain can penetrate. Withinside they are lined with the skins of ermines and sables, which are the most costly of all furs; for the latter, if of a size to trim a dress, is valued at two thousand bezants of gold, provided it be perfect; but if otherwise, only one thousand. It is esteemed by Tartars the queen of furs. The animal, which in their language is named *rondes*, is about the size of a marten. With these two kinds of skin, the halls as well as the sleeping-rooms are handsomely fitted up in compartments, arranged with much taste and skill. The tent-ropes, or cords by which they stretch the tents, are all of silk.

Near to the grand tent of his Majesty are situated those of his ladies, also very handsome and splendid. They have in like manner their gerfalcons, their hawks, and other birds and beasts, with which they partake in the amusement. The number of persons collected in these encampments is quite incredible, and a spectator might conceive himself to be in the midst of a populous city, so great is the assemblage from every part of the empire. The Great Khan is attended on the occasion by the whole of his family and household; that is to say, his physicians, astronomers, falconers, and every other description of officer.

In these parts of the country he remains until the spring, during which period he never ceases to frequent the lakes and rivers, where he takes storks, swans, herons, and a variety of other birds. His people also being detached to several different places, procure for him a large quantity of game. In this manner, during the season of his diversion, he enjoys himself to a degree that no person who is not an eyewitness can conceive; the excellence and the extent of the sport being greater than it is possible to express.

It is strictly forbidden to every tradesman, mechanic, or husbandman throughout his Majesty's dominions, to keep a vulture, hawk, or any other bird used for the pursuit of game, or any sporting dog; nor is a nobleman or cavalier to presume to chase beast or bird in the neighbourhood of the place where his Majesty takes up his residence, the distance being limited to five miles, for example, on one side, ten on another, and perhaps fifteen in a third direction, unless his name be inscribed in a list kept by the grand falconer, or he has a special privilege to that effect. Beyond those limits it is permitted. There is an order, however, which prohibits every person throughout all the countries subject to the Great Khan, from daring to kill hares, roebucks, fallow deer, stags, or other animals of that kind, or any large birds, between the months of March and October. This is that they may increase and multiply; and as the breach of this order is attended with punishment, game of every description increases prodigiously.

When the usual time is elapsed, his Majesty returns to the capital by the road he went; continuing his sport during the whole of the journey.

Chapter 21

THE WAY THE YEAR OF THE GREAT KHAN IS DIVIDED

Upon the return of the Great Khan to his capital, he holds a grand and splendid court, which lasts three days, in the course of which he gives feasts and otherwise entertains those by whom he is surrounded. The amusements of these three days are indeed admirable. He then quits his palace and proceeds to that city which he has built, as I told you before, and which is called Shangtu, where he has that grand park and palace of cane, and where he keeps his gerfalcons.

To escape the heat he spends his summer there, for the location is a cool one. Here he remains from May until the end of August when he returns again to his capital and remains until February when he keeps the grand feast of the New Year.

The grand hunting expedition towards the sea takes place in the months of March, April and May. So thus the whole year is spent; six months at the capital, three months in hunting, and three months at the Cane Palace to avoid the heat. It is in this manner that he passes his time with the greatest enjoyment; not to speak of the many little journeys in this or that direction at his own pleasure.

Chapter 22

CONCERNING THE CITY OF KANBALU ❧ OF THE MULTITUDE OF ITS INHABITANTS ❧ AND OF THE COMMERCE OF THE PLACE

THE multitude of inhabitants, and the number of houses in the city of Kanbalu, as also in the suburbs without the city of which there are twelve, corresponding to the twelve gates, is greater than the mind can comprehend. The suburbs are even more populous than the city, and it is there that the merchants and others whose business leads them to the capital, take up their abode. Wherever, indeed, his Majesty holds his court, there these people flock from all quarters, in pursuit of their several objects.

In the suburbs there are also as handsome houses and stately buildings as in the city, with the exception only of the palace of the Great Khan. No corpse is suffered to be interred within the precincts of the city; and those of the Idolaters, with whom it is customary to burn their dead, are carried to the usual spot beyond the suburbs. There likewise all public executions take place. Women who live by prostituting themselves for money dare not, unless it be secretly, to exercise their profession in the city, but must confine themselves to the suburbs, where, as has already been stated, there reside above five-and-twenty thousand; nor is this number greater than is necessary for the vast concourse of merchants and other strangers, who, drawn there by the court, are continually arriving and departing.

To this city everything that is most rare and valuable in all parts of the world finds its way; and more especially does this apply to India, which furnishes precious stones, pearls, and various drugs and spices. From the provinces of Cathay itself, as well as from the other provinces of the Empire, whatever there is of value is brought here, to supply the demands of those multitudes who are induced to establish their residence in the vicinity of the court. The quantity of merchandise sold exceeds also the traffic of any other place; for no fewer than a thousand carriages and pack-horses, loaded with raw silk, make their daily entry; and gold tissues and silks of various kinds are manufactured to an immense extent.

In the vicinity of the capital are many walled and other towns, whose inhabitants live chiefly by the court, selling the articles which they produce in return for such as their own occasions require.

Chapter 23

THE OPPRESSIONS OF ACHMATH THE BAILO ✚ AND OF THE PLOT THAT WAS FORMED AGAINST HIM

You will hear further on about twelve persons appointed who have authority to dispose of lands, offices, and everything else at their discretion. Now one of these was a certain Saracen named Achmath, a shrewd and able man, who had more power and influence with the Great Khan than any of the others; and the Khan held him in such regard that he could do what he pleased. The fact was, as came out after his death, that Achmath had so wrought upon the Khan with his sorcery, that the latter had the greatest faith and reliance on everything he said, and in this way did everything that Achmath wished him to do.

This person disposed of all governments and offices, and passed sentence on all malefactors; and whenever he desired to have any one whom he hated put to death, whether with justice or without it, he would go to the Emperor and say: "Such an one deserves death, for he hath done this or that against your imperial dignity." Then the Lord would say: "Do as you think right," and so he would have the man forthwith executed.

Thus when people saw how unbounded were his powers, and how unbounded the reliance placed by the Emperor on everything he said, they did not venture to oppose him in anything. No one was so high in rank or power as to be free from the dread of him. If any one was accused by him to the Emperor of a capital offence, and desired to defend himself, he was unable to bring proofs in his own defence, for no one would stand by him, as no one dared to oppose Achmath. And thus the latter caused many to perish unjustly.

Moreover, there was no beautiful woman whom he might desire, but he got hold of her; if she were unmarried, forcing her to be his wife, if otherwise, compelling her to consent to his desires. Whenever he knew of any one who had a pretty daughter, certain ruffians of his would go to the father, and say: "What say you? Here is this pretty daughter of yours; give her in marriage to the Bailo

Achmath and we will arrange for his giving you such a government or such an office for three years." And so the man would surrender his daughter. And Achmath would go to the Emperor, and say: "Such a government is vacant, or will be vacant on such a day. So-and-So is a proper man for the post." And the Emperor would reply: "Do as you think best"; and the father of the girl was immediately appointed to the government. Thus either through the ambition of the parents, or through fear of the Minister, all the beautiful women were at his beck, either as wives or mistresses. Also he had some five-and-twenty sons who held offices of importance, and some of these, under the protection of their father's name, committed scandals like his own, and many other abominable iniquities. This Achmath also had amassed great treasure, for everybody who wanted office sent him a heavy bribe.

In such authority did this man continue for two-and-twenty years. At last the people of the country, to wit the Cathaians, utterly wearied with the endless outrages and abominable iniquities which he perpetrated against them, whether as regarded their wives or their own persons, conspired to slay him and revolt against the government. Amongst the rest there was a certain Cathaian named Chenchu, a commander of a thousand, whose mother, daughter, and wife had all been dishonoured by Achmath. Now this man, full of bitter resentment, entered into parley regarding the destruction of the Minister with another Cathaian whose name was Vanchu, who was a commander of ten thousand. They came to the conclusion that the time to do the business would be during the Great Khan's absence from Kanbalu. For after stopping there three months he used to go to Shangtu and stop there three months; and at the same time his son Chinkin used to go away to his usual haunts, and this Achmath remained in charge of the city; sending to obtain the Khan's orders from Shangtu when any emergency arose.

So Vanchu and Chenchu, having come to this conclusion, proceeded to communicate it to the chief people among the Cathaians, and then by common consent sent word to their friends in many other cities that they had determined on such a day, at the signal given by a beacon, to massacre all the men with beards, and that the other cities should stand ready to do the like on seeing the signal fires.

The reason why they spoke of massacring the bearded men was that the Cathaians naturally have no beard, whilst beards are worn by the Tartars, Saracens, and Christians. And you should know that all the Cathaians detested the Great Khan's rule because he set over them governors who were Tartars, or still more frequently Saracens, and these they could not endure, for they were treated by them just like slaves. You see the Great Khan had not succeeded to the dominion of Cathay by hereditary right, but held it by conquest; and thus having no confidence in the natives, he put all authority into the hands of Tartars, Saracens, or Christians who were attached to his household and devoted to his service, and were foreigners in Cathay.

Wherefore, on the day appointed, the aforesaid Vanchu and Chenchu having entered the palace at night, Vanchu sat down and caused a number of lights to be kindled before him. He then sent a messenger to Achmath the Bailo, who lived in the Old City, as if to summon him to the presence of Chinkin, the Great Khan's son, who it was pretended had arrived unexpectedly. When Achmath heard this he was much surprised, but made haste to go, for he feared the Prince greatly. When he arrived at the gate, he met a Tartar called Cogatai, who was Captain of the twelve thousand that formed the standing garrison of the City; and the latter asked him whither he was bound so late? "To Chinkin, who is just arrived." Quoth Cogatai, "How can that be? How could he come so privily that I know nought of it?" So he followed the Minister with a certain number of his soldiers. Now the notion of the Cathaians was that, if they could make an end of Achmath, they would have nought else to be afraid of. So as soon as Achmath got inside the palace, and saw all the illumination, he bowed down before Vanchu, supposing him to be Chinkin, and Chenchu who was standing ready with a sword straightway cut his head off.

As soon as Cogatai, the Tartar Captain, who had halted at the entrance, beheld this, he shouted "Treason!" and instantly discharged an arrow at Vanchu and shot him dead as he sat. At the same time he called his people to seize Chenchu, and sent a proclamation through the city that any one found in the streets would be instantly put to death. The Cathaians saw that the Tartars had discovered the plot, and that they had no longer any leader, since Vanchu was killed and Chenchu taken. So they kept still in their houses, and were unable to pass the signal for the rising of the other cities as had been settled.

Cogatai immediately dispatched messengers to the Great Khan giving an orderly report of the whole affair, and the Khan sent back orders for him to make a careful investigation, and to punish the guilty as their misdeeds deserved. In the morning Cogatai examined the Cathaians, and put to death a number whom he found to be ringleaders in the plot. The same thing was done in the other cities, when it was found that the plot extended to them also.*

---

* This chapter is not contained in the French manuscript but is found in an early Italian version probably taken from a Latin manuscript and known as the Ramusio text.

After the Great Khan had returned to Kanbalu he was very anxious to discover what had led to this affair and then he learned all about the endless iniquities of that accursed Achmath and his sons. It was proved that he and seven of his sons had forced no end of women to be their wives, besides those whom they had ravished. The Great Khan then ordered all the treasure that Achmath had accumulated in the Old City to be transferred to his own treasury in the New City, and it was found to be of enormous amount. He also ordered the body of Achmath to be dug up and cast into the streets for the dogs to tear; and commanded those of his sons who had followed the father's evil example to be flayed alive.*

These circumstances called the Khan's attention to the accursed doctrines of the Sect of the Saracens, which excuse every crime, yea, even murder itself, when committed on such as are not of their religion. And seeing that this doctrine had led the accursed Achmath and his sons to act as they did without any sense of guilt, the Khan was led to entertain the greatest disgust and abomination for it. So he summoned the Saracens and prohibited their doing many things which their religion enjoined. Thus, he ordered them to regulate their marriages by the Tartar Law, and prohibited their cutting the throats of animals killed for food, ordering them to rip the stomach in the Tartar way.

Now when all this happened Messer Marco was on the spot.

---

* This story is in strict accordance with the account found in Chinese Annals; but more than this, for the Chinese records speak of Marco Polo in high praise of his courageous frankness. "The Emperor having returned from Chaghan-No: to Shangtu. desired Polo, Assessor of the Privy Council, to explain the reasons which had led Wangchu to commit this murder. Polo spoke with boldness of the crimes and oppressions of Achmath, which had rendered him an object of detestation throughout the Empire. The Emperor's eyes were opened, and he praised the courage of Wangchu."

Chapter 24

OF THE KIND OF PAPER MONEY ISSUED BY THE GREAT KHAN AND MADE TO PASS CURRENT THROUGHOUT HIS DOMINIONS

In this city of Kanbalu is the mint of the Great Khan, who may truly be said to possess the secret of the alchemists, as he has the art of producing money by the following process.

He causes the bark to be stripped from those mulberry-trees the leaves of which are used for feeding silk-worms, and takes from it that thin inner rind which lies between the coarser bark and the wood of the tree. This being steeped, and afterwards pounded in a mortar, until reduced to a pulp, is made into paper, resembling, in substance, that which is manufactured from cotton, but quite black. When ready for use, he has it cut into pieces of money of different sizes, nearly square, but somewhat longer than they are wide. Of these, the smallest pass for a half tournois; the next size for a Venetian silver groat; others for two, five, and ten groats; others for one, two, three, and as far as ten bezants of gold. The coinage of this paper money is authenticated with as much form and ceremony as if it were actually of pure gold or silver; for to each note a number of officers, specially appointed, not only subscribe their names, but affix their seals also. When this has been regularly done by the whole of them, the principal officer, appointed by his Majesty, having dipped into vermilion the royal seal committed to his custody, stamps with it the piece of paper, so that the form of the seal tinged with the vermilion remains impressed upon it. In this way it receives full authenticity as current money, and the act of counterfeiting it is punished as a capital offence.

When thus coined in large quantities, this paper currency is circulated in every part of the Great Khan's dominions; nor dares any person, at the peril of his life, refuse to accept it in payment. All his subjects receive it without hesitation, because, wherever their business may call them, they can dispose of it again in the purchase of merchandise they may require; such as pearls, jewels, gold, or silver. With it, in short, every article may be procured.*

Several times in the course of the year, large caravans of merchants arrive with such articles as have just been mentioned, together with gold tissues, which they lay before the Great Khan. He thereupon calls together twelve experienced and skilful persons, selected for this purpose, whom he commands to examine the articles with great care, and to fix the value at which they should be purchased. Upon the sum at which they have been thus conscientiously appraised he allows a reasonable profit, and immediately pays for them with this paper. To this the owners can have no objection, because, as has been observed, it answers the purpose of their own disbursements; and even though they should be inhabitants of a country where this kind of money is not current, they invest the amount in other articles of merchandise suited to their own markets.

When any persons happen to be possessed of paper money which from long use has become damaged, they carry it to the mint, where, upon the payment of only three per cent, they receive fresh notes in exchange. Should any be desirous of procuring gold or silver for the purposes of manufacture, such as of drinking-cups, girdles, or other articles wrought of these metals, they in like manner

* "Early in the ninth century, bills of exchange came into use; and from the middle of the twelfth century paper money became quite common, and is still in general use all over China, notes being issued in some places for amounts less even than a shilling." Giles, *The Civilization of China.*

apply to the mint, and for their paper obtain the bullion they require.

All his Majesty's armies are paid with this currency, which is to them of the same value as if it were gold or silver. Upon these grounds, it may certainly be affirmed that the Great Khan has a more extensive command of treasure than any other sovereign in the universe.

Chapter 25

OF THE COUNCIL OF TWELVE BARONS APPOINTED FOR THE AFFAIRS OF THE ARMY ◄ AND OF THE TWELVE OTHERS FOR THE GENERAL CONCERNS OF THE EMPIRE

THE Great Khan selects twelve noblemen of high rank and consequence whose duty it is to decide upon every point respecting the army. This includes the removal of troops from one station to another; the change of officers commanding them; the employment of a force where it may be judged necessary; and the numbers which it may be proper to detach upon any particular service, according to the degree of its importance. Besides these objects, it is their business to distinguish between officers who have given proofs of valour in combat, and those who have shown themselves base and cowardly, in order to advance the former and to degrade the latter. Thus, if the commander of a thousand has been found to conduct himself in an unbecoming manner, this tribunal, considering him to be unworthy of the rank he held, reduce him to the command of an hundred men; or, on the contrary, if he has displayed such qualities as give claim to promotion, they appoint him commander of ten thousand. All this, however, is done with the knowledge and subject to the approval of his Majesty, to whom they report their opinion of the officer's merit or demerit, and who, upon confirming their decision, grants to him who is

promoted to the command of ten thousand men the tablet
or warrant belonging to his rank, as before described. He
also confers on him large presents, in order to excite others
to merit the same rewards. The tribunal composed of
these twelve nobles is named Thai, denoting a supreme
court, as being responsible to no other than the sovereign.

Besides this, there is another tribunal, likewise of twelve
nobles, appointed for the superintendence of everything
that respects the government of the thirty-four provinces
of the Empire. These have in Kanbalu a large and handsome palace or court, containing many chambers and halls.
For the business of each province there is a presiding law-
officer, together with several clerks, who have their respective apartments in the court, and there transact whatever
business is necessary to be done for the province to which
they belong, according to the directions they receive from the
tribunal of twelve. These have authority to make choice of
persons for the governments of the several provinces, whose
names are presented to the Great Khan for confirmation
of their appointments and delivery of the tablets of gold
or of silver appropriated to their ranks. They have also
the superintendence of every matter that regards the collection of the revenue, both from land and customs, together with its disposal, and have the control of every other
department of the state; with the exception only of what
relates to the army. This tribunal is named Sing, implying
that it is a second high court, and, like the other, responsible only to the Great Khan. But the former tribunal,
named Thai, which has the administration of military affairs,
is regarded as superior in rank and dignity to the latter.

Chapter 26

OF THE PLACES ESTABLISHED ON ALL THE GREAT ROADS FOR SUPPLYING POST-HORSES ❦ OF THE COURIERS ON FOOT ❦ AND OF THE MODE IN WHICH THE EXPENSE IS DEFRAYED

FROM the city of Kanbalu there are many roads leading to the different provinces, and upon each of these, that is to say, upon every great high road, at the distance of twenty-five or thirty miles, accordingly as the towns happen to be situated, there are stations, with houses of accommodation for travellers. These are called *yamb* or post-houses. They are large and handsome buildings, having several well-furnished apartments, hung with silk, and provided with everything suitable to persons of rank. Even kings may be lodged at these stations in a becoming manner, as every article required may be obtained from the towns and strong places in the vicinity; and for some of them the court makes regular provision.

At each station four hundred good horses are kept in constant readiness, in order that all messengers going and coming upon the business of the Great Khan, and all ambassadors, may have relays, and, leaving their jaded horses, be supplied with fresh ones. Even in mountainous districts, remote from the great roads, where there were no villages, and the towns are far distant from each other, his Majesty has equally caused buildings of the same kind to be erected, furnished with everything necessary, and provided with the usual supply of horses.

He sends people to dwell upon the spot, in order to cultivate the land, and attend to the service of the post; by which means large villages are formed. In consequence of these regulations, ambassadors to the court, and the royal messengers, go and return through every province and kingdom of the Empire with the greatest convenience and facility. In the management of all this the Great Khan exhibits a superiority over every other emperor, king, or human being.

In his dominions no fewer than two hundred thousand horses are thus employed in the department of the post, and ten thousand buildings, with suitable furniture, are kept up. It is indeed so wonderful a system, and so effective in its operation, as it is scarcely possible to describe. If it be questioned how the population of the country can supply sufficient numbers of these duties, and by what means they can be supported, we may answer, that all the Idolaters, and likewise the Saracens, keep six, eight, or ten women, according to their circumstances, by whom they have a prodigious number of children. Some of them have as many as thirty sons capable of following their fathers in arms; whereas with us a man has only one wife, and even although she should prove barren, he is obliged to pass his life with her, and is by that means deprived of the chance of raising a family. Hence it is that our population is so much inferior to theirs.

With regard to food, there is no deficiency of it, for these people, especially the Tartars, Cathaians, and inhabitants of the province of Manji in Southern China, subsist, for the most part, upon rice, panicum, and millet; which three grains yield, in their soil, an hundred measures for one. Wheat, indeed, does not yield a similar increase, and bread not being in use with them, it is eaten only in the form of vermicelli or of pastry. The former grains they boil in milk or stew with their meat. With them no spot of earth is suffered to lie idle, that can possibly be cultivated; and their cattle of different kinds multiply exceedingly, insomuch that when they take the field, there is scarcely an individual that does not carry with him six, eight, or more horses, for his own personal use. From all this may be seen the causes of so large a population, and the circumstances that enable them to provide so abundantly for their subsistence.

In the space between the post-houses, there are small villages settled at the distance of every three miles, which may contain about forty cottages. In these are stationed the foot messengers, likewise employed in the service of his Majesty. They wear girdles round their waists, to which several small bells are attached, in order that their coming may be perceived at a distance; and as they run only three miles, that is, from one of these foot-stations to another next adjoining, the noise serves to give notice of their approach, and preparation is accordingly made by a fresh courier to proceed with the packet instantly upon the arrival of the former. Thus it is so expeditiously conveyed from station to station, that in the course of two days and two nights his Majesty receives distant intelligence that in the ordinary mode could not be obtained in less than ten days. It often happens that in the fruit season, what is gathered in the morning at Kanbalu is conveyed to the Great Khan, at Shangtu, by the evening of the following day; although the distance is generally considered as ten days' journey.

At each of these three-mile stations there is a clerk, whose business it is to note the day and time at which the one courier arrives and the other departs; which is likewise done at all the post-houses. Besides this, officers are directed to pay monthly visits to every station, in order to examine into the management of them, and to punish those couriers who have neglected to use proper diligence. All these couriers are not only exempt from tax, but also receive from his Majesty good allowances.

The horses employed in this service are not attended with any direct expense; the cities, towns, and villages in the neighbourhood being obliged to furnish, and also to maintain them. By his Majesty's command the governors of the cities cause examination to be made by well informed persons, as to the number of horses the inhabitants, individually, are capable of supplying. The same is done with respect to the towns and villages; and according to their means the requisition is enforced; those on each side of the station contributing their due proportion. The charge of the maintenance of the horses is afterwards deducted by the cities out of the revenue payable to the Great Khan.

It must be understood, however, that of the four hundred horses the whole are not constantly on service at the station, but only two hundred, which are kept there for the space of a month. During this period the other half are at pasture; and at the beginning of the month, these in their turn take the duty, whilst the former have time to recover their flesh; each alternately relieving the other.

Where it happens that there is a river or a lake which the couriers on foot, or the horsemen, are under the necessity of passing, the neighbouring cities are obliged to keep three or four boats in continual readiness for that purpose; and where there is a desert of several days' journey, that does not admit of any habitation, the city on its borders is obliged to furnish horses to such persons as ambassadors to and from the court, that they may be enabled to pass the desert, and also to supply provisions to them and their suite. But cities so situated have a remuneration from his Majesty. Where the post stations lie at a distance from the great road, the horses are partly those of his Majesty, and are only in part furnished by the cities and towns of the district.

When it is necessary that the messengers should proceed with extraordinary dispatch, as in the cases of giving information of disturbance in any part of the country, the rebellion of a chief, or other important matter, they ride two hundred, or sometimes two hundred and fifty miles in the course of a day. On such occasions they carry with them the tablet of the gerfalcon as a signal of the urgency of their business and the necessity for dispatch. And when there are two messengers, they take their departure together from the same place, mounted upon good fleet horses; and they gird their bodies tight, bind a cloth round their heads, and push their horses to the greatest speed. They continue thus till they come to the next post-house, at twenty-five miles distant, where they find two other horses, fresh and in a state for work; they spring upon them without taking any repose, and changing in the same manner at every stage, until the day closes, they perform a journey of two hundred and fifty miles.

In cases of great emergency they continue their course during the night, and if there should be no moon, they are accompanied to the next station by persons on foot, who run before them with lights; when of course they do not make the same speed as in the day-time, the light-bearers not being able to exceed a certain pace. Messengers qualified to undergo this extraordinary degree of fatigue are held in high estimation.

Now we will leave this subject, and I will tell you of a great act of benevolence which the Great Khan performs twice every year.

Chapter 27

OF THE RELIEF AFFORDED BY THE EMPEROR TO ALL THE PROVINCES OF HIS EMPIRE ❦ IN TIMES OF DEARTH OR MORTALITY OF CATTLE

THE Great Khan sends every year his commissioners to ascertain whether any of his subjects have suffered in their crops from unfavourable weather, from storms of wind or violent rains, or by locusts, worms, or any other plague; and in such cases he not only refrains from exacting the usual tribute of that year, but furnishes them from his granaries with so much corn as is necessary for their subsistence, as well as for sowing their land.

With this view, in times of great plenty, he causes large purchases to be made of such kinds of grain as are most serviceable to them, which is stored in granaries provided for the purpose in the several provinces, and managed with such care as to ensure its keeping for three or four years without damage. It is his command, that these granaries be always kept full, in order to provide against times of scarcity; and when, in such seasons, he disposes of the grain for money, he requires for four measures no more than the purchaser would pay for one measure in the market. In like manner where there has been a mortality of cattle in any district, he makes good the loss to the sufferers from those belonging to himself, which he has received as his tenth of produce in other provinces. All his thoughts, indeed, are directed to the important object of assisting the people whom he governs, that they may be enabled to live by their labour and improve their substance. We must not omit to notice a peculiarity of the Great Khan, that where an accident has happened by lightning to any herd of cattle, flock of sheep, or other domestic animals, whether the

AN AGRICULTURAL COMMISSIONER

property of one or more persons, and however large the
herd may be, he does not demand the tenth of the increase
of such cattle during three years; and so also if a ship
laden with merchandise has been struck by lightning, he
does not collect from her any custom or share of her cargo,
considering the accident as an ill omen. God, he says, has
shown himself to be displeased with the owner of the
goods, and he is unwilling that property bearing the mark
of divine wrath should enter his treasury.

Chapter 28

OF THE TREES HE CAUSES TO BE PLANTED AT THE SIDES OF THE ROADS ◄ AND OF THE ORDER IN WHICH THEY ARE KEPT

THERE is another regulation adopted by the Great Khan,
equally ornamental and useful.   At both sides of the public
roads he causes trees to be planted, of a kind that become
large and tall, and being only two paces asunder, they serve
—besides the advantage of their shade in summer—to point
out the road—when the ground is covered with snow.
And this is of great assistance and affords much comfort
to travellers.   This is done along all the high roads, where
the nature of the soil allows; but when the road lies through
sandy deserts or over rocky mountains, where it is impossible to have trees, he orders stones to be placed and columns
to be erected, as marks for guidance.

He also appoints officers of rank, whose duty it is to see
that all these are properly arranged and the roads constantly
kept in good order.   Besides the motives that have been
mentioned it may be added that the Great Khan is the more
disposed to plant trees because astrologers tell him that
those who plant trees are rewarded with long life.

Chapter 29

OF THE KIND OF WINE MADE IN THE PROVINCE OF CATHAY

THE greater part of the inhabitants of the province of Cathay drink a sort of wine made from rice mixed with a variety of spices and drugs. This beverage, or wine as it may be termed, is so good and well flavoured that they do not wish for better. It is clear, bright, and pleasant to taste, and being taken very hot, has the quality of making one drunk sooner than any other wine.

Chapter 30

CONCERNING THE BLACK STONES DUG IN CATHAY USED FOR FUEL

THROUGHOUT this province there is found a sort of black stone, which they dig out of the mountains, where it runs in veins. When lighted, it burns like charcoal, and retains the fire much better than wood; insomuch that it may be preserved during the night, and in the morning be found still burning. These stones do not flame, excepting a little when first lighted, but during their ignition give out a considerable heat.*

It is true there is no scarcity of wood in the country, but the multitude of inhabitants is so immense, and their stoves and baths, which they are continually heating, so numerous, that the quantity could not supply the demand. There is no person who does not frequent a warm bath at least three times in the week, and during the winter daily, if it is in their power. Every man of rank or wealth has one in his house for his own use; and the stock of wood must soon

---

* The first mention of coal in Chinese literature is by Liu An who died B. C. 122. He called it "ice-charcoal."

prove inadequate to such consumption; whereas these stones may be had in the greatest abundance, and at a cheap rate.

Chapter 31

OF THE GREAT AND ADMIRABLE LIBERALITY EXERCISED BY THE GREAT KHAN TOWARDS THE POOR

It has been already stated that the Emperor distributes large quantities of grain to his subjects. We shall now speak of his great charity to and provident care of the poor in the city of Kanbalu. Upon his being informed of any respectable family, that had once lived in easy circumstances and by misfortunes reduced to poverty, or who, in consequence of infirmities, are unable to work for their living or to raise·a supply of any kind of grain: to a family in that situation he gives what is necessary for their year's consumption. At the customary period they present themselves before the officers who manage this department of his Majesty's expenses and who reside in a palace where that business is transacted. Here they deliver a statement in writing of the quantity furnished to them in the preceding year, according to which they receive also for the present.

In a similar way the Emperor provides clothing for his poor, which he has the means of doing from his tenths of wool, silk, and hemp. These materials he has woven into the different sorts of cloth, in a house erected for that purpose, where every artisan is obliged to work one day in the week for his Majesty's service. Garments made of stuffs thus manufactured he orders to be given to the poor families above described, as they are needed for their winter and their summer dresses. He also has clothing prepared for his armies, and in every city has a quantity of woollen cloth woven, which is paid for from the amount of the tenths levied at the place.

Chapter 32

OF THE MANY PERSONS WHO APPLY FOR RELIEF AT THE EMPEROR'S COURT

It should be known that the Tartars, when they followed their original customs, and had not yet adopted the religion of the idolaters, were not in the practice of bestowing alms, and when a poor man applied to them, they drove him away saying, "Begone with your complaint of a bad season which God has sent you; had He loved you, as He loves me, He would have provided for you."

But since the wise men of the idolaters, and especially the Bacsis, already mentioned, have represented to his Majesty that providing for the poor is a good work and highly acceptable to their deities, he has relieved their wants in the manner stated, and at his court none are denied food who come to ask it. Not a day passes in which there are not distributed, by the regular officers, twenty thousand vessels of rice, millet, and panicum. By reason of this admirable and astonishing liberality which the Great Khan exercises towards the poor, the people all adore him.

Chapter 33

OF THE ASTROLOGERS OF THE CITY OF KANBALU

There are in the city of Kanbalu, amongst Christians, Saracens, and Cathaians, about five thousand astrologers and soothsayers, for whose food and clothing the Emperor provides in the same manner as he does for the poor families above mentioned, and who are in the constant exercise of their art.

They have their astrolabes, upon which are described the planetary signs, the hours and their several aspects for the

THE OBSERVATORY OF PEKING

whole year. The astrologers of each distinct sect annually proceed to the examination of their respective tables, in order to ascertain the course of the heavenly bodies, and their relative positions.* They discover therein what the state of the weather shall be, from the paths of the planets in the different signs, and from this foretell the peculiar phenomena of each month. For instance, they predict that there shall be thunder and storms in a certain month, earthquakes; in another, strokes of lightning and violent rains; in another, diseases, mortality, wars, discords, conspiracies.

As they find the matter in their astrolabes, so they declare it will come to pass; adding, however, that God, according to his good pleasure, may do more or less than they have set down. They write their predictions for the year upon certain small squares, which are called *Tacuin,* and these they sell, for a groat apiece, to all persons who are desirous of peeping into the future. Those whose predictions are found to be the more generally correct are esteemed the most perfect masters of their art, and are consequently the most honoured.

When any person forms the design of executing some great work, of performing a distant journey in the way of commerce, or of commencing any other undertaking, and is desirous of knowing what success may be likely to attend it, he has recourse to one of these astrologers, and, informing him that he is about to proceed on such an expedition, inquires in what disposition the heavens appear to be at the time. The latter thereupon tells him, that before he can answer, it is necessary he should be informed of the year,

---

* By mistake two of the beautiful bronze astronomical instruments made for Kublai Khan were taken to Berlin after the Boxer Rebellion (1901). "I understand they have been restored in accordance with one of the provisions of the Treaty of Versailles. If so, this was probably the most important benefit which that treaty secured to the world." Bertrand Russell in *The Problem of China.*

the month, and the hour in which he was born; and that, having learned these particulars, he will then proceed to ascertain in what respect his horoscope corresponds with the aspect of the celestial bodies at the time of making the inquiry. Upon this comparison he grounds his prediction of the favourable or unfavourable termination of the adventure.

It should be observed that the Tartars compute their time by a cycle of twelve years; to the first of which they give the name of the Lion; to the second year, that of the Ox; to the third, the Dragon; to the fourth, the Dog; and so of the rest, until the whole of the twelve have elapsed.* When a person, therefore, is asked in what year he was born, he replies, In the course of the year of the Lion, upon such a day, at such an hour and minute; all of which has been carefully noted by his parents in a book. Upon the completion of the twelve years of the cycle, they return to the first, and continually repeat the same series.

Chapter 34

OF THE RELIGION OF THE TARTARS ❦ OF THE OPINIONS THEY HOLD AS TO THE SOUL ❦ AND OF SOME OF THEIR CUSTOMS

As has already been observed, these people are idolaters, and for deities, each person has a tablet fixed up against a high part of the wall of his chamber, upon which is written a name, that serves to denote the high, celestial, and sublime God. To this they pay daily adoration, with incense burning. Lifting up their hands and then striking their faces against the floor three times, they implore from Him the blessings of sound intellect and health of body;

---

* This cycle runs as follows:—1, Rat; 2, Ox; 3, Tiger; 4, Hare; 5, Dragon; 6, Serpent; 7, Horse; 8, Sheep; 9, Ape; 10, Cock; 11, Dog; 12, Swine.

but of Him they ask nothing else.   Below this, on the floor, they have a statue which they name Natigay, which they consider as the God of all terrestrial things or whatever is produced from the earth.   They give him a wife and children, and worship him in a similar manner, burning incense, raising their hands, and bending to the floor.   To him they pray for seasonable weather, abundant crops, increase of family, and the like.

They believe the soul to be immortal, after this fashion. Immediately upon the death of a man, it enters into another body, and that accordingly as he has acted virtuously or wickedly during his life, his future state will become, progressively, better or worse.   If he be a poor man, and has conducted himself worthily and decently, he will be re-born, in the first instance, from the womb of a gentlewoman, and become, himself, a gentleman; next, from the womb of a lady of rank, and become a nobleman; thus continually ascending in the scale of existence until he be united to the divinity.   But if, on the contrary, being the son of a gentleman, he has behaved unworthily, he will, in his next state, be a clown, and at length a dog, continually descending and going down lower and lower.

Their style of conversation is courteous; they salute each other politely and with cheerful countenance, have an air of good breeding, and eat their food with particular cleanliness.   To their parents they show the utmost reverence. Should it happen that a child acts disrespectfully or neglects to assist his parents when necessary, there is a public tribunal, whose especial duty it is to punish with severity this crime of filial ingratitude.

Malefactors guilty of various crimes, who are apprehended and thrown into prison, are executed by strangling. But such as remain for three years, being the time appointed by his Majesty for a general prison release, and are then liberated, have a mark branded upon one of their cheeks, that they may be recognized.

The present Great Khan has prohibited all species of gambling and other modes of cheating, to which the people of this country are addicted more than any others upon earth. As an argument for deterring them from this practice, he said: "I subdued you by the power of my sword, and consequently whatever you possess belongs of right to me: if you gamble, therefore, you are sporting with my property." He does not, however, take anything arbitrarily in virtue of this right.

The order and regularity observed by all ranks of people, when they present themselves before his Majesty, ought not to pass unnoticed. When they approach within half a mile of the place where he happens to be, they show their respect for his exalted character by assuming a humble, placid, and quiet demeanour, insomuch that not the least noise, nor the voice of any person calling out, or even speaking aloud, is heard. Every man of rank carries with him a small vessel, into which he spits, so long as he continues in the hall of audience, no one daring to spit on the floor; and this being done, he replaces the cover, and makes a salutation. They are accustomed likewise to take with them handsome buskins made of white leather, and when they reach the court, but before they enter the hall they put on these white buskins, and give those in which they had walked to the care of the servants. This practice is observed that they may not soil the beautiful carpets, which are curiously wrought with silk and gold, and exhibit a variety of colours.

Chapter 35

OF THE INTERIOR OF CATHAY ❦ THE RIVER NAMED PULISANGAN ❦ AND OF THE BRIDGE OVER IT

HAVING thus completed the account of the government and police of the province of Cathay and city of Kanbalu, as well as of the magnificence of the Great Khan, we shall now proceed to speak of other parts of the Empire. You must know then that the Great Khan sent Marco as his ambassador to the west. Leaving Kanbalu, he travelled westward during full four months; we shall now tell you all he saw on his travels as he went and returned.

Upon leaving the capital and travelling ten miles, you come to a river named Pulisangan, which discharges itself into the ocean, and is navigated by many vessels entering from thence, with considerable quantities of merchandise. Over this river there is a very handsome bridge of stone, perhaps unequalled by any other in the world. Its length is three hundred paces, and its width eight paces; so that ten mounted men can, without inconvenience, ride abreast. It has twenty-four arches, supported by twenty-five piers erected in the water, all of serpentine stone, and built with great skill.

On each side, and from one extremity to the other, there is a handsome parapet, formed of marble slabs and pillars arranged in a masterly style. At the beginning of the ascent the bridge is something wider than at the summit, but from the part where the ascent terminates, the sides run in straight lines and parallel to each other. Upon the upper level there is a massive and lofty column, resting upon a tortoise of marble, and having near its base a large figure of a lion, with a lion also on the top. Towards the slope of the bridge there is another handsome column or pillar, with its lion, at the distance of a pace and a half from the former; and all the spaces between one pillar and another, throughout the whole length of the bridge, are filled up with slabs of marble, curiously sculptured, and mortised into the next adjoining pillars, forming altogether a beautiful spectacle. These parapets serve to prevent accidents that might otherwise happen to passengers.

Chapter 36

OF THE CITY OF GOUZA

AFTER having passed this bridge, proceeding thirty miles in a westerly direction, through a country abounding with fine buildings, amongst vineyards and cultivated and fertile land, you arrive at a handsome and large city, named Gouza [Cho-chau], where there are many convents of the idolaters.

The inhabitants in general live by commerce and manual arts. They have manufactures of gold tissues and the finest kind of gauze. The inns for accommodating travellers are there numerous.

At the distance of a mile beyond this place, the roads divide; one going in a westerly, and the other in a southeasterly direction, the westerly road through the province of Cathay, and the other towards the province of Manji. From the city of Gouza it is a journey of ten days through Cathay to the kingdom of Tainfu; in the course of which you pass many fine cities and strong places, in which manufactures and commerce flourish, and where you see many vineyards and much cultivated land. From hence grapes are carried into the interior of Cathay, where the vine does not grow. Mulberry-trees also abound, the leaves of which enable the inhabitants to produce large quantities of silk

THE BRIDGE OF PULISANGEN

A degree of civilization prevails amongst all the people of this country, in consequence of their frequent intercourse with the towns, which are numerous and not far from each other. To these the merchants continually resort, carrying their goods from one city to another, as the fairs are successively held at each.

Chapter 37

THE KINGDOM OF TAINFU

AT the end of five days' journey beyond the ten that have been mentioned, it is said there is another city unusually large and handsome named Ach-baluch, to which the limits of his Majesty's hunting grounds extend, and within which no persons dare to sport, excepting the Princes of his own family, and those whose names are inscribed on the grand falconer's list. Beyond these limits, all persons qualified by rank are at liberty to pursue game.

It happens, however, that the Great Khan scarcely ever takes the amusement of the chase on this side of the country; and the consequence is, that the wild animals, especially hares, multiply to such a degree as to occasion the destruction of all the growing corn of the province. When this came to the knowledge of the Great Khan, he repaired thither, with the whole of his court, and innumerable multitudes of these animals were taken.

A considerable trade is carried on here, and a variety of articles are manufactured, particularly arms and other military stores, which are at this place conveniently situated for the use of the Emperor's armies. Vineyards are numerous, from which grapes in vast abundance are gathered. Other fruits also grow here in plenty, as does the mulberry-tree, together with the worms that yield the silk.

Leaving Tainfu, and travelling westward, seven days' journey, through a fine country in which there are many cities and strong places, where commerce and manufactures prevail, and whose merchants, travelling over various parts of the country, obtain considerable profits, you reach a city named Painfu, which is of a large size and very important. It likewise contains numerous merchants and artisans. Silk is produced here also in great quantity. We shall not say anything further of these places, but proceed to speak of the distinguished city of Kachanfu; first noticing, however, a noble castle named Thaigin.

Chapter 38

OF THE CASTLE OF THAIGIN

In a western direction from Painfu there is a large and handsome fortress named Thaigin, which is said to have been built, at a remote period, by a king who was called the Golden King. Within the walls of the fort stands a spacious and highly-ornamented palace, the hall of which contains paintings of all the renowned Princes who, from ancient times, have reigned at this place, forming together a superb exhibition.

A remarkable circumstance in the history of this king shall now be related. He was a powerful Prince, and was always waited upon by young women of great beauty, a vast number of whom he entertained at his court. When, for recreation, he went about the palace, he was drawn in his carriage by these damsels, which they could do with ease, as it was of a small size. They were devoted to his service, and performed every service that added to his convenience or amusement. In his government he was not wanting in vigour, and he ruled with dignity and justice.

The castle, according to the report of the people of the country, held a very strong position. He was, however, a vassal of Prester John; but, influenced by pride, he rebelled against him. When this came to the knowledge of Prester John, he was exceedingly grieved, and because of the strong situation of the castle, it was impossible to attack it. Matters had remained some time in this state, when seventeen cavaliers belonging to his retinue presented themselves before him, and declared their resolution to attempt the seizure of the Golden King, and bring him alive to his Majesty. To this they were encouraged by the promise of a large reward.

They accordingly took their departure and went to the Golden King and presented themselves saying that they had come from a distant country, made him an offer of their services. In his employment they so ably and diligently performed their duties that they gained the esteem of their new master, who showed them distinguished favour.

One day when the king was engaged in the chase, and had crossed a river which separated him from the rest of his party, who remained on the opposite side, these cavaliers perceived that the opportunity now presented itself of executing their design. They drew their swords, surrounded the king, and led him away by force towards the territory of Prester John, without its being possible for him to receive assistance from his own people.

Chapter 39

HOW PRESTER JOHN TREATED HIS PRISONER THE GOLDEN KING

WHEN they reached the court of Prester John, he gave orders for clothing his prisoner in the meanest apparel, and, with the view of humiliating him by the indignity, ordered him to be put to look after cattle.

In this wretched condition he remained for two years, strict care being taken that he should not effect his escape. At the expiration of that period, Prester John caused him to be again brought before him, trembling from apprehension that they were going to put him to death. But on the contrary, Prester John, after warning him against suffering pride and arrogance, granted him a pardon, directed that he should be dressed in royal apparel, and sent him back to his principality with an honourable escort. From that time forward he always preserved his loyalty, and lived on friendly terms with Prester John. The foregoing is what was related to me on the subject of the Golden King.

Chapter 40

OF THE VERY LARGE AND NOBLE RIVER CALLED THE KARA-MORAN

Upon leaving the fortress of Thaigin, and travelling about twenty miles, you come to a river called the Karamoran [Yellow River], which is of such magnitude, both in respect to width and depth, that no solid bridge can be erected upon it. Its waters are discharged into the ocean. On its banks are many cities and castles, in which a number of trading people reside, who carry on an extensive commerce. The country bordering upon it produces ginger, and silk also in large quantities.

Of birds the multitude is incredible, especially of pheasants, which are sold at the rate of three for the value of a Venetian groat. Here likewise grows a species of large cane, in infinite abundance, some of a foot, and others a foot and a half in circumference, which are employed by the inhabitants for a variety of useful purposes.

Having crossed this river and travelled three days' journey, you arrive at a city named Ka-chan-fu, whose inhabitants are idolaters. They carry on a considerable traffic, and work at a variety of manufactures. The country produces in great abundance, silk, ginger, and many drugs that are nearly unknown in our part of the world. Here they weave gold tissues, as well as every other kind of silken cloth. We shall speak in the next place of the noble and celebrated city of Ken-zan-fu, in the kingdom of the same name.

Chapter 41

OF THE CITY OF KEN-ZAN-FU

DEPARTING from Ka-chan-fu, and proceeding eight days' journey in a westerly direction, you continually meet with cities and commercial towns, and pass many gardens and cultivated grounds, with abundance of the mulberry tree that contributes to the production of silk. The inhabitants in general worship idols, but there are also found here Nestorian Christians, Turkomans, and Saracens.

The wild beasts of the country afford excellent sport, and a variety of birds also are taken.

At the end of eight days you arrive at the city of Kenzan-fu, which was anciently the capital of an extensive, noble, and powerful kingdom, the seat of many kings, highly descended and distinguished in arms. At the present day it is governed by a son of the Great Khan, named Mangalu, upon whom his father has conferred the sovereignty.

It is a country of great commerce, and eminent for its manufactures. Raw silk is produced in large quantities, and

tissues of gold and every other kind of silk are woven
there.   At this place likewise they prepare every article
necessary for the equipment of an army.   All species of
provisions are in abundance, and to be procured at a moderate price.   The inhabitants in general worship idols, but
there are some Christians, Turkomans, and Saracens.

In a plain, about five miles from the city, stands a beautiful palace belonging to King Mangalu, embellished with
many fountains and rivulets, both within and on the outside of the buildings.   There is also a fine park, surrounded
by a high wall, with battlements, enclosing an extent of
five miles, where all kinds of wild animals, both beasts and
birds, are kept for sport.   In its centre is this spacious palace,
which, for symmetry and beauty, cannot be surpassed.   It
contains many marble halls and chambers, ornamented with
paintings and beaten gold and the finest azure.   Mangalu,
pursuing the footsteps of his father, governs his principality with strict equity, and is beloved by his people.   He
also takes much delight in hunting and hawking.

Chapter 42

OF THE BOUNDARIES OF CATHAY AND MANJI

TRAVELLING westward three days, from the residence of
Mangalu, you still find towns and castles, whose inhabitants
subsist by commerce and manufactures, and where there is
an abundance of silk.   At the end of these three days you
enter upon a region of mountains and valleys, which lie
within the province of Kun-kin.

This tract, however, has no want of inhabitants, who
are worshippers of idols, and cultivate the earth.   They
live also by the chase, the land being much covered with
woods.   In these are found many wild beasts, such as tigers,

bears, lynxes, fallow deer, antelopes, stags, and many other animals, which are made to turn to good account. This region extends to the distance of twenty days' journey, during which the way lies entirely over mountains and through valleys and woods, but containing towns where travellers may find convenient accommodation.

Chapter 43

CONCERNING THE PROVINCE OF MANJI

THIS journey of twenty days towards the west being performed, you arrive at a place called Ach-baluch Manji, which signifies, the white city on the confines of Manji, where the country becomes level, and is very populous. The inhabitants live by trade and manual arts. Large quantities of ginger are produced here, which is conveyed through all the province of Cathay, with great profit to the merchants. The country yields wheat, rice, and other grain plentifully, and at a reasonable rate.

This plain, thickly covered with habitations, continues for two stages, after which you again come to high mountains, valleys, and forests. Travelling twenty days still further to the west, you continue to find the country inhabited, by people who worship idols, and subsist upon the produce of the soil, as well as that of the chase. Here also, besides the wild animals above enumerated, there are great numbers of that species which produces the musk.

Chapter 44

OF THE PROVINCE OF SIN-DIN-FU ❧ AND OF THE GREAT RIVER KIANG

HAVING travelled those twenty stages through a mountainous country, you reach a plain on the confines of Manji, where there is a district named Sin-din-fu, by which name also the large and noble city, its capital, is called. It was formerly the seat of many rich and powerful kings. The circumference of the city is twenty miles; but at the present day it is divided in the following manner.

The late old king had three sons; and it being his wish that each of them should reign after his death, he divided the city amongst them, separating one part from the other by walls, although the whole continued to be surrounded by one general enclosure.

These three brothers accordingly became kings, and each had for his portion a considerable tract of country, the territory of their father having been extensive and rich. But, upon its conquest by the Great Khan, he conquered these three princes, and took for himself their inheritance.

The city is watered by many considerable streams, which, descending from the distant mountains, surround and pass through it in a variety of directions. Some of these rivers are half a mile in width, others are two hundred paces, and very deep. A great bridge crosses one of these rivers within the city. From one extremity to the other there is a row of marble pillars on each side, which support the roof, which is constructed of wood, ornamented with paintings of a red colour, and covered with tiles. Throughout the whole length also there are neat apartments and shops, where all sorts of trades are carried on. One of the buildings, larger than the rest, is occupied by the officers who collect duties and a toll from persons who pass the bridge. From this bridge, it is said, his Majesty receives daily the sum of a hundred bezants of gold.

These rivers, uniting their streams below the city, contribute to form the mighty river called the Kiang [Yang-tzu Kiang], whose course, before it discharges itself into the ocean, is equal to a hundred days' journey.

On these rivers and in the parts adjacent are many towns and fortified places, and the vessels are numerous, in which large quantities of merchandise are transported to and from the city. The people of the province are idolaters. Departing from thence you travel five days, partly along a plain, and partly through valleys, where you see many respectable mansions, castles, and small towns. The inhabitants subsist by agriculture. In the city there are manufactures, particularly of very fine cloths and crapes or gauzes. This country, like the districts already mentioned, is infested with lions, bears, and other wild animals. At the end of these five days' journey, you reach the desolated country of Thebeth.

Chapter 45

OF THE PROVINCE OF THEBETH

THE province named Thebeth was laid entirely waste at the time that Mangu Khan carried his wars into that country. To the distance of twenty days' journey you see numberless towns and castles in a state of ruin; and in consequence of the want of inhabitants, wild beasts, and especially tigers, have multiplied to such a degree that merchants and other travellers are exposed there to great danger during the night.

They are not only under the necessity of carrying their provisions along with them, but are obliged, upon arriving at their halting places, to employ the utmost care, and to take the following precautions, that their horses may not be devoured. In this region, and particularly in the neighbourhood of rivers, are found bamboos of the length of ten paces, three palms in circumference, and three palms also in the space between each knot or joint. Several of these, in their green state, the travellers tie together, and place them, when evening approaches, at a certain distance from their quarters, with a fire lighted around them. The action of the heat upon the green wood causes the joints to burst with loud explosions. The noise is so loud as to be heard at the distance of two miles, and this terrifies the wild beasts, making them fly from the neighbourhood.

The merchants also provide themselves with iron shackles, in order to fasten the legs of their horses, which would otherwise, when alarmed by the noise, break their halters and run away. From the neglect of this precaution, it has happened that many owners have lost their cattle. Thus you travel for twenty days through a desolated country, finding neither inns nor provisions, unless perhaps once in three or four days, when you take the opportunity of replenishing your stock of necessaries. At the end of that period you begin to discover a few castles and strong towns, built upon rocky heights, or upon the summits of mountains, and gradually enter an inhabited and cultivated district, where there is no longer any danger from beasts of prey.

A scandalous custom, which could only proceed from the blindness of idolatry, prevails amongst the people of these parts, who are disinclined to marry young women so long as they are in their virgin state, but require, on the contrary, that they should have had previous commerce with many of the other sex. This, they assert, is pleasing to their deities, and believe that a woman who has not had the company of men is worthless.

Accordingly, upon the arrival of a caravan of merchants, and as soon as they have set up their tents for the night,

T I B E T

those mothers who have marriageable daughters conduct
them to the place, and entreat the strangers to accept of
their daughters and enjoy their society so long as they remain
in the neighbourhood.   Such as have most beauty to recommend them are of course chosen, and the others return
home disappointed.   Those chosen continue with the travellers until the period of their departure.   They then
restore them to their mothers, and never attempt to carry
them away.   It is expected, however, that the merchants
should make them presents of trinkets, rings, or other complimentary tokens of regard, which the young women take
home with them.

They wear all these ornaments about the neck or other
part of the body, and she who exhibits the greatest number
of them is considered to have attracted the attention of the
greatest number of men, and is on that account in higher
esteem with the young men who are looking out for wives.*
At the wedding, she accordingly makes a display of them to
the assembly, and he regards them as a proof that their
idols have rendered her lovely in the eyes of men.   From
thenceforward no person can dare to meddle with her who
has become the wife of another, and this rule is never
infringed.

These idolatrous people are treacherous and cruel, and
holding it no crime to rob, are the greatest brigands in the
world.   They subsist by the chase and by fowling, as well
as upon the fruits of the earth.

Here are found the animals that produce the musk, and
such is the quantity, that the scent of it is diffused over the
whole country.   Once in every month the secretion takes

---

* Want of chastity is still esteemed in Japan as well as among some uncivilized races.
This "testimony to the value of a bride's attractions" is discussed in Westermarck's *History
of Human Marriage.*

place, and it forms itself, as has already been said, into a sort of imposthume, or boil full of blood, near the navel. Throughout every part of this region the animal abounds, and the odour generally prevails.* They are called *gudderi* in the language of the natives, and are taken with dogs.

These people use no coined money, nor even the paper money of the Great Khan, but for their currency employ salt. Their dress is homely, being of leather, undressed skins, or of canvas. They have a language peculiar to the province of Thebeth, which borders on Manji.

Chapter 46

FURTHER DISCOURSE CONCERNING THEBETH

THEBETH was formerly a country of so much importance as to be divided into eight kingdoms, containing many cities and castles. Its rivers, lakes, and mountains are numerous. In the rivers gold-dust is found in very large quantities. Coral is in great demand, the women wear it about their necks, and with it ornament their idols. There are manufactures of camlet and of gold cloth, and many drugs are produced in the country that have not been brought to ours.

Among these people you find the best enchanters, who by their infernal art perform the most extraordinary and delusive marvels that were ever seen or heard. They cause tempests to arise, accompanied with flashes of lightning and thunderbolts, and produce many other miraculous effects.

They are altogether an ill-conditioned race. They have dogs of the size of asses, strong enough to hunt all sorts of wild beasts, particularly the wild oxen, and are extremely

* In recent years Paris perfumery houses have sent agents to the Upper Yangtze to buy this product. Its export from Tibet, for the year 1902, has been estimated at one million ounces of silver. See *Encyclopædia Sinica.*

large and fierce. Some of the best lanner falcons are bred here, and also sakers, very swift of flight, and the natives have good sport with them.

This province of Thebeth is subject to the Great Khan, as well as all the other kingdoms and provinces that have been mentioned. Next to this is the province of Kain-du.

Chapter 47

OF THE PROVINCE OF KAIN-DU

KAIN-DU is a western province, which was formerly sub-ject to its own princes; but, since it has been brought under the dominion of the Great Khan, it is ruled by the governors whom he appoints. We are not to understand, however, that it is situated in the western part of Asia, but only that it lies westward with respect to our course from the north-eastern quarter. It contains many cities and castles, and the capital city, standing at the commencement of the prov-ince, is likewise named Kain-du. Near to it there is a large lake of salt water, in which are found abundance of pearls, of a white colour, but not round. So great indeed is the quantity, that, if his Majesty permitted every individual to search for them, their value would become trifling; but the fishery is prohibited to all who do not obtain his licence.

A mountain in the neighbourhood yields the turquoise stone, the mines of which cannot be worked without the same permission.

The inhabitants of this district are in the shameful and odious habit of considering it no mark of disgrace that those who travel through the country should have connexion with their wives, daughters, or sisters; but, on the contrary, when strangers arrive, each householder endeavours to con-duct one of them home with him. Here he gives all the

females of the family to him, leaves him in the situation
of master of the house, and takes his departure. While
the stranger is in the house, he places a signal at the win-
dow, as his hat or some other thing; and as long as this
signal is seen in the house, the husband remains absent.
And this custom prevails throughout that province. This
they do in honour of their idols, believing that by such
acts of kindness and hospitality to travellers a blessing is
obtained, and that they shall be rewarded with a plentiful
supply of the fruits of the earth.

The money or currency they make use of is thus prepared. Their gold is formed into small rods, and passes
according to its weight, without any stamp. This is their
greater money: the smaller is of the following description.
In this country there are salt-springs, from which they
manufacture salt by boiling it in small pans. When the
water has boiled for an hour, it becomes a kind of paste,
which is formed into cakes of the value of twopence each.
These, which are flat on the lower, and convex on the
upper side, are placed upon hot tiles, near a fire, in order
to dry and harden. On this latter species of money the
stamp of the Great Khan is impressed, and it cannot be
prepared by any other than his own officers. Eighty of
the cakes are made to pass for a saggio of gold. But
when these are carried by the traders amongst the inhabitants of the mountains and other parts little frequented,
they obtain a saggio of gold for sixty, fifty, or even forty
of the salt cakes, in proportion as they find the natives less
civilized, further removed from the towns, and more accustomed to remain on the same spot.

The same merchants travel in like manner through the
mountainous and other parts of the province of Thebeth,
last spoken of, where the money of salt has equal currency.

Their profits are considerable, because these country people consume the salt with their food, and regard it as an indispensable necessary; whereas the inhabitants of the cities use for the same purpose only the broken fragments of the cakes, putting the whole cakes into circulation as money.

Here also the animals, which yield the musk, are taken in great numbers, and the article is proportionably abundant. Many fish, of good kinds, are caught in the lake. In the country are found tigers, bears, deer, stags, and antelopes. There are numerous birds also, of various sorts. The wine is not made from grapes, but from wheat and rice, with a mixture of spices, which is an excellent beverage.

This province likewise produces cloves. The tree is small; the branches and leaves resemble those of the laurel, but are somewhat longer and narrower. Its flowers are white and small, as are the cloves themselves, but as they ripen they become dark-coloured. Ginger grows there and also cassia in abundance, besides many other drugs, of which no quantity is ever brought to Europe.

Upon leaving the city of Kain-du, the journey is ten days to the opposite boundary of the province; in the course of which you meet with respectable habitations, many fortified posts, and also places adapted to hunting and fowling. The inhabitants follow the customs and manners that have already been described. At the end of these ten days, you come to the great river Brius, which bounds the province, and in which are found large quantities of gold-dust. It discharges itself into the ocean. We shall now leave this river, as nothing further that is worthy of observation presents itself, and shall proceed to speak of the province of Karazan.

Chapter 48

OF THE GREAT PROVINCE OF KARAZAN ☙ AND OF YACHI ITS PRINCIPAL CITY

HAVING passed the river above mentioned, you enter the province of Karazan, which is of such extent as to be divided into seven governments. It is situated towards the west; the inhabitants are idolaters. It is subject to the dominion of the Great Khan, who has constituted as its king his son named Cen-Temur, a rich, magnificent, and powerful prince, endowed with consummate wisdom and virtue, and by whom the kingdom is ruled with great justice. In travelling from this river five days' journey, in a westerly direction, you pass through a country fully inhabited, and see many castles. The inhabitants live upon flesh meat and upon the fruits of the earth. Their language is peculiar to themselves, and is difficult to be acquired. The best horses are bred in this province.

At the end of these five days you arrive at its capital city, which is named Yachi, and is large and noble. In it are found merchants and artisans, with a mixed population, consisting of idolaters, Nestorian Christians, and Saracens or Mahometans; but the first is the most numerous class. The land is fertile in rice and wheat. The people, however, do not use wheaten bread, which they esteem unwholesome, but eat rice. Of other grain, with the addition of spices, they make wine, which is clear, light-coloured, and most pleasant to the taste. For money they employ the white porcelain shell, found in the sea, and these they also wear as ornaments about their necks. Eighty of the shells are equal in value to a saggio of silver or two Venetian groats, and eight saggi of good silver, to one of pure gold. In this country also there are salt-springs, from which all the salt used by the inhabitants is procured. The duty levied on this salt produces a large revenue to the Emperor.

The natives do not consider it as an injury done to them, when others have connexion with their wives, provided the act be voluntary on the woman's part. Here there is a lake nearly a hundred miles in circuit, in which great quantities of various kinds of fish are caught; some of them being of a large size.

The people are accustomed to eat the undressed flesh of fowls, sheep, oxen, and buffaloes, but cured in the following manner. They cut the meat into very small particles, and then put it into a pickle of salt, with the addition of several of their spices. It is thus prepared for persons of the higher class, but the poorer sort only steep it, after mincing, in a sauce of garlic, and then eat it as if it were dressed.

Chapter 49

OF A FURTHER PART OF THE PROVINCE NAMED KARAZAN

LEAVING the city of Yachi, and travelling ten days in a westerly direction, you reach the chief city of the province of Karazan. The country belongs to the dominion of the Great Khan, and the royal functions are exercised by his son, named Kogatin. Gold is found in the rivers, both in small particles and in lumps; and there are also veins of it in the mountains. In consequence of the large quantity obtained, they give a saggio of gold for six saggi of silver. They likewise use porcelain shells in currency; which, however, are not found in this part of the world, but are brought from India. As I have said before, these people never take virgins for their wives.

Here are found snakes and huge serpents [crocodiles], ten paces in length, and ten spans in the girt of the body.

At the fore part, near the head, they have two short legs, having three claws with eyes larger than a fourpenny loaf and very glaring. The jaws are wide enough to swallow a man, the teeth are large and sharp, and their whole appearance is so formidable, that neither man, nor any kind of animal, can approach them without terror. Others are met with of a smaller size, being eight, six, or five paces long.

The following method is used for capturing them. In the day-time, by reason of the great heat, they lurk in caverns, but at night, they come out to seek their food, and whatever beast they meet with and can lay hold of, they devour. After eating they drag themselves towards some lake, spring of water, or river, in order to drink. By their motion in this way along the shore, and their vast weight, they make a deep impression, as if a heavy beam had been drawn along the sands. Those whose employment it is to hunt them observe the track by which they are most frequently accustomed to go, and fix into the ground several pieces of wood, armed with sharp iron spikes, which they cover with the sand in such a manner as not to be perceptible. When therefore the animals make their way towards the places they usually haunt, they are wounded by these instruments, and speedily killed.

The crows, as soon as they perceive them to be dead, set up their scream; and this serves as a signal to the hunters, who advance to the spot, and proceed to separate the skin from the flesh, taking care immediately to secure the gall, which is most highly valued in medicine. In cases of the bite of a mad dog, a pennyweight of it, dissolved in wine, is administered. It is also useful in accelerating delivery, when the labour pains of women have come on. A small quantity of it being applied to carbuncles, pustules, or other eruptions on the body, they are presently dispersed; and it is efficacious in many other complaints.

The flesh also of the animal is sold at a dear rate, being thought to have a higher flavour than other kinds of meat, and by all persons it is esteemed a delicacy. In this province the horses are of a large size, and whilst young, are carried for sale to India. It is the practice to deprive them of one joint of the tail, in order to prevent them from lashing it from side to side, and to occasion its remaining pendent; as the whisking it about, in riding, appears to them a vile habit.

These people ride with long stirrups, as the French do in our part of the world; whereas the Tartars, and almost all other people, wear them short, so that they may with ease rise in their stirrups above the horse, when they shoot their arrows. They have complete armour of buffalo-leather, and carry lances, shields, and cross-bows. All their arrows are poisoned.

I was assured, as a certain fact, that many persons, and especially those who harbour bad designs, always carry poison about them, with the intention of swallowing it, in the event of their being captured, and exposed to torture. Rather than suffer it, they effect their own destruction. But their rulers, who are aware of this practice, are always provided with the dung of dogs, which they oblige the accused to swallow, causing a vomiting of the poison. Thus an antidote is ready against the arts of these wretches.

Before the time of their becoming subject to the dominion of the Great Khan, these people were addicted to the following brutal custom. When any stranger of superior quality, who united personal beauty with distinguished valour, happened to take up his abode at the house of one of them, he was murdered during the night; not for the sake of his money, but in order that the spirit of the deceased, endowed with his talents and intelligence, might remain with the family, and all their concerns might prosper. Accordingly the individual was accounted fortunate who possessed in this manner the soul of any noble personage; and many lost their lives in consequence. But from the time of his Majesty's beginning to rule the country, he has taken measures for suppressing the horrid practice, and as severe punishments have been inflicted, it has ceased to exist.

Chapter 50

OF THE PROVINCE OF KARDANDAN AND THE CITY OF VOCHANG

PROCEEDING five days' journey in a westerly direction from Karazan, you enter the province of Kardandan, belonging to the dominion of the Great Khan, and of which the principal city is named Vochang. The currency of this country is gold by weight, and also porcelain shells. An ounce of gold is exchanged for five ounces of silver, and a saggio of gold for five saggi of silver. There being no silver mines in this country, but much gold, the merchants who import silver obtain a large profit.

Both the men and the women of this province have the custom of covering their teeth with thin plates of gold, which are fitted with great nicety to the shape of the teeth, and remain on them continually. The men also form dark stripes or bands round their arms and legs, by puncturing them in the following manner. They have five needles joined together, which they press into the flesh until blood is drawn; and they then rub the punctures with a black colouring matter, which leaves an indelible mark. To bear these dark stripes is considered as an ornamental and honourable distinction.

They pay little attention to anything but horsemanship, the sports of the chase, and whatever belongs to the use of arms and a military life; leaving the entire management of their domestic concerns to their wives, who are assisted in their duties by slaves, either purchased or made prisoners in war.

These people have the following singular usage. As soon as a woman has been delivered of a child, and, rising from her bed, has washed and swathed the infant, her husband immediately takes the place she has left, has the child laid beside him, and nurses it for forty days. In the meantime, the friends and relations of the family pay to him their visits of congratulation; whilst the woman attends to the business of the house, carries victuals and drink to the husband in his bed, and suckles the infant at his side.*

These people eat their meat raw, or prepared in the manner that has been described, and along with it eat rice. Their wine is manufactured from rice, with a mixture of spices, and is a good beverage.

In this district they have neither temples nor idols, but pay their worship to the elder or ancestor of the family, from whom, they say, as they derive their existence, so to him they are indebted for all that they possess. They have no knowledge of any kind of writing, nor is this to be wondered at, considering the rude nature of the country, which is a mountainous tract, covered with the thickest forests. During the summer season, the atmosphere is so gloomy

---

* This delightful practice has also been noted in India, Borneo, Siam, Africa and sections of South America. This hatching on the part of the father has been named *"Couvade."* It is illustrated in an old Chinese painting now in the Victoria and Albert Museum, London, and reproduced in the museum's catalogue of Chinese Art.

and unwholesome, that merchants and other strangers are obliged to leave the district, in order to escape from death.

When the natives have transactions of business with each other, which require them to execute any obligation for the amount of a debt or credit, their chief takes a square piece of wood, and divides it in two. Notches are then cut on it, denoting the sum in question, and each party receives one of the corresponding pieces, as is practised in respect to our tallies. Upon the expiration of the term, and payment made by the debtor, the creditor delivers up his counterpart, and both remain satisfied.

Neither in this province, nor in the cities of Kain-du, Vochang, or Yachi, are to be found persons professing the knowledge of the leech. When a person of consequence is attacked with a disorder, his family send for those sorcerers who offer sacrifices to the idols, to whom the sick person gives an account of the nature of his complaint.

The sorcerers thereupon give directions for the attendance of persons who perform on a variety of loud instruments, in order that they may dance and sing hymns in honour and praise of their idols. This they continue to do, until the evil spirit has taken possession of one of them, when their musical exertions cease. They then inquire of the person so possessed the cause of the man's indisposition, and the means that should be used for effecting his cure. The evil spirit answers by the mouth of him into whose body he has entered, that the sickness has been occasioned by an offence given to a certain deity. Upon which the sorcerers address their prayers to that deity, beseeching him to pardon the sinner, on the condition that when cured he shall offer a sacrifice of his own blood. But if the demon perceives that there is no prospect of a recovery, he pronounces the deity to be so grievously offended that no sacrifice can appease him. If, on the contrary, he judges that a cure is likely to take place, he requires that an offering be made of so many sheep with black heads; that so many sorcerers, with their wives, be assembled, and that the sacrifice be performed by their hands; by which means, he says, the favour of the deity may be gained.

The relations comply immediately with all that has been demanded, the sheep are slain, their blood is sprinkled towards the heavens, the sorcerers, male and female, light up and perfume with incense the whole house of the sick person, making a smoke with wood of aloes. They cast into the air the water in which the flesh has been seethed, together with some of the liquor brewed with spices; and then laugh, sing, and dance about, with the idea of doing honour to their idol or divinity. Then they proceed to feast on the meat that had been offered in sacrifice, and to drink the spiced liquor, of which a libation had been made, with signs of great hilarity.

Having finished their meal, and received their fees, they return to their homes; and if, through God's providence, the patient recovers, they attribute his cure to the idol for whom the sacrifice was performed; but if he happens to die, they then declare that the rites had been rendered ineffective by those who dressed the victuals, having presumed to taste them before the deity's portion had been presented to him.

It must be understood that ceremonies of this kind are not practised upon the illness of every individual, but only perhaps once or twice in the course of a month, for noble or wealthy personages. They are common, however, to all the idolatrous inhabitants of the whole provinces of Cathay and Manji, amongst whom a physician is a rare character.

And thus do the demons sport with the blindness of these deluded and wretched people.

Chapter 51

OF THE MANNER IN WHICH THE GREAT KHAN EFFECTED THE CONQUEST OF THE KINGDOM OF MIEN ❦ AND BANGALA

WE should speak of a memorable battle that was fought in this kingdom. It happened that in the year 1272 the Great Khan sent an army into the countries of Vochang and Karazan, for their protection and defence against any attack that foreigners might attempt to make. At this period he had not as yet appointed his own sons to the governments.

When the king of Mien and Bangala, in India, who was powerful in the number of his subjects, in extent of territory, and in wealth, heard that an army of Tartars had arrived at Vochang, he advanced immediately to attack it, in order that by its destruction the Great Khan should be deterred from again attempting to station a force upon the borders of his dominions. For this purpose he assembled a very large army, including a multitude of elephants upon whose backs were placed battlements or castles, of wood, capable of containing twelve or sixteen men. With these, and a large army of horse and foot, he took the road to Vochang, where the Great Khan's army lay, and encamping at no great distance from it, intended to give his troops a few days of rest.

Chapter 52

OF THE BATTLE THAT WAS FOUGHT BY THE GREAT KHAN'S ARMY

As soon as the approach of the king of Mien, with so great a force, was known to Nestardin, who commanded the troops of the Great Khan, although a brave and able officer, he felt much alarmed, not having under his orders more than twelve thousand men, whereas the enemy had sixty thousand, besides the elephants. He did not, however, betray any sign of apprehension, but descending into the plain of Vochang, took a position in which his flank was covered by a thick wood. In case of a furious charge by the elephants his troops might be able to retire in this wood. And from here, in security, could annoy them with their arrows.

Calling together the principal officers of his army, he ordered them not to display less valour on the present occasion than they had done in all their preceding engagements, reminding them that victory did not depend upon the number of men, but upon courage and discipline. He told them that the troops of the king of Mien and Bangala were raw and unpracticed in the art of war, not having had the opportunities of acquiring experience that had fallen to their lot; that instead of being discouraged by the superior number of their foes, they ought to feel confidence in their own strength; that their very name was a subject of terror, not merely to the enemy before them, but to the whole world. Then he concluded by promising to lead them to certain victory.

When the enemy learned that the Tartars had descended into the plain, they immediately advanced to about a mile from the Tartars.

At a given command they advanced boldly with their whole army towards that of the Tartars, which remained firm, making no movement, but allowed them to approach their entrenchments. They then rushed out with great spirit and the utmost eagerness to engage; but it was soon found that the Tartar horses, unused to the sight of such huge animals, with their castles, were terrified, and wheeling about endeavoured to fly; nor could their riders by any exertions restrain them, whilst the king, with the whole of his forces, was every moment gaining ground. As soon as the prudent commander perceived this unexpected disorder, without losing his presence of mind, he instantly adopted the measure of ordering his men to dismount and their horses to be taken into the wood, where they were fastened to the trees. When dismounted, the men, without loss of time, advanced on foot towards the line of elephants, and commenced a brisk discharge of arrows.

At the same time those who were stationed in the castles, and the rest of the king's army, shot volleys in return with great activity; but their arrows did not make the same impression as those of the Tartars, whose bows were drawn with a stronger arm. So incessant were the discharges of the latter, and all their weapons being directed against the elephants, these were soon covered with arrows, and, suddenly giving way, fell back upon their own people in the rear, who were thereby thrown into confusion. It soon became impossible for their drivers to manage them.

Smarting under the pain of their wounds, and terrified by the shouting of the assailants, they were no longer governable, but without guidance or control ran about in all directions, until at length, impelled by rage and fear, they rushed into a part of the wood not occupied by the Tartars. The consequence of this was, that the branches of large trees wrecked the battlements or castles that were upon their backs, and destroyed those who sat upon them. Upon seeing the rout of the elephants the Tartars acquired fresh courage, and filing off by detachments, with perfect order and regularity, they remounted their horses, and joined their several divisions. Then the fierce and dreadful combat was renewed.

On the part of the king's troops there was no want of valour, and he himself went amongst the ranks entreating them to stand firm, and not to be alarmed by the accident that had befallen the elephants. But the Tartars, by their great skill in archery, were too powerful for them. The arrows having been expended on both sides, the men grasped their swords and iron maces, and violently encountered each other. Then in an instant were to be seen many horrible wounds, limbs dismembered, and multitudes falling to the ground, maimed and dying; with such effusion of blood as was dreadful to behold. So great also was the exchange of blows, and such the shoutings and the shrieks, that the noise seemed to ascend to the skies.

The king of Mien, acting as a valiant chief, was present wherever the greatest danger appeared, animating his soldiers, and beseeching them to maintain their ground with resolution. He ordered fresh squadrons from the reserve to advance to the support of those that were exhausted; but perceiving at length that it was impossible any longer to sustain the conflict or to hold out against the Tartars, he found himself compelled to take to flight with the wreck of his army, numbers of whom were afterwards slain in the pursuit.

The losses in this battle, which lasted from the morning till noon, were severely felt on both sides; but the Tartars were finally victorious. A point perhaps of great importance is that the king ought not to have made his attack on the Tartars in a position where their flank was supported by a wood, but should have endeavoured to draw them into the open country, where they could not have resisted the attack of the armed elephants, and where, by extending the cavalry of his two wings, he might have surrounded them.

The Tartars having collected their force after the

slaughter of the enemy, returned towards the wood into
which the elephants had fled for shelter, in order to take
possession of them, where they found that the men who
had escaped from the overthrow were employed in cutting
down trees and barricading the passages, in order to defend
themselves. But the Tartars soon slew many of them, and
with the assistance of the persons accustomed to the management of elephants, they captured two hundred or more
of them.

After this battle the Great Khan has always employed
elephants in his armies. The consequences of the victory
were, that he acquired possession of the whole of the territories of the king of Bangala and Mien, and annexed them
to his dominions.

Chapter 53

OF AN UNINHABITED REGION ❦ AND OF THE KINGDOM OF MIEN

LEAVING the province of Kardandan, you enter upon a
vast descent, which you travel without variation for two
days and a half, in the course of which no habitations are to
be found. You then reach a spacious plain, whereon, three
days in every week, a number of trading people assemble,
many of whom come down from the neighbouring mountains, bringing their gold to be exchanged for silver, which
the merchants who repair thither from distant countries
carry with them for this purpose; and one saggio of gold is
given for five of silver.

The inhabitants are not allowed to act as the exporters of
their own gold, but must dispose of it to the merchants, who
furnish them with such articles as they require; and as none
but the natives themselves can gain access to the places of
their residence, so high and strong are the situations, and

so difficult of approach, it is on this account that the transactions of business are conducted in the plain.

Beyond this, in a southerly direction, towards the confines of India, lies the province of Mien [Burma]. The
journey occupies fifteen days, through a country without
people or dwellings, and forests abounding with elephants,
rhinoceroses, and other wild beasts.

Chapter 54

OF THE CITY OF MIEN ❦ AND OF THE TWO TOWERS ❦ ONE
OF SILVER AND ONE OF GOLD

AFTER the journey of fifteen days you reach the city of
Mien, which is large, magnificent, and the capital of the
kingdom [Burma]. The inhabitants have a language peculiar to themselves.

It is related that there formerly reigned in this country a
rich and powerful monarch, who, when his death was drawing near, gave orders for erecting two pyramidal towers
beside his tomb. One of these pyramids was covered with
a plate of gold an inch in thickness, so that nothing besides
the gold was visible; and the other with a plate of silver,
of the same thickness. Around the balls, at the top were
suspended small bells of gold and of silver, which sounded
when put in motion by the wind. The whole formed a
splendid object for each tower was ten paces in height.

The tomb was in like manner covered with a plate, partly
of gold and partly of silver. This the king commanded
to be prepared for the honour of his soul, and in order that
his memory might not perish.

The Great Khan having resolved upon taking possession
of this city, sent thither a valiant officer to effect it, and
the army, at its own desire, was accompanied by some of
the jugglers or sorcerers, of whom there were always a great

number about the court. When these entered the city, they observed the two pyramids so richly ornamented, but would not meddle with them until his Majesty's pleasure respecting them should be known. The Great Khan, upon being informed that they had been erected in pious memory of a former king, would not suffer them to be violated nor injured in the smallest degree; the Tartars being accustomed to respect any article connected with the dead. In this country were found many elephants, large and handsome wild oxen, with stags, fallow deer, and other animals in great abundance.

Chapter 55

OF THE PROVINCE OF BANGALA

THE province of Bangala [Bengal] is situated on the south and was not yet brought under the dominion of the Great Khan at the time of Marco Polo's residence at his court. Operations against it occupied his army for a considerable period, the country being strong and its king powerful, as has been related.

It has its peculiar language. The people are worshippers of idols. Oxen are found here almost as tall as elephants, but not so big. The inhabitants live upon flesh, milk, and rice, of which they have abundance. Much cotton is grown in the country, and trade flourishes. Spikenard, galangal, ginger, sugar, and many sorts of drugs are amongst the productions of the soil; to purchase which the merchants come from various parts of India.

They likewise make purchases of eunuchs, of whom there are numbers in the country, as slaves; and as every prince and person of rank is desirous of having them for the custody of their women, the merchants obtain a large profit

THE CITY OF MIEN

by carrying these slaves to other kingdoms, and there disposing of them. This province is thirty days' journey in extent, and at the eastern extremity of it lies a country named Kangigu.

Chapter 56

OF THE PROVINCE OF KANGIGU

Kangigu is a province situated towards the east, and is governed by a king. The people are idol worshippers, have a peculiar language, and made a voluntary submission to the Great Khan, to whom they pay an annual tribute. The king is so devoted to sensual pleasures, that he has about three hundred wives, and when he hears of any handsome woman, he takes and marries her.

Gold is found here in large quantities, and also many kinds of drugs; but, being an inland country, distant from the sea, the products are of little value. There are elephants in abundance, and other beasts.

The inhabitants live upon flesh, rice, and milk. They have no wine made from grapes, but prepare it from rice and a mixture of drugs. Both men and women have their bodies marked with the needle all over, in figures of beasts and birds; and there are among them practitioners whose sole employment it is to execute these ornaments upon the hands, the legs, and the breast. When a black colouring stuff has been rubbed over these punctures, it is impossible, either by water or otherwise, to efface the marks. The man or woman who exhibits the greatest profusion of these figures, is esteemed the most handsome.

Chapter 57

OF THE PROVINCE OF AMU

AMU, also, is situated towards the east, and its inhabitants are subjects of the Great Khan. They live upon the flesh of their cattle and the fruits of the earth and have a peculiar language. The country produces many horses and oxen, which are sold to merchants, and conveyed to India. Buffaloes also, as well as oxen, are numerous in consequence of the extent and excellence of the pastures.

Both men and women wear rings, of gold and silver, upon their wrists, arms, and legs; but the ornaments of the females are the more costly.

The distance between this province and that of Kangigu is twenty-five days' journey, and thence to Bangala is twenty days' journey. We shall now speak of a province named Tholoman, situated eight days' journey from the former.

Chapter 58

OF THOLOMAN

THE province of Tholoman lies towards the east, and its inhabitants are idolaters. They have a peculiar language, and are also subjects of the Great Khan. The people are tall and good-looking; their complexions inclining rather to brown than fair. They are just in their dealings, and brave in war.

Many of their towns and castles are situated upon lofty mountains. They burn the bodies of their dead; and the bones that are not reduced to ashes, they put into wooden boxes, and carry to the mountains, where they conceal them in caverns of the rocks, in order that no wild animal may disturb them.

Abundance of gold is found here. For the ordinary small currency they use the porcelain shells that come from India; and this sort of money prevails also in the two provinces of Kangigu and Amu, already mentioned. Their food and drink are flesh, rice and milk.

Chapter 59

OF THE CITIES OF CHINTIGUI ❧ SIDIN-FU ❧ GIN-GUI ❧ AND PAZAN-FU

You travel for twelve days by a river, on each side of which lie many towns and castles, and at length you reach the large and handsome city of Chintigui. The inhabitants are traders and artisans. They make cloth of the bark of certain trees, which looks well, and is the ordinary summer clothing of both sexes. The men are brave warriors. They have no other kind of money than the stamped paper of the Great Khan.

In this province the tigers are so numerous, that the inhabitants, from apprehension of their ravages, cannot venture to sleep at night out of their towns; and those who navigate the river dare not go to rest with their boats moored near the banks. These animals have been known to plunge into the water, swim to the vessel, and drag the men out.

In this country are likewise found the largest and fiercest dogs that can be met with. So courageous and powerful are they, that a man, with a couple of them, may be an over-match for a tiger. Armed with a bow and arrows, and thus attended, should he meet a tiger, he sets on his bold dogs, who instantly advance to the attack. The animal instinctively seeks a tree, against which to place himself, in order that the dogs may not be able to get behind him, and that he may have his enemies in front. With this intent, as soon as he perceives the dogs, he makes towards the tree, but with a slow pace, and by no means running, that he may not show any signs of fear, which his pride would not allow. During this deliberate movement, the dogs fasten upon him, and the man shoots him with his arrows. He, in his turn, endeavours to seize the dogs, but they are too nimble for him, and draw back. By this time he has been wounded by so many arrows, and so often bitten by the dogs, that he falls through weakness and from loss of blood. By these means it is that he is captured.

There is here an extensive manufacture of silks, which are exported in large quantities to other parts by the navigation of the river, which flows through towns and castles. The people subsist entirely by trade. At the end of twelve days, you arrive at the city of Sidin-fu, of which an account has been already given. From thence, in twenty days, you reach Gin-gui, in which we were, and in four days more the city of Pazan-fu, which belongs to Cathay, and lies towards the south, in returning by the other side of the province. The inhabitants worship idols, and burn the bodies of their dead. They are subjects of the Great Khan, and his paper money is current among them. They gain their living by trade and manufacture, having silk in abundance, of which they weave tissues mixed with gold, and also very fine scarfs. This city has many towns and castles under its jurisdiction: a great river flows beside it, by means of which large quantities of merchandise are conveyed to the city of Kanbalu [Peking]; for by the digging of many canals it is made to communicate with the capital. But we shall take our leave of this, and, proceeding three days' journey, speak of another city named Chan-glu.

Chapter 60

OF THE CITY OF CHAN-GLU

CHAN-GLU is a large city situated towards the south, and is in the province of Cathay. It is under the dominion of the Great Khan. The inhabitants worship idols, and burn the bodies of their dead. The stamped paper of the Emperor is current amongst them.

In this city and the district surrounding it they make great quantities of salt, by the following process: in the country is found a salty earth; upon this, when laid in large heaps, they pour water, which in its passage through the mass imbibes the particles of salt, and is then collected in channels and is conveyed to very wide pans, not more than four inches in depth. In these it is well boiled, and then left to crystallize. The salt thus made is white and good, and is exported to various parts. Great profits are made by those who manufacture it, and the Great Khan derives from it a considerable revenue.

This district produces abundance of well-flavoured peaches, of such a size that one of them will weigh two pounds troy-weight. We shall now speak of another city, named Chan-gli.

Chapter 61

OF THE CITY OF CHAN-GLI ❧ AND THAT OF TUDIN-FU ❧ AND OF A REBELLION

CHAN-GLI also is a city of Cathay, situated towards the south and belonging to the Great Khan; the inhabitants in like manner make use of the Khan's paper currency. Its distance from Chan-glu is five days' journey, in the course of which you pass many cities and castles likewise in the dominions of the Great Khan. They are places of great commerce, and the customs levied at them amount to a large sum.

Through this city passes a wide and deep river, which affords conveyance to vast quantities of merchandise, consisting of silk, drugs, and other valuable articles. We shall now take leave of this place, and give an account of another city named Tudin-fu.

When you depart from Chan-gli, and travel southwards six days' journey, you pass many towns and castles of great importance and grandeur, whose inhabitants worship idols, and burn the bodies of their dead. They subsist by trade and manufactures, and have provisions in abundance. At the end of these six days you arrive at a city named Tudin-fu, which was formerly a magnificent capital, but the Great Khan reduced it to his subjection by force of arms. It is rendered a delightful residence by the gardens which surround it, and is filled with handsome shrubs and excellent fruits. Silk is produced here in wonderfully large quantities. It has under its jurisdiction eleven cities and considerable towns of the empire, all places of great trade, and having abundance of silk. It was the seat of government of its own king, before the period of its reduction by the Great Khan.

In 1273 the Emperor appointed one of his officers of the highest rank, named Lucansor, to the government of this city, with a command of seventy thousand horse, for the protection of that part of the country. This man upon finding himself master of a rich and highly productive district, and at the head of so powerful a force, became intoxicated with pride, and formed schemes of rebellion against his sovereign. With this view he induced principal persons of the city to become partakers in his evil

designs, and by these means succeeded in producing a revolt
throughout all the towns and fortified places of the province.

As soon as the Great Khan became acquainted with these
proceedings, he dispatched to that quarter an army of a
hundred thousand men, under the orders of two others
of his nobles, one of whom was named Angul and the other
Mongatai. When the approach of this force became known
to Lucansor, he lost no time in assembling an army no less
numerous than that of his opponents, and brought them as
speedily as possible to action. There was much slaughter
on both sides, but at length Lucansor was killed, and his
troops betook themselves to flight. Many were slain in
the pursuit, and many were made prisoners. These were
conducted to the presence of the Great Khan, who caused
the principals to be put to death, and pardoning the others
took them into his own service, to which they ever afterwards remained loyal.

Chapter 62

OF THE CITY OF SINGUI-MATU

TRAVELLING from Tudin-fu three days, in a southerly
direction, you pass many considerable towns and strong
places, where commerce and manufactures flourish. The
country abounds with game, both beasts and birds, and produces an ample supply of the necessaries of life.

At the end of three days you arrive at the city of Singui-
matu, which is noble, large, and handsome, and rich in
merchandise and manufactures; all the inhabitants of this
city are idolaters, and are subjects of the Great Khan and
use paper money; within it, but on the southern side, passes
a large and deep river, which the inhabitants divided into
two branches [canals] one of which, taking its course to the

east, runs through Cathay, whilst the other, taking a westerly course, passes towards the province of Manji. This river is navigated by so many vessels that the number might seem incredible. It serves to join both provinces. It is indeed surprising to observe the multitude and the size of the vessels that are continually passing and repassing, laden with merchandise of the greatest value.

Chapter 63

CONCERNING THE CITIES LINGUI AND PINGUI

On leaving Singui-matu and travelling towards the south for sixteen days, you unceasingly meet with commercial towns and with castles. At the end of eight days' journey you find a city named Lingui. It is a very noble and great city; the men are warlike; and it has manufactures and commerce.

There are plenty of animals, and abundance of everything for eating and drinking. After leaving Lingui you proceed three days' journey to the south, passing plenty of cities and castles, all under the Great Khan. All the inhabitants are idolaters, and burn their dead. At the end of these three days you find a good city called Pingui, where there are all the necessaries of life, and this city furnishes a great revenue to the Great Khan. You go thence two days' journey to the south, through fair and rich countries, to a city called Cingui, which is very large, and abounding in commerce and manufactures. All its inhabitants are idolaters and burn their dead; they use paper money, and are subjects also of the Great Khan. They have much grain and wheat. In the country through which you pass subsequently, you find cities, towns, and castles, and very handsome and useful dogs, and abundance of wheat. The people resemble those just described.

Chapter 64

OF THE GREAT RIVER CALLED THE KARA-MORAN AND OF THE CITIES OF KOI-GAN-ZU AND KUAN-ZU

AT the end of two days' journey you reach, once more, the great river Kara-moran [Yellow River], which has its source in the territories that belonged to Prester John. It is a mile wide and of vast depth, and upon its waters great ships freely sail with their full loading. Large fish in considerable quantitites are caught there.

At a place in this river, about a mile distant from the sea, there is a station for fifteen thousand vessels, each of them capable of carrying fifteen horses and twenty men, besides the crews to navigate them, and the necessary stores and provisions. These the Great Khan causes to be kept in a constant state of readiness for the conveyance of an army to any of the Indian Isles that may happen to be in rebellion, or for expeditions to any more distant region. These vessels are moored close to the bank of the river, not far from a city named Koi-gan-zu, on the opposite side to which is another named Kuan-zu but the former is a large place, and the latter a small one.

Upon crossing this river you enter the noble province of Manji; but it must not be understood that a complete account has been given of the province of Cathay. Not the twentieth part have I described. Marco Polo, in travelling through the province, has only noted such cities as lay in his route, omitting those situated on the one side and the other, as well as many intermediate places, because a relation of them all would be a work of too great length, and prove fatiguing to the reader. Leaving these parts we

shall therefore proceed to speak, in the first instance, of
the manner in which the province of Manji was acquired,
and then of its cities, the magnificence and riches of which
shall be set forth in the subsequent part of our discourse.

Chapter 65

OF THE MOST NOBLE PROVINCE OF MANJI ❦ AND OF THE MANNER IN WHICH IT WAS CONQUERED BY THE GREAT KHAN

THE province of Manji is the most magnificent and the
richest that is known in the eastern world. It was subject
to a prince who was styled Facfur, and who surpassed in
power and wealth any other except the Great Khan himself. His disposition was pacific, and his actions benevolent.
So much was he beloved by his people, and such the
strength of his kingdom, enclosed by rivers of the largest
size, that his being molested by any power upon earth was
regarded as an impossible event. The effect of this opinion
was, that he neither paid any attention himself to military
affairs, nor encouraged his people to become acquainted with
military exercises.

The cities of his dominions were remarkably well fortified, being surrounded by deep ditches, a bow-shot in width,
and full of water. He did not keep up any force in cavalry,
because he was not apprehensive of attack. The means of
increasing his enjoyments and multiplying his pleasures
were the chief employment of his thoughts. He maintained at his court, and kept near his person, about a
thousand beautiful women, in whose society he took delight.
He was a friend to peace and to justice, which he administered strictly. The smallest act of oppression, or injury of
any kind, committed by one man against another, was punished in a proper manner. Such indeed was the impression

THE RIVER KARAMORAN

of his justice, that when shops, filled with goods, happened, through the negligence of the owners, to be left open, no person dared to enter them, or to rob them of the smallest article.

Travellers of all descriptions might pass through every part of the kingdom, by night as well as by day, freely and without apprehension of danger. He was religious, and charitable to the poor and needy. Children whom their wretched mothers exposed in consequence of their inability to rear them, he caused to be saved and taken care of, to the number of twenty thousand annually. When the boys attained a sufficient age, he had them instructed in some handicraft, and afterwards married them to young women who were brought up in the same manner.

Very different from the temper and habits of Facfur were those of Kublai Khan, emperor of the Tartars, whose whole delight consisted in thoughts of a warlike nature, of the conquest of countries, and of extending his renown. After having annexed to his dominions a number of provinces and kingdoms, he now directed his views to the subduing that of Manji, and for this purpose assembled a numerous army of horse and foot, the command of which he gave to a general named Chin-san Bay-an, which signifies in our language, the "Hundred-eyed." This occurred in the year 1268.

A number of vessels were put under his orders, with which he proceeded to the invasion of Manji. Upon landing there, he immediately summoned the inhabitants of the city of Koi-gan-zu to surrender to the authority of his sovereign. Upon their refusal to comply, instead of giving orders for an assault, he advanced to the next city, and when he there received a similar answer, proceeded to a third and a fourth, with the same result. Deeming it no longer

prudent to leave so many cities in his rear, even though he
expected to be soon joined by another army of equal force
which the Great Khan was to send to him from the interior,
he resolved upon the attack of one of these cities. By great
exertions and consummate skill he succeeded in carrying
the place, and put every individual found in it to the
sword.

As soon as the intelligence of this event reached the
other cities, it struck their inhabitants with such terror, that
of their own accord they hastened to declare their submission. This being effected, he advanced, with the united
force of his two armies, against the royal city of Kinsai,
the residence of King Facfur, who felt all the agitation and
dread of a person who had never seen a battle, nor been
engaged in any sort of warfare. Alarmed for the safety
of his person, he made his escape to a fleet of vessels that lay
in readiness for the purpose, and left the charge of the city
to his queen, with directions for its being defended to the
utmost. He felt assured that her sex would be a protection to her, in the event of her falling into the hands of
the enemy. Proceeding to sea, and reaching certain islands
which were strongly fortified, he remained there till his
death.

After the queen had been left in the manner related, it
is said to have come to her knowledge that the king had
been told by his astrologers that he could never be deprived
of his sovereignty by any other than a chief who should
have a hundred eyes. On the strength of this declaration
she felt confident, notwithstanding that the city became daily
more and more endangered, that it could not be lost, because
it seemed a thing impossible that any mortal could have
that number of eyes. Inquiring, however, the name of the
general who commanded the enemy's troops, and being told

it was Chin-san Bay-an, which means a hundred eyes, she was seized with horror at hearing it pronounced, as she felt certain that this must be the person who, according to the saying of the astrologers, would drive her husband from his throne. Overcome by fear, she no longer attempted to make resistance, but immediately surrendered.

Being thus in possession of the capital, the Tartars soon brought the remainder of the province under their subjection. The queen was sent to the presence of Kublai Khan, where she was honourably received by him, and an allowance was by his orders assigned, that enabled her to support the dignity of her rank. Having stated the manner in which the conquest of Manji was effected, we shall now speak of the different cities of that province, and first of Koi-gan-zu.

Chapter 66

OF THE CITY OF KOI-GAN-ZU

KOI-GAN-ZU is a very handsome and wealthy city, lying in a direction between south-east and east, at the entrance of the province of Manji, where a prodigious number of vessels are continually passing, its situation being near the bank of the river Kara-moran [Yellow River].

Large consignments of merchandise are forwarded to this city, in order that the goods may be transported, by means of this river, to various other places. Salt is manufactured here in great quantities, not only for the consumption of the city itself, but for exportation to other parts; and from this salt the Great Khan derives an ample revenue.

Chapter 67

OF THE TOWN OF PAU-GHIN ❧ AND OF THE CITY OF KAIN

UPON leaving Koi-gan-zu, you travel one day's journey towards the south-east, by a handsome stone causeway, leading into the province of Manji. On both sides of the causeway there are very extensive marshy lakes, the waters of which are deep, and may be navigated. There is no other road by which the province can be entered. It is, however, accessible by means of shipping; and in this manner it was that the officer who commanded the Great Khan's armies invaded it, by effecting a landing with his whole force.

At the end of the day's journey, you reach a considerable town named Pau-ghin. The inhabitants worship idols, burn their dead, use paper money, and are the subjects of the Great Khan. They gain their living by trade and manufacture: they have much silk, and weave gold tissues. The necessaries of life are there in abundance.

At the distance of a day's journey from Pau-ghin, towards the south-east, stands the large and well-built city of Kain. Trade and manufactures flourish here. They have fish in abundance, and game also, both beasts and birds. Pheasants, in particular, are in such plenty, that for a bit of silver equal in value to a Venetian groat you may purchase three of these birds, of the size of pea-fowls.

Chapter 68

OF THE CITIES OF TIN-GUI AND CHIN-GUI ❧ OF THE CITY OF YAN-GUI ❧ OF WHICH MARCO POLO HELD THE GOVERNMENT

AT the end of a day's journey from the last-mentioned place, in the course of which many villages and much tilled land are met with, you reach a city named Tin-gui, not of any great size, but plentifully furnished with all the necessaries of life. The people are merchants, and have many trading vessels. Both beasts and birds are here found in plenty. The situation of this city is towards the south-east, and on the left hand—that is, on the eastern side of it, at the distance of three days' journey—you find the sea. In the intermediate space there are many salt-works, where large quantities of salt are manufactured.

You next come to the large and well-built town of Chingui, from whence salt is exported sufficient for the supply of all the neighbouring provinces. On this article the Great Khan raises a revenue, the amount of which would scarcely be credited. Here also the inhabitants worship idols, use paper money, and are the subjects of his Majesty.

Proceeding in a south-easterly direction from Chin-gui, you come to the important city of Yan-gui [Yang-chau], which, having twenty-four towns under its jurisdiction, must be considered as a place of great consequence. It belongs to the dominion of the Great Khan. The people are idolaters, and subsist by trade and manual arts. They manufacture arms and all sorts of warlike accoutrements; in consequence of which many troops are stationed in this part of the country.

The city is the place of residence of one of the twelve nobles before spoken of, who are appointed by his Majesty to the government of the provinces; and in the place of one of these, Marco Polo, by special order of the Great Khan, acted as governor of this city during the space of three years.

Chapter 69

OF THE PROVINCE OF NAN-GHIN

NAN-GHIN [Nan-king] is the name of a large and distinguished province of Manji, situated towards the west. The people are idolaters, use paper money in currency, are subjects of the Great Khan, and are largely engaged in commerce. They have raw silk, and weave tissues of silver and gold in great quantitites, and of various patterns. The country produces abundance of corn, and is stored as well with domestic cattle as with beasts and birds that are the objects of the chase, and plenty of tigers. It supplies the sovereign with an ample revenue, and chiefly from the imposts levied upon the rich articles in which the merchants trade. We shall now speak of the noble city of Sa-yan-fu.

Chapter 70

OF THE CITY OF SA-YAN-FU ❦ THAT WAS TAKEN BY THE MEANS OF NICOLO AND MAFFEO POLO

SA-YAN-FU is a considerable city of the province of Manji, having under its jurisdiction twelve wealthy and large towns. It is a place of great commerce and extensive manufactures. The inhabitants burn the bodies of their dead, and are idolaters. They are the subjects of the Great Khan, and use his paper currency. Raw silk is there produced in great quantity, and the finest silks, intermixed with gold, are woven. Game of all kinds abounds. The place is amply furnished with everything that belongs to a great city, and by its uncommon strength it was enabled to stand a siege of three years; refusing to surrender to the Great Khan, even after he had obtained possession of the province of Manji.

The difficulties experienced in the siege were chiefly occa-

sioned by the army's not being able to approach it, excepting
on the northern side, the other sides being surrounded with
water.   When the operations were reported to his Majesty,
he felt extremely hurt that this place alone should obsti-
nately hold out, after all the rest of the country had bowed
to obedience.

The above facts having come to the knowledge of the
brothers Nicolo and Maffeo, who were then resident at the
imperial court, they immediately presented themselves to
the Emperor, and proposed to him that they should be
allowed to construct machines, such as were made use of in
the West, capable of throwing stones three hundred pounds
in weight.   With these machines the buildings of the city
might be destroyed and the inhabitants killed.   Their request was granted by the Great Khan, who, warmly approving of the scheme, gave orders that the ablest smiths
and carpenters should be placed under their direction;
amongst whom were some Nestorian Christians, who proved
to be able mechanics.

In a few days they completed their mangonels, according
to the instructions furnished by the two brothers; and a trial
being made of them in the presence of the Great Khan, and
of his whole court, an apportunity was afforded of seeing
them cast stones, each of which weighed three hundred
pounds.   They were then put on board of vessels, and conveyed to the army.

When set up in front of the city of Sa-yan-fu, the first
stone projected by one of them fell with such weight and
violence upon a building, that a great part of it was crushed,
and fell to the ground.   So terrified were the inhabitants
by this mischief, which to them seemed to be the effect of a
thunderbolt from heaven, that they immediately decided
upon surrendering.   Persons authorized to act were accord-

ingly sent and their submission was accepted on the same terms and conditions as had been granted to the rest of the province.

This prompt result of their ingenuity increased the reputation and credit of these two Venetian brothers in the opinion of the Great Khan and of all his courtiers.

Chapter 71

OF THE CITY OF SIN-GUI ◀ AND OF THE VERY GREAT RIVER
KIANG

LEAVING the city of Sa-yan-fu, and proceeding fifteen days' journey towards the south-east, you reach the city of Sin-gui, which, although not large, is a place of great commerce. The number of vessels that belong to it is prodigious, in consequence of its being situated near the Kiang [Yang-tzu Kiang], which is the largest river in the world, its width being in some places ten, in others eight, and in others six miles. Its length, to the place where it discharges itself into the sea, is upwards of one hundred days' journey. It is indebted for its great size to the vast number of other navigable rivers that empty their waters into it, which have their sources in distant countries.

A great number of cities and large towns are situated upon its banks, and more than two hundred, with sixteen provinces, partake of the advantages of its navigation, by which the transport of merchandise is to an extent that might appear incredible to those who have not had an opportunity of witnessing it. When we consider, indeed, the length of its course, and the multitude of rivers communicating, it is not surprising that the quantity and value of articles for the supply of so many places, lying in all directions, should be incalculable. The principal commodity, however, is salt, which is not only conveyed by means of the Kiang, and the rivers connected with it, to the towns upon their banks, but afterwards from thence to all places in the interior of the country.

On one occasion, when Marco Polo was at the city of Sin-gui, he saw there no less than fifteen thousand vessels; and yet there are other towns along the river where the number is still greater. All these vessels are covered with a kind of deck, and have a mast with one sail. Their burden is in general about four thousand cantari, or quintals, of Venice, and from that upwards to twelve thousand cantari [500 tons], which some of them are capable of loading. They do not employ hempen rope excepting for the masts and sails. They have canes of the length of fifteen paces, such as have been already described, which they split, in their whole length, into very thin pieces, and these, by twist-ing them together, they form into ropes three hundred paces long. So skilfully are they manufactured, that they are equal in strength to rope made of hemp.

With these ropes the vessels are tracked along the rivers, by means of ten or twelve horses to each. At many places near the banks of this river there are hills and small rocky eminences, upon which are erected idol temples and other edifices, and you find a continual succession of villages and inhabited places.

Chapter 72

OF THE CITY OF KAYN-GUI

KAYN-GUI is a small town on the southern bank of the before-mentioned river, where annually is collected a very large quantity of corn and rice, the greatest part of which is conveyed from thence to the city of Kanbalu, for the supply of the establishment of the Emperor. This place

is in the line of communication with the province of Cathay,
by means of rivers, lakes, and a wide and deep canal which
the Great Khan has caused to be dug, in order that vessels
may pass from one great river to the other, and from the
province of Manji, by water, as far as Kanbalu, without
making any part of the voyage by sea.

This magnificent work is deserving of admiration; and
not so much from the manner in which it is conducted
through the country, or its vast extent, as from its utility
and the benefit it produces to those cities which lie in its
course.   On its sides, likewise, are constructed strong and
wide embankment roads, upon which the travelling by land
also is rendered perfectly convenient.

In the midst of the river, opposite to the city of Kayn-
gui, there is an island entirely of rock, upon which are built
a grand temple and monastery, where two hundred monks,
as they may be termed, reside, and perform service to the
idols.   This is the supreme head of many other temples
and monasteries.   We shall now speak of the city of Chan-
ghian-fu.

Chapter 73
OF THE CITY OF CHAN-GHIAN-FU

CHAN-GHIAN-FU is a city of the province of Manji, the
inhabitants of which are idolaters, subjects of the Great
Khan, and use his paper money.   They gain their living by
trade and manufacture, and are wealthy.   They weave
tissues of silk and gold.   The sports are there most excellent
in every species of game, and provisions are abundant.

There are in this city three churches of Nestorian Christians, which were built in the year 1278, when his Majesty
appointed a Nestorian, named Mar-Sachis, to the govern-

ment of it for three years. By him these churches were established, where there had not been any before; and they still subsist. Leaving this place, we shall now speak of Tin-gui-gui.

Chapter 74

OF THE CITY OF TIN-GUI-GUI

DEPARTING from Chan-ghian-fu, and travelling four days towards the south-east, you pass many towns and fortified places, the inhabitants of which are idolaters, live by arts and commerce, are the subjects of the Great Khan, and use his paper money. At the end of these four days, you reach the city of Tin-gui-gui, which is large and handsome, and produces much raw silk, of which tissues of various qualities and patterns are woven. The necessaries of life are here in plenty, and the variety of game affords excellent sport.

The inhabitants, however, are a vile, inhuman race. At the time that Chin-san Ba-yan, or the hundred-eyed, subdued the country of Manji, he dispatched certain Alans who are Christians, along with a party of his own people, to take this city. As soon as they appeared before it, they were suffered to enter without resistance. The place being surrounded by a double wall, one of them within the other, the Alans occupied the first enclosure, where they found a large quantity of wine, and having previously suffered much from fatigue and privation, they were eager to quench their thirst, and, without any consideration, proceeded to drink to such excess, that becoming intoxicated, they fell asleep.

The people of the city, who were within the second enclosure, as soon as they perceived that their enemies lay slumbering on the ground, took the opportunity of murdering them, not allowing one to escape. When Chin-san Ba-yan learned the fate of his detachment, his indignation and anger were raised to the highest pitch, and he sent another army to attack the place. When it was captured, he gave orders for putting to the sword all the inhabitants, great and small, without distinction of sex, as an act of retaliation.

Chapter 75

OF THE CITIES OF SIN-GUI ❧ AND VA-GIU

SIN-GUI [Soochow] is a large and magnificent city, the circumference of which is twenty miles. The people have vast quantities of raw silk, and manufacture it, not only for their own consumption, all of them being clothed in dresses of silk, but also for other markets.* There are amongst them some very rich merchants, and the number of inhabitants is so great as to be a subject of astonishment. They are, however, a cowardly race, and solely occupied with their trade and manufactures. In these indeed they display considerable ability, and if they were as enterprising, manly, and warlike, as they are ingenious, so vast is their number, that they might not only subdue the whole of the province, but might carry their views still further.

They have amongst them many physicians of eminent skill, who can ascertain the nature of a disorder, and know how to apply the proper remedies. There are also persons distinguished as professors of learning, or, as we should term them, philosophers, and others who may be called magicians or enchanters.

On the mountains near the city, rhubarb grows in the

---

* Soochow is still a silk centre. The weavers are divided into two powerful guilds called the *Nankin* and the *Suchau,* and between them keep busy seven thousand looms.

highest perfection, and is from thence distributed throughout the province.   Ginger is likewise produced in large
quantities, and is sold at so cheap a rate, that forty pounds
weight of the fresh root may be had for the value, in their
money, of a Venetian silver groat.

Under the jurisdiction of Sin-gui there are sixteen respectable and wealthy cities and towns, where trade and
arts flourish.   By the name of Sin-gui is to be understood
"The City of the Earth," as by that of Kin-sai, "The City
of Heaven."   Leaving Sin-gui, we shall now speak of
another city, distant from it only a day's journey, named
Va-giu, where, likewise, there is a vast abundance of raw
silk, and where there are many merchants as well as artisans.
Silks of the finest quality are woven here, and are afterwards carried to every part of the province.   No other circumstances presenting themselves as worthy of remark, we
shall now proceed to the description of the principal city and
metropolis of the province of Manji, named Kin-sai.

Chapter 76

OF THE NOBLE AND MAGNIFICENT CITY OF KIN-SAI

UPON leaving Va-giu you pass, in the course of three
days' journey, many towns, castles, and villages, all of them
well inhabited and opulent.   The people have abundance of
provisions.   At the end of three days you reach the noble
and magnificent city of Kin-sai [= capital; Hang-chau], a
name that signifies "The Celestial City," and which it merits
from its pre-eminence to all others in the world, in point
of grandeur and beauty, as well as from its abundant delights, which might lead an inhabitant to imagine himself in
paradise.

This city was frequently visited by Marco Polo, who carefully and diligently observed and inquired into every circumstance respecting it, all of which he recorded in his notes, from whence the following particulars are briefly stated. According to common estimation, this city is an hundred miles in circuit. Its streets and canals are extensive, and there are squares, or market-places, which being necessarily proportioned in size to the prodigious concourse of people by whom they are frequented, are exceedingly spacious. It is situated between a lake of fresh and very clear water on the one side, and a river of great magnitude on the other, the waters of which, by a number of canals, large and small, are made to run through every quarter of the city, carrying with them all the filth into the lake, and ultimately to the sea. This furnishes a communication by water, in addition to that by land, to all parts of the town. The canals and the streets being of sufficient width to allow of boats on the one, and carriages in the other, to pass easily with articles necessary for the inhabitants.

It is commonly said that the number of bridges, of all sizes, amounts to twelve thousand. Those which are thrown over the principal canals and are connected with the main streets, have arches so high, and built with so much skill, that vessels with their masts can pass under them. At the same time, carts and horses can pass over, so well is the slope from the street graded to the height of the arch. If they were not so numerous, there would be no way of crossing from one place to another.

Beyond the city, and enclosing it on that side, there is a ditch about forty miles in length, very wide, and full of water that comes from the river before mentioned. This was excavated by the ancient kings of the province, in order that when the river should overflow its banks, the superfluous water might be diverted into this channel. This

THE CITY OF KINSAI

serves at the same time as a measure of defence. The earth
dug out from thence was thrown to the inner side, and has
the appearance of many hillocks, surrounding the place.

There are within the city ten principal squares or market-
places, besides innumerable shops along the streets. Each
side of these squares is half a mile in length, and in front
of them is the main street, forty paces in width, and running
in a direct line from one extremity of the city to the other.
It is crossed by many low and convenient bridges. These
market-squares are at the distance of four miles from each
other. In a direction parallel to that of the main street,
but on the opposite side of the squares, runs a very large
canal, on the nearer bank of which capacious warehouses are
built of stone, for the accommodation of the merchants who
arrive from India and other parts with their goods and
effects. They are thus conveniently situated with respect
to the market-places. In each of these, upon three days in
every week, there is an assemblage of from forty to fifty
thousand persons, who attend the markets and supply them
with every article of provision that can be desired.

There is an abundant quantity of game of all kinds, such
as roebucks, stags, fallow deer, hares, and rabbits, together
with partridges, pheasants, francolins, quails, common fowls,
capons, and such numbers of ducks and geese as can scarcely
be expressed; for so easily are they bred and reared on the
lake, that, for the value of a Venetian silver groat, you
may purchase a couple of geese and two couple of ducks.

There, also, are the shambles, where they slaughter cattle
for food, such as oxen, calves, kids, and lambs, to furnish
the tables of rich persons and of the great magistrates. As
to the people of the lower classes, they eat every kind of
meat, without any discrimination.

At all seasons there is in the markets a great variety of

herbs and fruits, and especially pears of an extraordinary size, weighing ten pounds each, that are white in the inside, like paste, and have a very fragrant smell. There are peaches also, in their season, both of the yellow and white kind, and of a delicious flavour. Grapes are not produced there, but are brought in a dried state, and very good, from other parts. This applies also to wine, which the natives do not hold in estimation, being accustomed to their own liquor prepared from rice and spices. From the sea, which is fifteen miles distant, there is daily brought up the river, to the city, a vast quantity of fish; and in the lake also there is abundance, which gives employment at all times to persons whose sole occupation it is to catch them. The sorts are various according to the season of the year. At the sight of such an importation of fish, you would think it impossible that it could be sold; and yet, in the course of a few hours, it is all taken off, so great is the number of inhabitants, even of those classes which can afford to indulge in such luxuries, for fish and flesh are eaten at the same meal.

Each of the ten market-squares is surrounded with high dwelling-houses, in the lower part of which are shops, where every kind of manufacture is carried on, and every article of trade is sold; such, amongst others, as spices, drugs, trinkets, and pearls. In certain shops nothing is vended but the wine of the country, which they are continually brewing, and serve out fresh to their customers at a moderate price. The streets connected with the market-squares are numerous, and in some of them are many cold baths, attended by servants of both sexes. The men and women who frequent them, have from their childhood been accustomed at all times to wash in cold water, which they reckon highly conducive to health. At these bathing places, however, they have apartments provided with warm water, for the use of strangers, who cannot bear the shock of the cold. All are in the daily practice of washing their persons, and especially before their meals.

In other streets are the quarters of the courtesans who are here in such numbers as I dare not venture to report. Not only near the squares, which is the situation usually appropriated for their residence, but in every part of the city they are to be found, adorned with much finery, highly perfumed, occupying well-furnished houses, and attended by many female domestics. These women are accomplished, and are perfect in the arts of caressing and fondling which they accompany with expressions adapted to every description of person. Strangers who have once tasted of their charms, remain in a state of fascination, and become so enchanted by their wanton arts, that they can never forget the impression. Thus intoxicated with sensual pleasures, when they return to their homes they report that they have been in Kin-sai, or The Celestial City, and look forward to the time when they may be enabled to revisit this paradise.

In other streets are the dwellings of the physicians and the astrologers, who also give instructions in reading and writing, as well as in many other arts. They have apartments also amongst those which surround the market-squares. On opposite sides of each of these squares there are two large edifices, where officers appointed by the Great Khan are stationed, to take immediate notice of any differences that may happen to arise between the foreign merchants, or amongst the inhabitants of the place. It is their duty likewise to see that the guards upon the several bridges in their respective vicinities are duly placed, and in cases of neglect, to punish the offenders at their discretion.

On each side of the principal street, already mentioned as

extending from one end of the city to the other, there are houses and mansions of great size, with their gardens, and near to these, the dwellings of the artisans, who work in shops, at their several trades; and at all hours you see such multitudes of people passing and repassing, on their various avocations, that the providing food in sufficiency for their maintenance might be deemed an impossibility. It is observed, however, that on every market-day, the squares are crowded with tradespeople, who cover the whole space with the articles brought by carts and boats, for all of which they find sale. From the single article of pepper, some notion may be formed of the whole quantity of provisions, meat, wine, groceries, and the like, required for the consumption of the inhabitants of Kin-sai. Marco Polo learned from an officer employed in the Great Khan's customs, the daily amount of pepper bought was forty-three loads, each load being two hundred and forty-three pounds.

The inhabitants of the city are idolaters, and they use paper money as currency. The men as well as the women have fair complexions, and are handsome. The greater part of them are always clothed in silk, in consequence of the vast quantity of that material produced in the territory of Kin-sai, exclusively of what the merchants import from other provinces.

Amongst the handicraft trades exercised in the place, there are twelve considered to be superior to the rest, as being more generally useful. There are a thousand workshops for each craft, and each shop furnishes employment for ten, fifteen, or twenty workmen, and in a few instances as many as forty, under their respective masters. The opulent masters in these shops do not labour with their own hands, but, on the contrary, assume airs of gentility and affect parade. Their wives equally abstain from work.

They have much beauty, as has been remarked, and are brought up with delicate and languid habits. The costliness of their dresses, in silks and jewelry, can scarcely be imagined. Although the laws of their ancient kings ordained that each citizen should exercise the profession of his father, yet they were allowed, when they acquired wealth, to avoid manual labour, provided they kept up the establishment, and employ persons to work at their paternal trades.

Their houses are well built and richly adorned with carved work. So much do they delight in ornaments of this kind, in paintings, and fancy buildings, that the sums they lavish on such objects are enormous.

The natural disposition of the native inhabitants of Kinsai is peaceful, and by the example of their former kings, who were themselves unwarlike, they have been accustomed to habits of tranquillity. The management of arms is unknown to them, nor do they keep any in their houses. They conduct their mercantile and manufacturing concerns with perfect candour and honesty. They are friendly towards each other, and persons who inhabit the same street, both men and women, from the mere circumstance of neighbourhood, appear like one family.

In their domestic manners they are free from jealousy or suspicion of their wives, to whom great respect is shown, and any man would be accounted infamous who should presume to use indecent expressions to a married woman. To strangers also, who visit their city in the way of commerce, they give proofs of cordiality, inviting them freely to their houses, showing them friendly attention, and furnishing them with the best advice and assistance in their mercantile transactions. On the other hand, they dislike the sight of soldiery, not excepting the guards of the Great

Khan, for they remind them that they were deprived of the government of their native kings and rulers.

On the borders of the lake are many handsome and spacious edifices belonging to men of rank and great magistrates. There are likewise many idol temples, with their monasteries, occupied by a number of monks, who perform the service of the idols. Near the central part are two islands, upon each of which stands a superb building, with an incredible number of apartments and separate pavilions. When the inhabitants of the city have occasion to celebrate a wedding, or to give a sumptuous entertainment, they resort to one of these islands, where they find ready for their purpose every article that can be required, such as vessels, napkins, table linen, and the like, which are provided and kept there at the common expense of the citizens, by whom also the buildings were erected. It may happen that at one time there are a hundred parties assembled there, at wedding or other feasts, all of whom, notwithstanding, are accommodated with separate rooms or pavilions, so judiciously arranged that they do not interfere with each other.

In addition to this, there are upon the lake a great number of pleasure vessels or barges, calculated for holding ten, fifteen, to twenty persons, being from fifteen to twenty paces in length, with a wide and flat flooring, and not liable to heel to either side in passing through the water. Such persons as take delight in the amusement, and mean to enjoy it, either in the company of their women or that of their male companions, engage one of these barges, which are always kept in the nicest order, with proper seats and tables, together with every other kind of furniture necessary for giving an entertainment. The cabins have a flat roof or upper deck, where the boatmen take their place, and by means of long poles, which they thrust to the bottom of the lake, which is not more than one or two fathoms in depth, they shove the barges along, until they reach the desired spot. These cabins are painted inside with various colours and with a variety of figures; all parts of the vessel are likewise adorned with painting. There are windows on each side, which may either be kept shut, or opened, to give an opportunity to the company, as they sit at table, of looking out in every direction and feasting their eyes on the variety and beauty of the scenes as they pass them. And truly the gratification afforded in this manner, upon the water, exceeds any that can be derived from the amusements on the land; for as the lake extends the whole length of the city, on one side, you have a view, as you stand in the boat, at a certain distance from the shore, of all its grandeur and beauty, its palaces, temples, convents, and gardens, with trees of the largest size growing down to the water's edge, whilst at the same time you enjoy the sight of other boats of the same description, continually passing you, filled in like manner with parties in pursuit of amusement. In fact, the inhabitants of this place, as soon as the labours of the day have ceased, or their mercantile transactions are closed, think of nothing else than of passing the remaining hours in parties of pleasure, with their wives or their mistresses, either in these barges, or about the city in carriages, of which it will here be proper to give some account, as constituting one of the amusements of these people.

Chapter 77

FURTHER PARTICULARS CONCERNING THE GREAT CITY OF KIN-SAI

It must be observed, in the first place, that the streets of Kin-sai are all paved with stone and bricks, and so likewise are all the principal roads extending from thence through the province of Manji, by means of which passengers can travel to every part without soiling their feet. But as the couriers of his Majesty, who go on horseback with great speed, cannot make use of the pavement, a part of the road, on one side, is on their account left unpaved.

The main street of the city is paved with stone and brick to the width of ten paces on each side, the intermediate part being filled up with small gravel, and provided with arched drains for carrying off the rain-water that falls, into the neighbouring canals, so that it remains always dry. On this gravel carriages continually pass and repass. They are of a long shape, covered at top, have curtains and cushions of silk, and are capable of holding six persons. Both men and women who feel disposed to take their pleasure, are in the daily practice of hiring them for that purpose, and accordingly at every hour you may see vast numbers of them driven along the middle part of the street. Some of them proceed to visit certain gardens, where the company are introduced, by those who have the management of the place, to shady recesses contrived by the gardeners for that purpose. Here the men indulge themselves all day in the society of their women, returning home, when it becomes late, in the manner they came.

It is the custom of the people of Kin-sai, upon the birth of a child, for the parents to make a note, immediately, of the day, hour, and minute at which the delivery took place.

They then inquire of an astrologer under what sign or aspect of the heavens the child was born; and his answer is likewise committed carefully to writing. When therefore he is grown up, and is about to engage in any mercantile adventure, voyage, or treaty of marriage, this document is carried to the astrologer, who, having examined it, and weighed all the circumstances, pronounces certain oracular words, in which these people, who sometimes find them justified by the event, place great confidence. Of these astrologers, or rather magicians, great numbers are to be met with in every market-place, and no marriage is ever celebrated until an opinion has been pronounced upon it by one of that profession.

It is also their custom, upon the death of any great and rich personage, to observe the following ceremonies. The relations, male and female, clothe themselves in coarse dresses, and accompany the body to the place appointed for burning it. The procession is likewise attended by performers on various musical instruments, which are sounded as it moves along, and prayers to their idols are chanted in a loud voice. When arrived at the spot, they throw into the flame many pieces of cotton-paper, upon which are painted representations of male and female servants, horses, camels, silk wrought with gold, as well as of gold and silver money. This is done, in the belief that the deceased will possess in the other world all these conveniences, in their natural state of flesh and bones, together with the money and the silks. As soon as the pile has been consumed, they sound all the instruments of music at the same time, producing a loud and long-continued noise. They imagine that by these ceremonies their idols are induced to receive the soul of the man whose corpse has been reduced to ashes.

In every street of this city there are stone buildings or towers. In case of a fire breaking out in any quarter, an accident by no means unusual, as the houses are mostly constructed of wood, the inhabitants may remove their effects to these towers for security.

By a regulation which his Majesty has established, there is a guard of ten watchmen stationed, under cover, upon all the principal bridges, of whom five do duty by day and five by night. Each of these guards is provided with a sonorous wooden instrument as well as one of metal, together with a water device, by means of which the hours of the day and night are ascertained. As soon as the first hour of the night is expired, one of the watchmen gives a single stroke upon the wooden instrument, and also upon the metal gong, which announces to the people of the neighbouring streets that it is the first hour. At the expiration of the second, two strokes are given; and so on progressively, increasing the number of strokes as the hours advance. The guard is not allowed to sleep, and must be always on the alert. In the morning, as soon as the sun begins to appear, a single stroke is again struck, as in the evening, and so onwards from hour to hour.

Some of these watchmen patrol the streets, to observe whether any person has a light or fire burning after the hour appointed for extinguishing them. Upon making the discovery, they affix a mark to the door, and in the morning the owner of the house is taken before the magistrates, by whom, if he cannot assign a legitimate excuse for his offence, he is punished. Should they find any person abroad at an unseasonable hour, they arrest and confine him, and in the morning he is carried before the same tribunal. If they notice any person who from lameness or other infirmity is unable to work, they place him in one of the hospitals,

of which there are several in every part of the city, founded
by the ancient kings, and liberally endowed. When cured,
he is obliged to work at some trade.

Immediately upon the appearance of fire breaking out in
a house, they give the alarm by beating on the wooden
machine, when the watchmen from all the bridges within
a certain distance assemble to extinguish it, as well as to save
the effects of the merchants and others, by removing them
to the stone towers that have been mentioned. The goods
are also sometimes put into boats, and conveyed to the islands
in the lake. Even on such occasions the inhabitants dare
not stir out of their houses, when the fire happens in the
night, and only those can be present whose goods are actually
being removed, together with the guard collected to assist,
which seldom amounts to a smaller number than from one
to two thousand men.

In cases also of tumult or insurrection amongst the citizens, the services of this police guard are necessary; but,
independently of them, his Majesty always keeps on foot
a large body of troops, both infantry and cavalry, in the
city and its vicinity, the command of which he gives to his
ablest officers.

For the purposes of nightly watch, there are mounds of
earth thrown up, at the distance of above a mile from each
other, on the top of which a wooden frame is constructed,
with a sounding board, which being struck with a mallet by
the guard stationed there, the noise is heard to a great distance. If precautions of this nature were not taken upon
occasions of fire, there would be danger of half the city being consumed; and their use is obvious also in the event of
popular commotion, as, upon the signal being given, the
guards at the several bridges arm themselves, and repair to
the spot where their presence is required.

When the Great Khan reduced to his obedience the province of Manji, which until that time had been one kingdom, he thought proper to divide it into nine parts, over each of which he appointed a king or viceroy, who should act as supreme governor of that division, and administer justice to the people. These make a yearly report to commissioners acting for his Majesty, of the amount of the revenue, as well as of every other matter pertaining to their jurisdiction. Upon the third year they are changed, as are all other public officers.

One of these nine viceroys resides and holds his court in the city of Kin-sai, and has authority over more than a hundred and forty cities and towns, all large and rich. Nor is this number to be wondered at, considering that in the whole of the province of Manji there are no fewer than twelve hundred, containing a large population of industrious and wealthy inhabitants. In each of these, according to its size and other circumstances, his Majesty keeps a garrison, consisting, in some places, of a thousand, in others of ten or twenty thousand men, accordingly as he judges the city to be, in its own population, more or less powerful. It is not to be understood that all these troops are Tartars. On the contrary, they are chiefly natives of the province of Cathay. The Tartars are universally horsemen, and cavalry cannot be quartered about those cities which stand in the low, marshy parts of the province, but only in firm, dry situations, where such troops can be properly exercised. To the former, he sends Cathaians, and such men of the province of Manji as appear to have a military turn; for it is his practice to make an annual selection amongst all his subjects of such as are best qualified to bear arms. But the soldiers drawn from the province of Manji he does not employ in the duty of their native cities. On the con-

trary, he marches them to other places at a distance of
perhaps twenty days' journey, where they remain for four
or five years, at the expiration of which they are allowed to
return to their homes, and others are sent to replace them.
This regulation applies equally to the Cathaians.

The greater part of the revenues of the cities, paid into
the treasury of the Great Khan, is appropriated to the maintenance of these garrisons. When it happens that a city is
in a state of rebellion, and it is not an uncommon occurrence
for these people, actuated by some sudden exasperation, or
when intoxicated, to murder their governors, a part of the
garrison of a neighbouring city is immediately dispatched
with orders to destroy the place where such guilty excesses
have been committed. For such purposes, the city of Kin-
sai constantly supports a garrison of thirty thousand soldiers; and the smallest number stationed at any place is
one thousand.

It now remains to speak of a very fine palace that was
formerly the residence of King Facfur, whose ancestors
enclosed an extent of ground ten miles in compass, and
divided it into three parts. That in the centre was entered by a lofty portal, on each side of which was a magnificent colonnade, on a flat terrace, the roofs of which were
supported by rows of pillars, highly ornamented with the
most beautiful azure and gold. The colonnade opposite to
the entrance, at the further side of the court, was still
grander than the others, its roof being richly adorned, the
pillars gilt, and the walls on the inner side ornamented
with exquisite paintings, representing the histories of former
kings.

Here, annually, King Facfur was accustomed to hold
his court, and to entertain at a feast his principal nobles, the
chief magistrates, and the prominent citizens of Kin-sai.

Under these colonnades might be seen, at one time, ten
thousand persons suitably accommodated at table. This
festival lasted ten or twelve days, and the magnificence displayed on the occasion, in silks, gold, and precious stones,
exceeded all imagination; for every guest endeavoured to
exhibit as much finery as his circumstances would possibly
allow.

Behind the colonnade last mentioned, or that which
fronted the grand portal, there was a wall, with a passage,
that divided this exterior court of the palace from an interior
court, which formed a kind of large cloister, and led to
various apartments for the use of the king and queen.
From this cloister you entered a covered passage or corridor,
six paces in width, and of such a length as to reach to the
margin of the lake. On each side of this there were corresponding entrances to ten courts, in the form of long
cloisters, and each cloister or court had fifty apartments,
with their respective gardens, the residence of a thousand
young women, whom the king retained in his service.

Accompanied sometimes by his queen, and on other occasions by a party of these females, it was his custom to take
amusement on the lake, in barges covered with silk, and to
visit the temples on its borders. The other two divisions
of this estate were laid out in groves, pieces of water, beautiful gardens stored with fruit-trees, and also enclosures for
all sorts of animals that are the objects of sport, such as
antelopes, deer, stags, hares, and rabbits. Here likewise
the king amused himself, in company with his damsels,
some in carriages and some on horseback. No male person
was allowed to be of these parties, but on the other hand,
the females were practised in the art of coursing with
dogs, and pursuing the animals that have been mentioned.
When fatigued with these exercises, they retired into the

THE PLEASURE BOAT

groves on the banks of the lake, and there quitting their dresses, rushed into the water in a state of nudity, playfully swimming about, some in one direction and some in another, whilst the king remained a spectator of the exhibition. After this they returned to the palace.

Sometimes he ordered his repast to be provided in one of these groves, where the foliage of lofty trees afforded a thick shade, and was there waited upon by the same damsels. Thus was his time consumed amidst the weakening charms of his women, and in profound ignorance of whatever related to military affairs. The consequence of this was, that his depraved habits enabled the Great Khan to deprive him of his splendid possessions, and to expel him from his throne as has been already stated.

All these particulars were communicated to me, when I was in that city, by a rich merchant of Kin-sai, then very old, who had been a confidential servant of King Facfur, and was acquainted with every circumstance of his life. Having known the palace in its original state, he was desirous of conducting me to view it. Being at present the residence of the Great Khan's viceroy, the colonnades are preserved in the style in which they had formerly subsisted, but the chambers of the females had been suffered to go to ruin, and the foundations only were visible. The wall likewise that enclosed the park and gardens was fallen to decay, and neither animals nor trees were any longer to be found there.

At the distance of twenty-five miles from this city, in a direction to the northward of east, lies the sea, where there is an extremely fine port, frequented by all the ships that bring merchandise from India.

Marco Polo, happening to be in the city of Kin-sai at the time of making the annual report to his Majesty's

commissioners of the amount of revenue and the number
of inhabitants, had an opportunity of observing that the
latter were registered at one hundred and sixty tomans of
fire-places, that is to say, of families dwelling under the
same roof; and as a toman is ten thousand, it follows that
the whole city must have contained one million six hundred
thousand families.

Every father of a family, or housekeeper, is required
to affix a writing to the door of his house, specifying the
name of each individual of his family, whether male or
female, as well as the number of his horses. When any
person dies, or leaves the dwelling, the name is struck out,
and upon the occasion of a birth, it is added to the list. By
these means the great officers of the province and governors
of the cities are at all times acquainted with the exact number of the inhabitants. The same regulation is observed
throughout the province of Cathay as well as of Manji.
In like manner, all the keepers of inns and public hotels
inscribe in a book the names of those who take up their
occasional abode with them, marking the day and the hour
of their arrival and departure; a copy of which is trans-
mitted daily to those magistrates who have been spoken
of as stationed in the market-squares. It is a custom in the
province of Manji, with the indigent class of the people,
who are unable to support their families, to sell their children to the rich, in order that they may be fed and brought
up in a better manner than their own poverty would admit.

Chapter 78

OF THE REVENUES OF THE GREAT KHAN

WE shall now speak of the revenue which the Great Khan
draws from the city of Kin-sai and the places within its

jurisdiction, constituting the ninth division or kingdom of Manji. In the first place, upon salt, the most productive article, he levies a yearly duty of eighty tomans of gold, each toman being eighty thousand saggi, and each saggio fully equal to a gold florin, and consequently amounting to six million four hundred thousand ducats. This vast produce is occasioned by the distance of the province to the sea, and the number of salt lakes or marshes, in which, during the heat of summer, the water becomes crystallized, and from whence a quantity of salt is taken, sufficient for the supply of five of the other divisions of the province.

There is here cultivated and manufactured a large quantity of sugar, which pays, as do all other groceries, three and one-third per cent. The same is also levied upon the wine, or fermented liquor, made of rice. The twelve classes of artisans, of whom we have already spoken, as having each a thousand shops, and also the merchants, as well those who import the goods into the city, in the first instance, as those who carry them from thence to the interior, or who export them by sea, pay, in like manner, a duty of three and one-third per cent. But goods coming by sea from distant countries and regions, such as from India, pay ten per cent. So likewise all native articles of the country, as cattle, the vegetable produce of the soil, and silk, pay a tax to the king.

The account being made up in the presence of Marco Polo, he had an opportunity of seeing that the revenue of his Majesty, exclusively of that arising from salt, already stated, amounted in the year to the sum of two hundred and ten tomans, or sixteen million eight hundred thousand ducats.

Chapter 79

OF THE CITY OF TA-PIN-ZU ❦ AND OTHERS

LEAVING the city of Kin-sai, and travelling one day's journey towards the south-east, continually passing houses, villas, and delightful gardens, where every kind of vegetable is produced in abundance, you arrive at the city of Ta-pin-zu, which is very handsome and large, and belongs to the jurisdiction of Kin-sai. The inhabitants worship idols, use paper money, burn the bodies of their dead, are subjects of the Great Khan, and gain their subsistence by trade and manual arts. This place not demanding any more particular notice, we shall proceed to speak of the city of Uguiu.

From Ta-pin-zu, travelling three days towards the south-east, you come to the city of Uguiu, and still further, in the same direction, two days' journey, you pass in continual succession so many towns, castles, and other inhabited places, and such is their vicinity to each other, that to a stranger they have the appearance of one extended city. All of them are dependent upon Kin-sai. The people are idolaters, and the country supplies the necessaries of life in great abundance. Here are found canes of greater bulk and length than those already noticed, being four spans in girth and fifteen paces long.

Proceeding further, three days' journey in the same direction, you reach the town of Gen-gui, and still advancing to the south-east, you never cease to meet with towns full of inhabitants, who are employed at their trades, and cultivate the soil. In this part of the province of Manji there are not any sheep to be seen, but many oxen, cows, buffaloes, and goats, and of swine a vast number. At the end of the fourth day you arrive at the city of Zen-gian, built upon a hill that stands insulated in the river, which, by dividing itself into two branches, appears to embrace it. These streams take opposite directions, one of them pursuing its course to the south-east, and the other to the north-west. The cities last mentioned are likewise under the dominion of the Great Khan, and dependent upon Kin-sai. The people worship idols, and subsist by trade. There is in the country abundance of game, both beasts and birds. Proceeding further, three days' journey, you reach the large and noble city of Gie-za, which is the last within the jurisdiction of Kin-sai. Having passed this city, you enter upon another kingdom or viceroyalty of Manji, named Kon-cha.

Chapter 80

OF THE KINGDOM OF KON-CHA ❦ AND ITS CAPITAL CITY NAMED FU-GIU

Upon leaving the last city of the kingdom of Kin-sai, named Gie-za, you enter that of Kon-cha, the principal city of which is named Fu-giu. In the course of six days' journey through this country, in a south-east direction, over hills and along valleys, you continually pass towns and villages, where the necessaries of life are in abundance, and there is much field sport, particularly of birds. The people are subjects of the Great Khan, and are engaged in commerce and manufactures.

In these parts there are tigers of great size and strength. Ginger and also galangal are produced in large quantities, as well as other drugs. For money equal in value to a Venetian silver groat you may have eighty pounds weight of fresh ginger, so common is its growth. There is also a vegetable which has all the properties of the true saffron, as well the smell as the colour, and yet it is not really saffron. It is held in great estimation, and being an ingredient in all their dishes, it bears, on that account, a high price.

The people in this part of the country are addicted to eating human flesh, esteeming it more delicate than any other, provided the death of the person has not been occasioned by disease. When they advance to combat they throw loose their hair about their ears, and they paint their faces of a bright blue colour. They arm themselves with lances and swords, and all march on foot excepting their chief, who rides on horse-back. They are a most savage race of men, insomuch that when they slay their enemies in battle, they are anxious to drink their blood, and afterwards they devour their flesh. Leaving this subject, we shall now speak of the city of Kue-lin-fu.

The journey of six days being accomplished, you arrive at the city of Kue-lin-fu, which is of considerable size, and contains three very handsome bridges, upwards of a hundred paces in length, and eight paces in width. The women of the place are very handsome, and live in a state of luxurious ease. There is much raw silk produced here, and it is manufactured into silk pieces of various sorts. Cottons are also woven, of coloured threads, which are carried for sale to every part of the province of Manji. The people employ themselves extensively in commerce, and export quantities of ginger and galangal.

I have been told, but did not myself see the animal, that there are found at this place a species of domestic fowls which have no feathers; their skins clothed with black hair, resembling the fur of cats. Such a sight must be extraordinary.* They lay eggs like other fowls, and they

---

* These birds are known to poultry-fanciers as the *Fleecy Persian*. The Chinese call them "velvet-hair fowls," but only a white variety exists today.

are good to eat. The multitude of tigers renders travelling through the country dangerous, unless a number of persons go in company.

Chapter 81

OF THE CITY OF UN-GUEN

UPON leaving the city of Kue-lin-fu, and travelling three days, during which you are continually passing towns and castles, of which the inhabitants are idolaters, have silk in abundance, and export it in considerable quantities, you reach the city of Un-guen.

This place is remarkable for a great manufacture of sugar, which is sent from thence to the city of Kanbalu for the supply of the court. Previously to its being brought under the dominion of the Great Khan, the natives were unacquainted with the art of manufacturing sugar of a fine quality, and boiled it in such an imperfect manner, that when left to cool it remained in the state of a dark-brown paste. But at the time this city became subject to his Majesty's government, there happened to be at the court some persons from Babylon who were skilled in the process, and who, being sent thither, instructed the inhabitants in the mode of refining the sugar by means of the ashes of certain woods.

Travelling fifteen miles further in the same direction, you come to the city of Kan-giu, which belongs to the kingdom or viceroyalty of Kon-cha, one of the nine divisions of Manji. In this place is stationed a large army for the protection of the country, and to be always in readiness to act, in the event of rebellion.

Through the midst of it passes a river, a mile in breadth, upon the banks of which, on either side, are extensive and handsome buildings. In front of these, great numbers of ships are seen lying, having merchandise on board, and especially sugar, of which large quantities are manufactured here also. Many vessels arrive at this port from India, freighted by merchants who bring with them rich assortments of jewels and pearls, upon the sale of which they obtain a considerable profit. This river empties into the sea, at no great distance from the port named Zai-tun. The ships coming from India ascend the river as high up as the city, which abounds with every sort of provision, and has delightful gardens, producing exquisite fruits.

Chapter 82

OF THE CITY AND PORT OF ZAI-TUN ❤ AND THE CITY OF TIN-GUI

Upon leaving the city of Kan-giu and crossing the river to proceed in a south-easterly direction, you travel during five days through a well-inhabited country, passing towns, castles, and substantial dwellings, well supplied with all kinds of provisions. The road lies over hills, across plains, and through woods, in which are found many of those shrubs from whence the camphor is procured. The country abounds also with game. The inhabitants are subjects of the Great Khan, and within the jurisdiction of Kan-giu.

At the end of five days' journey, you arrive at the noble and handsome city of Zai-tun, which has a port on the sea-coast celebrated for the resort of shipping, loaded with merchandise, that is afterwards distributed through every part of the province of Manji. The quantity of pepper imported there is so considerable, that what is carried to Alexandria, to supply the demand of the western parts of the world, is trifling in comparison, perhaps not more than the hundredth part. It is indeed impossible to convey an idea of the number of merchants and the accumulation of goods in this place, which is held to be one of the largest ports in the world. The Great Khan derives a vast revenue from this place, as every merchant is obliged to pay ten per cent. upon the amount of his investment. The ships are freighted by them at the rate of thirty per cent. for fine goods, forty-four for pepper, and for sandalwood, and other drugs, as well as articles of trade in general, forty per cent. It is computed by the merchants, that their charges, including customs and freight, amount to half the value of the cargo; and yet upon the half that remains to them their profit is so considerable, that they are always disposed to return to the same market with a further stock of merchandise.

The country is delightful. The people are idolaters, and have all the necessaries of life in plenty. Their disposition is peaceable, and they are fond of ease and indulgence. Many persons arrive in this city from the interior parts of India for the purpose of having their persons ornamented by puncturing with needles in the manner before described, as it is celebrated for the number of its artists skilled in that practice.

The river that flows by the port of Zai-tun is large and rapid, and is a branch of that which passes the city of Kin-sai. At the place where it separates from the principal channel stands the city of Tin-gui. Of this place there is nothing further to be observed, than that cups or bowls and dishes of porcelainware are there manufactured. The process was explained to be as follows. They collect a certain kind of earth, as it were, from a mine, and laying it in a great heap, suffer it to be exposed to the wind, the rain, and the sun, for thirty or forty years, during which time it is never disturbed. By this it becomes refined and

fit for being wrought into the vessels above mentioned. Such
colours as may be thought proper are then laid on, and
the ware is afterwards baked in ovens or furnaces. Those
persons, therefore, who cause the earth to be dug, collect
it for their children and grandchildren. Great quantities of
the manufacture are sold in the city, and for a Venetian
groat you may purchase eight porcelain cups.*

We have now described the viceroyalty of Kon-cha, one
of the nine divisions of Manji, from whence the Great
Khan draws as ample a revenue as even from that of Kin-
sai. Of the others we shall not attempt to speak, because
Marco Polo did not himself visit any of their cities, as he has
done those of Kin-sai and Kon-cha. It should be observed
that throughout the province of Manji one general language prevails, and one uniform manner of writing, yet in
the different parts of the country there is a diversity of
dialect, similar to what is found between the Genoese, the
Milanese, the Florentine, and the dialects of other Italian
states, whose inhabitants, although they have each their peculiar speech, can make themselves reciprocally understood.

Not having yet completed the subjects upon which Marco
Polo purposed to write, he will now bring this Second Book
to a close, and will commence another with a description
of the countries and provinces of India, dividing it into
the Greater, the Lesser, and the Middle India. These parts
he visited whilst employed in the service of the Great
Khan, who ordered him thither upon different occasions
of business, and afterwards again when, accompanied by his
father and uncle, on their returning journey escorting the
queen destined for King Argon.

* Porcelain is mentioned in Chinese books of the Han dynasty (B. C. 206—A. D. 220),
but it was about a hundred years after Marco Polo during the Ming dynasty that the
great porcelain age of China flourished.

He will have the opportunity of relating many extraordinary circumstances observed by himself personally in those countries, but at the same time will not omit to notice others of which he was informed by persons worthy of credit, or which were pointed out to him in the sea-chart of the coasts of India.

BOOK III

JAPAN THE ARCHIPELAGO, SOUTHERN INDIA, AND THE COASTS AND ISLANDS OF THE INDIAN SEA

Chapter 1

HAVING TREATED, IN THE preceding parts of our work, of various provinces and regions, we shall now take leave of them, and proceed to the account of India.

We shall commence with a description of the ships employed by the merchants, which are built of fir-timber. They have a single deck, and below this the space is divided into about sixty small cabins, fewer, or more, according to the size of the vessels, each of them affording accommodation for one merchant. They are provided with a good helm. They have four masts, with as many sails, and some of them have two masts, which can be set up and lowered again, as may be found necessary. Some ships of the larger class have as many as thirteen bulk-heads or divisions in the hold, formed of thick planks mortised into each other. The object of these is to guard against accidents which may occasion the vessel to spring a leak, such as striking on a rock or receiving a stroke from a whale,

a circumstance that not unfrequently occurs; for, when sailing at night, the motion through the waves causes a white
foam that attracts the notice of the hungry animal.   Expecting food, it rushes violently to the spot, strikes the
ship, and often staves in some part of the bottom.   The
water, running in at the place where the injury has been
sustained, makes its way to the well, which is always kept
clear.   The crew, upon discovering the situation of the leak,
immediately remove the goods from the division affected
by the water, which, in consequence of the boards being so
well fitted, cannot pass from one division to another.   They
then repair the damage, and return the goods to their place
in the hold.

The ships are all double-planked; that is, they have a
course of sheathing-boards laid over the planking in every
part.   These are caulked with oakum both inside and without, and are fastened with iron nails.   They are not coated
with pitch, as the country does not produce that substance,
but the bottoms are smeared over with the following preparation.   The people take quick-lime and hemp, which latter
they cut small, and with these, when pounded together,
they mix oil procured from a certain tree, making of the
whole a kind of unguent, which retains its viscous properties more firmly, and is a better material than pitch.

Ships of the largest size require a crew of three hundred
men; others, two hundred; and some, one hundred and
fifty only, according to their greater or less bulk.   They
carry from five to six thousand baskets, or mat bags, of
pepper.

In former times they were of greater size than they are
at present; but the violence of the sea having in many
places broken up the islands, and especially in some of the
principal ports, there is a want of depth of water for vessels

INDIA

of such draught. They are on that account built of a smaller size.

The vessels are likewise moved with oars or sweeps, each of which requires four men to work it. Those of the larger class are accompanied by two or three large barks, capable of containing about one thousand baskets of pepper, and are manned with sixty, eighty, or one hundred sailors. These small craft are often employed to tow the larger, when working their oars, or even under sail, provided the wind be on the quarter, but not when right aft, because, in that case, the sails of the larger vessel must becalm those of the smaller. The ships also carry with them as many as ten small boats, for the purpose of carrying out anchors, for fishing, and a variety of other services. They are slung over the sides, and lowered into the water when there is occasion to use them. The barks are in like manner provided with their small boats.

When a ship, having been on a voyage for a year or more, stands in need of repair, the practice is to give her a course of sheathing over the original boarding, forming a third course, which is caulked and paid in the same manner as the others. When she needs further repairs this is repeated, even to the number of six layers, after which she is condemned as unserviceable and not seaworthy.

Having thus described the shipping, we shall proceed to the account of India; but in the first instance we shall speak of certain islands in the part of the ocean where we are at present, and shall commence with the island named Zipangu.

Chapter 2

OF THE ISLAND OF ZIPANGU ⬛ AND THE GREAT KHAN'S ATTACK AGAINST IT

ZIPANGU [Japan] is an island in the eastern ocean, situated at the distance of about fifteen hundred miles from the main-land, or coast of Manji.

It is of considerable size; its inhabitants have fair complexions, are well made, and are civilized in their manners. Their religion is the worship of idols. They are independent of every foreign power, and governed only by their own kings. They have gold in the greatest abundance, its sources being inexhaustible, but as the king does not allow its being exported, few merchants visit the country. Nor is it frequented by much shipping from other parts.

The extraordinary richness of the sovereign's palace, according to what we are told by those who have access to the place is a wonderful sight. The entire roof is covered with a plating of gold, in the same manner as we cover houses, or more properly churches, with lead. The ceilings of the halls are of the same precious metal; many of the apartments have small tables of pure gold, of considerable thickness; and the windows also have golden ornaments. So vast, indeed, are the riches of the palace, that it is impossible to convey an idea of them.

In this island there are pearls also, in large quantities, of a pink colour, round in shape, and of great size equal in value to, or even exceeding that of the white pearls.

It is customary with one part of the inhabitants to bury their dead, and with another part to burn them. The former have a practice of putting one of these pearls into the mouth of the corpse. There are also found there a number of precious stones.

So great was the wealth of this island, that a desire was excited in the breast of the Great Khan Kublai, now reigning, to make the conquest of it, and to annex it to his dominions. In order to effect this, he fitted out a numerous fleet, and embarked a large body of troops, under the command of two of his principal officers, one of whom was named Abbacatan, and the other Vonsancin. The expedition sailed from the ports of Zai-tun and Kin-sai, and, crossing the intermediate sea, reached the island in safety.

A jealousy, however, arose between the two commanders, one of whom treated the plans of the other with contempt and resisted the execution of his orders. Because of this they were unable to gain possession of any city or fortified place, with the exception of one only, which was carried by assault, the garrison having refused to surrender.

It happened, after some time, that a north wind began to blow with great force, and the ships of the Tartars, which lay near the shore of the island, were driven foul of each other. It was then determined, in a council of the officers on board, that they ought to disengage themselves from the land; and accordingly, as soon as the troops were re-embarked, they set out to sea. The gale, however, increased to so violent a degree that a number of the vessels foundered. The people belonging to them, by floating upon pieces of the wreck, saved themselves upon an island lying about four miles from the coast of Zipangu.

The other ships, which, not being so near to the land, did not suffer from the storm, and in which the two chiefs were embarked, together with the principal officers, or those whose rank entitled them to command a hundred thousand or ten thousand men, directed their course homewards, and returned home to the Great Khan.

Chapter 3

WHAT CAME OF THE GREAT KHAN'S EXPEDITION ❦ AND OF THOSE LEFT ON THE ISLAND

THOSE of the Tartars who remained upon the island where they were wrecked, and who amounted to about thirty thousand men, finding themselves left without shipping, abandoned by their leaders, and having neither arms nor provisions, expected nothing less than to become captives or to perish, especially as the island afforded no habitations where they could take shelter and refresh themselves.

As soon as the gale ceased and the sea became smooth and calm, the people from the main island of Zipangu came over with a large force, in numerous boats, in order to make prisoners of these shipwrecked Tartars, and having landed, proceeded in search of them, but in a straggling, disorderly manner. The Tartars, on their part, being concealed from view by high land in the centre of the island, whilst the enemy were hurrying in pursuit of them by one road, made a circuit of the coast by another. This brought them to the place where the fleet of boats was at anchor. Finding these all abandoned, but with their colours flying, they instantly seized them, and pushing off from the island, sailed for the principal city of Zipangu, into which, from the appearance of the colours, they were suffered to enter unmolested. Here they found few of the inhabitants besides women, whom they retained for their own use, and drove out all others.

When the king learned of what had taken place, he was much afflicted, and immediately gave directions for a strict blockade of the city, which was so effectual that not any person was suffered to enter or to escape from it, during six months that the siege continued. At the expiration of this time, the Tartars, despairing of succour, surrendered upon the condition of their lives being spared.

These events took place in the course of the year 1279.* The Great Khan having learned some years after that the unfortunate issue of the expedition was to be attributed to the dissension between the two commanders, caused the head of one of them to be cut off. The other he sent to the savage island of Zorza, where it is the custom to execute criminals in the following manner. They are wrapped round both arms, in the hide of a buffalo fresh taken from the beast, which is sewed tight. As this dries, it compresses the body to such a degree that the sufferer is incapable of moving or in any manner helping himself, and thus miserably perishes.

Chapter 4

OF THE NATURE OF THE MANY IDOLS WORSHIPPED IN ZIPANGU ◀ AND OF THE PEOPLE BEING ADDICTED TO EATING HUMAN FLESH

IN this island of Zipangu [Japan] and the others in its vicinity, their idols are fashioned in a variety of shapes, some of them having the heads of oxen, some of swine, of dogs, goats, and many other animals. Some exhibit the appearance of a single head, with two faces; others of three heads, one of them in its proper place, and one upon each shoulder. Some have four arms, others ten, and some an hundred, those which have the greatest number being regarded as the most powerful, and therefore entitled to the most particular worship.

---

*Chinese Annals give this date as 1280 and describe the expedition as the sixth attempt on the part of Kublai Khan to conquer Japan. He also contemplated still another attack in 1283 but public sentiment among his people checked his ambition.

When they are asked by Christians wherefore they give to their deities these diversified forms, they answer that their fathers did so before them. "Those who preceded us," they say, "left them such, and such shall we transmit them to our posterity."

The various ceremonies practiced before these idols are so wicked and diabolical that it would be nothing less than an abomination to give an account of them in this book. The reader should, however, be informed that the idolatrous inhabitants of these islands, when they seize the person of an enemy who has not the means of effecting his ransom for money, invite to their house all their relations and friends. Putting their prisoner to death they cook and eat the body, in a convivial manner, asserting that human flesh surpasses every other in the excellence of its flavour.

It is to be understood that the sea in which the island of Zipangu is situated is called the Sea of Chin [China], and so extensive is this eastern sea, that according to the report of experienced pilots and mariners who frequent it, and to whom the truth must be known, it contains no fewer than seven thousand four hundred and forty islands, mostly inhabited. It is said that of the trees which grow in them, there are none that do not yield a fragrant smell. They produce many spices and drugs, particularly lignum-aloes and pepper, in great abundance, both white and black.

It is impossible to estimate the value of the gold and other articles found in the islands; but their distance from the continent is so great, and the navigation attended with so much trouble and inconvenience, that the vessels engaged in the trade, from the ports of Zai-tun and Kin-sai, do not reap large profits, for they are obliged to consume a whole year in their voyage, sailing in the winter and returning in the summer.

In these regions only two winds prevail; one of them during the winter, and the other during the summer season; so that they must avail themselves of the one for the outward, and of the other for the homeward-bound voyage. These countries are far remote from the continent of India. In terming this sea the Sea of Chin [China], we must understand it, nevertheless, to be a part of the ocean; for as we speak of the English Sea, or of the Egean Sea, so do the eastern people of the Sea of Chin and of the Indian Sea. We shall here cease to treat further of these countries and islands, as well on account of their lying so far out of the way, as of my not having visited them personally, and of their not being under the dominion of the Great Khan. We return now to Zai-tun.

Departing from the port of Zai-tun, and steering a westerly course, but inclining to the south, for fifteen hundred miles, you pass the gulf named Keinan, which extends to the distance of two months' navigation, along its northern shore, where it bounds the southern part of the province of Manji, and from thence to where it approaches the countries of Ania, Toloman, and many others already mentioned. Within this gulf there are a multitude of islands, for the most part well inhabited. About the coasts much gold-dust is collected from the sea, at those places where the rivers discharge themselves. Copper also and many other articles are found there, and with these a trade is carried on, the one island supplying what another does not produce. They traffic also with the people of the continent, exchanging their gold and copper for such necessaries as they may require. In the most of these islands grain is raised in abundance. This gulf is so extensive and the inhabitants so numerous, that it appears like another world.

Chapter 5

OF THE COUNTRY OF ZIAMBA • OF THE KING OF THAT COUNTRY • AND OF HIS BECOMING TRIBUTARY TO THE GREAT KHAN

WE now resume our former subject. Upon leaving Zai-tun and navigating fifteen hundred miles across this gulf, as has been mentioned, you arrive at a country named Ziamba [Indo-China], which is of great extent, and rich. It is governed by its own kings, and has its peculiar language. The inhabitants are worshippers of idols. An annual tribute, in elephants and nothing but elephants, is paid to the Great Khan, the occasion and circumstances of which shall be related.

About the year 1278, Kublai, having received accounts of the great wealth of this kingdom, resolved upon the measure of sending a large force, both of infantry and cavalry, to effect its conquest. The country was accordingly invaded by a powerful army, placed under the command of one of his generals, named Sogatu. The king, whose name was Accambale, and who was far advanced in years, feeling himself incapable of making resistance in the field to the forces of the Great Khan, retired to his strongholds, which afforded him security, and he there defended himself valiantly.

The open towns, however, and habitations on the plains, were in the meantime overrun and laid waste, and the king, perceiving that his whole territory would be ruined by the enemy, sent ambassadors to the Great Khan for the purpose of pleading for the old king, who had always preserved his dominions in a state of peace, and was anxious to save his people from destruction. The king was willing to pay yearly an honorary tribute of elephants and sweet-scented wood.

Upon receiving this proposal, the Great Khan, from motives of compassion, immediately sent orders to Sogatu for his retreat from thence with the force under his command, and directed him to proceed to the conquest of other countries. From that time the king has annually presented to the Great Khan, in the form of tribute, twenty of the largest and handsomest elephants to be found in his districts. Thus it was that the king of Ziamba became the subject of the Great Khan.

Having related the foregoing, we shall now mention some circumstances respecting this king and his country. In the first place it should be noticed that in his dominions no young woman can be given in marriage, until she has been first proved by the king. Those who prove agreeable to him he retains for some time, and when they are dismissed, he furnishes them with a sum of money, in order that they may be able to obtain, according to their rank in life, advantageous matches. Marco Polo, in the year 1285, visited this place, at which period the king had three hundred and twenty-six children, male and female. Most of the former had distinguished themselves as valiant soldiers. The country abounds with elephants. There are also many forests of ebony of a fine black, which is worked into various handsome articles of furniture. No other circumstance requires particular mention. Leaving this place, we shall now speak of the island called Java Major.

Chapter 6

OF THE ISLAND OF JAVA

DEPARTING from Ziamba, and steering between south and south-east, fifteen hundred miles, you reach an island of very great size, named Java. According to the reports of some well-informed navigators, it is the greatest in the world, and has a compass above three thousand miles. It is under the dominion of one king only, nor do the inhabitants pay tribute to any other power. They are worshippers of idols.

The country abounds with rich commodities. Pepper, nutmegs, spikenard, galangal, cubebs, cloves and all the other valuable spices and drugs, are the produce of the island; which occasion it to be visited by many ships laden with merchandise, that yields to the owners considerable profit.

The quantity of gold collected there exceeds all calculation and belief. From thence it is that the merchants of Zai-tun and of Manji in general have imported, and to this day import, that metal to a great amount, and from thence also is obtained the greatest part of the spices that are distributed throughout the world. That the Great Khan has not brought the island under subjection to him, must be attributed to the length of the voyage and the dangers of the navigation.

Chapter 7

OF THE ISLANDS OF SONDUR AND KONDUR ❦ AND OF THE COUNTRY OF LOCHAC

Upon leaving the island of Java, and steering a course between south and south-west, seven hundred miles, you arrive at two islands. The larger is named Sondur, and the other Kondur. Both being uninhabited, it is unnecessary to say more respecting them.

Having run the distance of fifty miles from these islands, in a south-easterly direction, you reach an extensive and rich province, that forms a part of the main land, and is named Lochac. Its inhabitants are idolaters. They have a language peculiar to themselves, and are governed by their own king, who pays no tribute to any other, the situation of the country being such as to protect it from any hostile attack. Were it assailable, the Great Khan would not have delayed to bring it under his dominion.

In this country brazil wood [dyewood], is produced in large quantities. Gold is abundant to a degree scarcely credible; elephants are found there; and the objects of the chase, either with dogs or birds, are in plenty.

From hence are exported all those porcelain shells, which, being carried to other countries, are there circulated for money, as has been already noticed. Besides these circumstances there is nothing further that requires mention, unless it be that the country is wild and mountainous, and is little frequented by strangers, whose visits the king discourages, in order that his treasures and other secret matters of his realm may be as little known to the rest of the world as possible.

Chapter 8

OF THE ISLAND OF PENTAN ❧ AND OF THE KINGDOM OF MALAIUR

DEPARTING from Lochac, and keeping a southerly course for five hundred miles, you reach an island named Pentan [Bentan], the coast of which is wild and uncultivated, but the woods abound with sweet-scented trees. Between the province of Lochac and this island of Pentan, the sea, for the space of sixty miles, is not more than four fathoms in depth, which obliges those who navigate it to lift the rudders of their ships.

After sailing these sixty miles, in a south-easterly direction, and then proceeding thirty miles further, you arrive at an island, in itself a kingdom, named Malaiur, which is

likewise the name of its chief city. The people are governed by a king, and have their own peculiar language.
The town is large and well-built. A considerable trade is
there carried on in spices and drugs, with which the place
abounds. Nothing else that requires notice presents itself.
Proceeding onwards from thence, we shall now speak of
Java Minor.

Chapter 9

OF THE ISLAND OF JAVA MINOR

Upon leaving the island of Pentan, and steering in the
direction of south-east for about one hundred miles, you
reach the island of Java the Lesser [Sumatra]. Small,
however, as it may be termed by comparison, it is not less
than two thousand miles in circuit.

In this island there are eight kingdoms, governed by so
many kings, and each kingdom has its own proper language,
distinct from those of all the others. The people are
idolaters. It contains abundance of riches, and all sorts
of spices, sappan-wood for dyeing, and various other kinds
of drugs, which, on account of the length of the voyage and
the danger of the navigation, are not imported into our
country, but which find their way to the provinces of Manji
and Cathay.

We shall now treat separately of what relates to the
inhabitants of each of these kingdoms; but in the first
place it is proper to observe that the island lies so far to
the southward as to render the north star invisible. Six
of the eight kingdoms were visited by Marco Polo; and
these he will describe, omitting the other two, which he had
not an opportunity of seeing.

We shall begin with the kingdom of Felech, which is one
of the eight. Its inhabitants are for the most part idolaters,

J A V A

but many of those who dwell in the seaport towns have been converted to the religion of Mahomet, by the Saracen merchants who constantly frequent them. Those who inhabit the mountains live in a beastly manner. They eat human flesh, and indiscriminately all other sorts of flesh, clean and unclean. Their worship is directed to a variety of objects, for each individual adores throughout the day the first thing that presents itself to his sight when he rises in the morning.

Upon leaving the last-mentioned kingdom, you enter that of Basman, which is independent of the others, and has its peculiar language. The people profess obedience to the Great Khan, but pay him no tribute, and their distance is so great, that his troops cannot be sent to these parts. The whole island, indeed, is nominally subject to him, and when ships pass that way the opportunity is taken of sending him rare and curious articles, and especially a particular sort of falcon.

In the country are many wild elephants and rhinoceroses, which latter are much inferior in size to the elephant, but their feet are similar. Their hide resembles that of the buffalo. In the middle of the forehead they have a single horn; but with this weapon they do not injure those whom they attack, employing only for this purpose their tongue, which is armed with long, sharp spines. Their head is like that of a wild boar, and they carry it low towards the ground. They take delight in muddy pools, and are filthy in their habits. They are not of that description of animals [unicorn] which suffer themselves to be taken by maidens, as our people suppose, but are quite of a contrary nature. There are found in this district monkeys of various sorts, and vultures as black as crows, which are of a large size, and pursue the quarry in a good style.

It should be known that what is reported respecting the dried bodies of diminutive human creatures, or pigmies, brought from India, is an idle tale, such men being manufactured in this island in the following manner. The country produces a species of monkey, of a tolerable size, and having a countenance resembling that of a man. Those persons who make it their business to catch them, shave off the hair, leaving it only about the chin, and those other parts where it naturally grows on the human body. They then dry and preserve them with camphor and other drugs; and having prepared them in such a mode that they have exactly the appearance of little men, they put them into wooden boxes, and sell them to trading people, who carry them to all parts of the world. But this is merely an imposition. Neither in India, nor in any other country, however wild, have pigmies been found of a form so diminutive as these exhibit. Sufficient having been said of this kingdom, which presents nothing else remarkable, we shall now speak of another, named Samara.

Chapter 10

OF THE KINGDOMS NAMED SAMARA AND DRAGOIAN

LEAVING Basman, you enter the kingdom of Samara, being another of those into which the island is divided. In this Marco Polo resided five months, during which, exceedingly against his inclination, he was detained by contrary winds. The north star is not visible here, nor even the stars that are in the wain. The people are idolaters; they are governed by a powerful prince, who professes himself the vassal of the Great Khan.

As it was necessary to continue for so long a time at this island Marco Polo established himself on shore, with a party of about 2,000 men. In order to guard against mischief from the savage natives, who seek for opportunities of seizing stragglers, putting them to death, and eating them, he caused a large and deep ditch to be dug around him on the land side, in such manner that each of its extremities terminated in the port, where the shipping lay. The ditch he strengthened by erecting several blockhouses or redoubts of wood, the country affording an abundant supply of that material. Being defended by this kind of fortification, he kept the party in complete security during the five months of their residence. Such was the confidence inspired amongst the natives, that they furnished supplies of victuals and other necessary articles according to an agreement made with them.

No finer fish for the table can be met with in any part of the world than are found here. There is no wheat produced, but the people live upon rice. Wine is not made; but from a species of tree resembling the date-bearing palm [gomuti palm] they procure an excellent beverage in the following manner. They cut off a branch, and put over the opening a vessel to receive the juice as it distils from the wound. This is filled in the course of a day and a night. So wholesome are the qualities of this liquor, that it affords relief in dropsical complaints, as well as in those of the lungs and of the spleen. When these shoots that have been cut are perceived not to yield any more juice, they contrive to water the trees, by bringing from the river, in pipes or channels, so much water as is sufficient for the purpose; and upon this being done, the juice runs again as it did at first. Some trees naturally yield it of a reddish, and others of a pale colour.

The Indian nuts [coco-nuts] also grow here, of the size of a man's head, containing an edible substance that is sweet

and pleasant to the taste, and white as milk. The cavity
of this pulp is filled with a liquor clear as water, cool,
and better flavoured and more delicate than wine or any
other kind of drink whatever. The inhabitants feed upon
flesh of every sort, good or bad, without distinction.

Dragoian is a kingdom governed by its own prince, and
having its peculiar language. Its inhabitants are uncivilized,
worship idols, and acknowledge the authority of the Great
Khan. They observe this horrible custom, in cases where
any member of the family is afflicted with a disease:—The
relations of the sick person send for the magicians, whom
they require, upon examination of the symptoms, to declare
whether he will recover or not. These, according to the
opinion suggested to them by the evil spirit, reply, either
that he will or will not recover. If the decision be that he
cannot, the relations then call in certain men, whose
peculiar duty it is and who perform their business with dex-
terity, to close the mouth of the patient until he be suffocated. This being done, they cut the body in pieces, in
order to prepare it as victuals. When it has been so dressed,
the relations assemble, and eat the whole of it, not leaving
so much as the marrow in the bones. Should any particle
of the body be suffered to remain, it would breed vermin,
and they believe these vermin, for want of further sustenance, would perish, and their death would prove the
occasion of grievous punishment to the soul of the deceased.
They afterwards proceed to collect the bones, and having
deposited them in a small, neat box, carry them to some
cavern in the mountains, where they may be safe against the
disturbance of wild animals. If they have it in their power
to seize any person who does not belong to their own
district, and who cannot pay for his ransom, they put him
to death, and devour him.

Chapter 11

OF THE KINGDOMS NAMED LAMBRI AND FANFUR

LAMBRI, in like manner, has its own king and its peculiar language. The country produces camphor, with a variety of other drugs. They sow brazil and when it springs up and begins to throw out shoots, they transplant it to another spot, where it is suffered to remain for three years. It is then taken up by the roots, and used as a dye-stuff. Marco Polo brought some of the seeds of this plant with him to Venice, and sowed them there; but the climate not being sufficiently warm, none of them came up.

In this kingdom are found men with tails, a span in length, like those of the dog, but not covered with hair.* The greater number of them are formed in this manner, but they dwell in the mountains, and do not inhabit towns. The rhinoceros is a common inhabitant of the woods, and there is abundance of all sorts of game, both beasts and birds.

Fanfur is a kingdom of the same island, governed by its own prince. In this part of the country a species of camphor, much superior in quality to any other, is produced. It is named the camphor of Fanfur, and is sold for its weight in gold.

There is not any wheat nor other corn, but the food of the inhabitants is rice, with milk, and the wine extracted from trees in the manner that has been described in the chapter respecting Samara. They have also a tree [sago tree] from which, by a singular process, they obtain a kind of meal. The stem is lofty, and as thick as can be grasped

---

* From time to time stories of tailed men have sprung up in Africa, Borneo, the islands in the Indian Sea and China, but to date none has ever been captured. Mediæval Europe had stories about Englishmen having short tails.

by two men. When from this the outer bark is stripped, the inner substance is found to be about three inches in thickness, and the central part is filled with pith, which yields a meal or flour. The pith is put into vessels filled with water, and is stirred about with a stick, in order that the fibres and other impurities may rise to the top, and the pure part subside to the bottom. When this has been done, the water is poured off, and the flour which remains, divested of all extraneous matter, is applied to use, by making it into cakes and various kinds of pastry. Of this, which resembles barley bread in appearance and taste, Marco Polo has frequently eaten, and some of it he brought home with him to Venice.

The wood of the tree, found here, may be compared to iron in this respect, that when thrown into water it immediately sinks. It admits of being split in an even direction from one end to the other, like the bamboo cane. Of this the natives make short lances: were they to be of any considerable length, their weight would render it impossible to carry or to use them. They are sharpened at one end, and rendered so hard by fire that they are capable of penetrating any sort of armour, and in many respects are preferable to iron.

What we have said on the subject of this kingdom, one of the divisions of the island, is sufficient. Of the other kingdoms composing the remaining part we shall not speak, because Marco Polo did not visit them. Proceeding further, we shall next describe a small island named Nocueran.

Chapter 12

OF THE ISLAND OF NOCUERAN

UPON leaving Java minor and the kingdom of Lambri, and sailing about one hundred and fifty miles, you arrive at two islands, one of which is named Nocueran [Nicobar], and the other Angaman.

Nocueran is not under the government of a king, and the people are little removed from the conditions of beasts. Both males and females go naked, without a covering to any part of the body. They are idolaters. Their woods abound with the noblest and most valuable trees, such as the white and the red sandal, those which bear the Indian coco-nuts, cloves, and sappan. Besides this they have a variety of drugs. Proceeding further, we shall speak of Angaman.

Chapter 13

OF THE ISLAND OF ANGAMAN

ANGAMAN is a very large island [Andaman Islands], not governed by a king. The inhabitants are idolaters, and are a most brutish and savage race, having heads, eyes, and teeth resembling those of the canine species. Their dispositions are cruel, and every person, not being of their own nation, whom they can lay their hands upon, they kill and eat. They have abundance and variety of drugs. Their food is rice and milk, and flesh of every description. They have Indian nuts, apples, and many other fruits different from those which grow in our country.

Chapter 14

OF THE ISLAND OF ZEILAN

TAKING a departure from the island of Angaman, and steering a course something to the southward of west, for a thousand miles, the island of Zeilan [Ceylon] presents itself. This, for its actual size, is better than any other island in the world. It is in circuit two thousand four hundred miles, but in ancient times it was still larger, its circumference then measuring full three thousand six hundred miles, as you find in the charts of the mariners of those seas. But the northern gales, which blow with violence, have in a manner corroded the mountains, so that they have in some parts fallen and sunk in the sea, and the island, from that cause, no longer retains its original size.

It is governed by a king whose name is Sender-naz. The people worship idols, and are independent of every other state. Both men and women go nearly in a state of nudity, only wrapping a cloth round the middle part of their bodies. They have no grain besides rice and sesame, of which latter they make oil. Their food is milk, rice, and flesh, and they drink the wine drawn from trees, which has already been described. There is here the best dye-wood that can anywhere be met with.

The island produces more beautiful and valuable rubies than are found in any other part of the world, and likewise sapphires, topazes, amethysts, garnets, and many other precious and costly stones. The king is reported to possess the grandest ruby that ever was seen, being a span in length, and the thickness of a man's arm, brilliant beyond description, and without a single flaw. It has the appearance of a glowing fire, and upon the whole is so valuable that no estimation can be made of its worth in money. The Great

Khan, Kublai, sent ambassadors to this monarch, with a request that he would yield to him the possession of this ruby; in return for which he should receive the value of a city. The answer he made was to this effect: that he would not sell it for all the treasure of the universe; nor could he on any terms suffer it to go out of his dominions, being a jewel handed down to him by his predecessors on the throne. The Great Khan failed therefore to acquire it.

The people of this island are no soldiers but, on the contrary, are poor and cowardly creatures. When there is occasion to employ soldiers, they are brought from other countries.

Chapter 15

THE HISTORY OF SOGOMON BARCHAN ◀ AND THE BEGINNING OF IDOLATRY

In this island of Zeilan [Ceylon] there is a very high mountain, so rocky and precipitous that the ascent to the top is impracticable, as it is said, excepting by the assistance of iron chains employed for that purpose. By means of these some persons attain the summit, where the tomb of Adam, our first parent, is reported to be found. Such is the account given by the Saracens. But the idolaters assert that it contains the body of Sogomon Barchan [Buddha], the founder of their religious system, and whom they revere as a great saint.

He was the son of a king of the island, who devoted himself to an holy life, refusing to accept of kingdoms or any other worldly possessions, although his father endeavoured, by the allurements of women, and every other imaginable gratification, to divert him from the resolution he had adopted. Every attempt to dissuade him was in vain, and the young man fled privately to this lofty mountain, where, in the observance of celibacy and strict abstinence, he at length terminated his mortal career.

By the idolaters he is regarded as a saint. The father, distracted with the most poignant grief, caused an image to be formed of gold and precious stones, bearing the resemblance of his son, and required that all the inhabitants of the island should honour and worship it as a deity. Such was the origin of the worship of idols in that country; but Sogomon Barchan [Buddha] is still regarded as superior to every other.

In this belief, people flock from various distant parts in pilgrimage to the mountain on which he was buried. Some of his hair, his teeth, and the basin he made use of, are still preserved, and shown with much ceremony. The Saracens, on the other hand, maintain that these belonged to the prophet Adam, and are in like manner led by devotion to visit the mountain.

It happened that in the year 1284, the Great Khan heard from certain Saracens who had been upon the spot, the fame of these relics belonging to our first parent, and felt so strong a desire to possess them, that he was induced to send an embassy to demand them of the king of Zeilan. After a long and tedious journey, his ambassadors at length reached the place of their destination, and obtained from the king two large back-teeth, together with some of the hair, and a handsome vessel of green stone. When the Great Khan received intelligence of the approach of the messengers, on their return with such valuable curiosities, he ordered all the people of Kanbalu to march out of the city to meet them, and they were conducted to his presence with great pomp and solemnity. Having mentioned these particulars respecting the mountain of Zeilan, we shall proceed to the kingdom of Maabar [India].

THE ISLAND OF CEYLON

Chapter 16

OF THE PROVINCE OF MAABAR

LEAVING the island of Zeilan, and sailing in a westerly direction sixty miles, you reach the great province of Maabar, which is not an island, but a part of the continent of the greater India, as it is termed, being the noblest and richest country in the world.

It is governed by four kings, of whom the principal is named Sender-bandi. Within his dominions is a fishery for pearls, in the gulf of a bay that lies between Maabar and the island of Zeilan, where the water is not more than from ten to twelve fathoms in depth, and in some places not more than two fathoms.

The business of the fishery is conducted in the following manner. A number of merchants form themselves into separate companies, and employ many vessels and boats of different sizes, well provided with anchors. They engage and carry with them persons who are skilled in the art of diving for the oysters in which the pearls are enclosed. These they bring up in bags made of netting that are fastened about their bodies, and then repeat the operation, rising to the surface when they can no longer hold their breath. And after a short interval they dive again. The greater proportion of the pearls obtained from the fisheries in this gulf, are round, and of a good lustre. The spot where the oysters are taken in the greatest number is called Betala, on the shores of the mainland.

The gulf being infested with a kind of large fish, which often prove destructive to the divers, the merchants take the precaution of being accompanied by certain enchanters belonging to a class of Bramins, who, by means of their mystical art, have the power of stupefying these fish, so as to prevent them from doing mischief. As the fishing takes place in the daytime only, they discontinue the effect of the charm in the evening; in order that dishonest persons who might be inclined to take the opportunity of diving at night and stealing the oysters, may be deterred. The enchanters are likewise skilled in the art of fascinating all kinds of beasts and birds.

The fishery commences in the month of April, and lasts till the middle of May. The privilege of engaging in it is farmed of the king, to whom a tenth part only of the produce is allowed. To the magicians they allow a twentieth part, and consequently they reserve to themselves a considerable profit. By the time the period above-mentioned is completed, the stock of oysters is exhausted; and the vessels are then taken to another place, distant full three hundred miles from this gulf, where they establish themselves in the month of September, and remain till the middle of October. Independently of the tenth of the pearls to which the king is entitled, he requires to have the choice of all such as are large and well-shaped; and as he pays liberally for them, the merchants are not disinclined to carry them to him for that purpose.

Chapter 17

CONTINUES TO SPEAK OF THE PROVINCE OF MAABAR

THE natives of this part of the country always go naked, excepting that they cover with a piece of cloth those parts of the body which modesty dictates.

The king is no more clothed than the rest, except that he has a piece of richer cloth, and is honourably distinguished by various kinds of ornaments, such as a collar set with jewels, sapphires, emeralds, and rubies, of immense value.

THE PEARLS OF MAABAR

He also wears, suspended from the neck and reaching to the breast, a fine silken string containing one hundred and four large handsome pearls and rubies. The reason for this particular number is, that he is required by the rules of his religion to repeat a prayer or invocation so many times daily, in honour of his gods; and this his ancestors never failed to perform. The daily prayer consists of these words, *pacauca, pacauca, pacauca,* which they repeat one hundred and four times. On each arm he wears three gold bracelets, adorned with pearls and jewels; on three different parts of the leg, golden bands ornamented in the same manner; and on the toes of his feet, as well as on his fingers, rings of great value. To this king it is indeed a matter of pride to display such splendid regalia, as the precious stones and the pearls are all found in his own kingdom.

He has at the least five hundred wives and concubines, and when he sees a woman whose beauty pleases him, he immediately signifies his desire to possess her. In this manner he appropriated the wife of his brother, who being a discreet and sensible man, was prevailed upon not to make much noise about it.

The king retains about his person many knights, who are called "the devoted servants of his majesty, in this world and the next." These attend upon his person at court, ride by his side in processions, and accompany him on all occasions. They exercise considerable authority in every part of the realm. Upon the death of the king, and when the ceremony of burning his body takes place, all these devoted servants throw themselves into the same fire, and are consumed with the royal corpse; intending by this act to bear him company in another life.

The following custom likewise prevails. When a king dies, the son who succeeds him does not meddle with the treasure which the former had amassed, under the impression that it would reflect upon his own ability to govern, if being left in full possession of the territory, he did not show himself as capable of enriching the treasury as his father was. In consequence of this prejudice it is supposed that immense wealth is accumulated by successive generations.

No horses being bred in this country, the king and his three royal brothers expend large sums of money annually in the purchase of them from merchants who carry them thither for sale, and become rich by the traffic. They import as many as five thousand at a time and for each of them obtain five hundred saggi of gold, being equal to one hundred marks of silver. At the end of the year perhaps not three hundred of these remain alive, and thus the necessity is occasioned for replacing them. But it is my opinion that the climate of the province is unfavourable to the race of horses, and that from this arises the difficulty in breeding or preserving them. For food they give them flesh dressed with rice, and other prepared meats, the country not producing any grain besides rice. A mare, although of a large size, and covered by a handsome horse, produces only a small ill-made colt, with distorted legs, and unfit to be trained for riding.

The following extraordinary custom prevails at this place. When a man who has committed a crime, for which he has been tried and condemned to suffer death, upon being led to execution, declares his willingness to sacrifice himself in honour of some particular idol, his relations and friends immediately place him in a kind of chair, and deliver to him twelve knives of good temper and well sharpened. In this manner they carry him about the city, proclaiming, with a loud voice, that this brave man is about to devote himself to a voluntary death, from motives of zeal for the worship of the idol. Upon reaching the place where the sentence of the law would have been executed, he snatches up two of the knives, and crying out, "I devote myself to death in honour of such an idol," hastily strikes one of them into each thigh, then one into each arm, two into the belly, and two into the breast. Having in this manner thrust all the knives but one into different parts of his body, repeating at every wound the words that have been mentioned, he plunges the last of them into his heart, and immediately expires. As soon as this scene has been acted, his relations proceed, with great triumph and rejoicing, to burn the body; and his wife, from motives of pious regard for her husband, throws herself upon the pile, and is consumed with him. Women who display this resolution are much applauded by the community, as, on the other hand, those who shrink from it are despised and reviled.*

The greater part of the idolatrous inhabitants of this kingdom show particular reverence to the ox; and none will from any consideration be induced to eat the flesh of oxen. But there is a particular class of men termed gaui, who although they may eat of the flesh, yet dare not to kill the animal. But when they find a carcase, whether it has died a natural death or otherwise, they eat of it.

All descriptions of people daub their houses with cow-dung. Their mode of sitting is upon carpets on the ground, and when asked why they sit in that manner, they reply that a seat on the earth is honourable; that as we are sprung from the earth, so we shall again return to it; that none can do it sufficient honour, and much less should any despise the earth. These gaui and all their tribe are the

---

* "An unsympathetic Government made suttee (*widow burning*) illegal in 1829; but it is said that cases of it still occur." See *India and the Future*, by William Archer.

descendants of those who slew Saint Thomas the Apostle, and on this account no member of this tribe can possibly enter the building where the body of the blessed apostle rests. Were the strength of ten men employed to convey him to the spot, they could not hold him here, so great is the supernatural power of the holy corpse.

The country produces no other grain than rice and sesame.

The people go to battle with lances and shields, but without clothing, and are most wretched soldiers. They do not kill cattle nor any kind of animals for food, but when desirous of eating the flesh of sheep or other beasts, or of birds, they procure the Saracens, who are not under the influence of the same laws and customs, to play the butcher.

Both men and women wash their whole bodies in water twice every day, that is, in the morning and the evening. Until this ablution has taken place they neither eat nor drink; and the person who should neglect this observance, would be regarded as a heretic. It ought to be noticed, that in eating they make use of the right hand only, nor do they ever touch their food with the left. For every cleanly and delicate work they employ the former, and reserve the latter for uncleanly and disagreeable necessities, such as cleansing the secret parts of the body. They drink out of a particular kind of vessel, and each individual from his own, never making use of the drinking pot of another person. When they drink they do not apply the vessel to the mouth, but hold it above the head, and pour the liquor into the mouth, not suffering the vessel on any account to touch the lips. In giving drink to a stranger, they do not hand their vessel to him, but, if he is not provided with one of his own, pour the wine or other liquor into his hands, from which he drinks it, as from a cup.

Criminals in this country are punished with strict justice. With regard to debtors the following customs prevail. If application for payment shall have been repeatedly made by a creditor, and the debtor puts him off from time to time with false promises, the former may attach his person by drawing a circle round him, from whence he dare not depart until he has satisfied his creditor, either by payment, or by giving adequate security. Should he attempt to make his escape, he renders himself liable to the punishment of death, as a violator of the rules of justice.

Messer Marco, when he was in this country on his return homeward, happened to be an eye-witness of a remarkable transaction of this nature. The king was indebted in a sum of money to a certain foreign merchant, and although frequently asked for payment, put him off for a long time with promises. One day when the king was riding on horseback, the merchant took the opportunity of describing a circle round him and his horse. As soon as the king perceived what had been done, he immediately halted and would ride no further until the demand of the merchant was fully satisfied. The bystanders beheld what passed and marvelled at the king, saying that he was most just for he himself submitted to the laws of justice.

These people abstain from drinking wine made from grapes; and should a person be detected drinking wine, so disreputable would it be held, that his evidence would not be received in court. A similar prejudice exists against persons frequenting the sea, who, they observe, can only be people of desperate fortunes, and whose testimony in court ought not to be admitted. They do not, however, hold gross sensuality to be a crime.

The heat of the country is most excessive, and the inhabitants on that account go naked. There is no rain excepting in the months of June, July, and August, and if it was not for the coolness imparted to the air during these three months by the rain, it would be impossible to support life.

In this country there are many experts in the science of physiognomy, which teaches the knowledge of the nature and qualities of men, and whether they tend to good or evil. These qualities are immediately recognized upon the appearance of the man or woman. They also know what events are to be expected by meeting certain beasts or birds. More attention is paid by these people to the flight of birds than by any others in the world, and from thence they predict good or bad fortune. In every day of the week there is one hour which they regard as unlucky, and in these hours they do not make purchases, nor transact any kind of business, being persuaded that it would not be attended with success. They judge of the hour of the day by the length of a man's shadow when he stands erect.

When an infant is born, be it a boy or a girl, the father or the mother makes a memorandum in writing of the day of the week on which the birth took place; also of the age of the moon, the name of the month, and the hour. This is done because every future act of their lives is regulated by astrology.

As soon as a son attains the age of thirteen years, they set him at liberty, and no longer suffer him to be an inmate in his father's house; giving him to the amount, in their money, of twenty to twenty-four groats. Thus provided, they consider him as capable of gaining his own livelihood, by engaging in some kind of trade and thence deriving a profit. These boys never cease to run about in all directions during the whole course of the day, buying an article in one place, and selling it in another. At the season when the pearl fishery is going on, they frequent the beach, and make purchases from the fishermen or others, of five, six, or more small pearls, according to their means, carrying them afterwards to the merchants, who, on account of the heat of the sun, remain sitting in their houses, and to whom they say: "These pearls have cost us so much; pray allow such a profit on them as you may judge reasonable." The merchants then give something beyond the price at which they had been obtained. In this manner they deal in many other articles, and become excellent and most acute traders. When business is over for the day, they carry to their mothers their food to be cooked and served, but they never eat anything at their father's expense.

Not only in this kingdom, but throughout India in general, all the beasts and birds are unlike those of our own country, excepting the quails, which perfectly resemble ours. There are bats as large as vultures, and vultures as black as crows, and much larger than ours. Their flight is rapid, and they do not fail to seize their prey.

In their temples there are many idols, the forms of which represent them of the male and the female sex; and to these, fathers and mothers dedicate their daughters. Having been so dedicated, they are expected to attend whenever the priests of the convent require them to contribute to the gratification of the idol. On such occasions they repair thither, singing and playing on instruments, and adding by their presence to the festivity. These young women are very numerous, and form large bands. Several times in the week they carry an offering of food to the idol to whose service they are devoted, and of this food they say the idol partakes. A table for the purpose is placed before it, and upon this the dishes remain for the space of a full hour, during which damsels never cease to sing, and play, and exhibit wanton gestures. This lasts as long as a person

of condition would require for making a convenient meal.
They then declare that the spirit of the idol is content with
its share of the entertainment provided, and, ranging themselves around it, they proceed to eat in their turn. This
they perform several times every year until they are
married.

The reason given for assembling the young women, and
performing the ceremonies that have been described, is
this:—The priests declare that the god is out of humour
with and incensed against the goddess, refusing to have connexion or even to converse with her; and that if some
measure were not adopted to restore peace and harmony
between them, all the concerns of the monastery would go
to ruin, as the grace and blessing of the divinities would be
withheld from them. For this purpose it is, they expect
the girls to appear in a state of nudity, with only a cloth
round their waists, to chaunt hymns to the god and goddess.
These people believe that the god often comforts himself
with the society of the goddess.

The natives make use of a kind of bedstead, or cot, of
very light cane-work, so ingeniously contrived that when
they repose on them, and are inclined to sleep, they can
draw close the curtains about them by pulling a string. This
they do in order to exclude the tarantulas, which bite grievously, as well as to prevent their being annoyed by fleas and
other small vermin; whilst at the same time the air, so
necessary for mitigating the excessive heat, is not excluded.
Indulgences of this nature, however, are enjoyed only by
persons of rank and fortune; others of the inferior class
lie in the open streets.

Chapter 18

OF THE PLACE WHERE LIETH THE HOLY BODY OF ST. THOMAS AND THE MIRACLES THEREOF

IN this province of Maabar is the body of the glorious martyr, Saint Thomas the Apostle, who there suffered martyrdom. It rests in a small city [near Madras] not frequented by many merchants, because it is a place not very accessible. A vast number both of Christians and Saracens resort thither. The latter regard him as a great Saint, and name him Ananias, signifying a "Holy Man."

The Christians who perform this pilgrimage collect earth from the spot where he was slain, which is of a red colour, and reverentially carry it away with them; often employing it afterwards in the performance of miracles, and giving it, when diluted with water, to the sick, by which many disorders are cured.

In the year of our Lord 1288, a powerful baron of the country, who at the time of gathering the harvest had accumulated a very great quantity of rice, and not having granaries sufficient to deposit it all, thought proper to make use of the religious house belonging to the church of Saint Thomas. This being against the will of those who had charge of it, they beseeched him not to occupy this building given over to the accommodation of pilgrims who came to visit the tomb. But the pagan baron refused to remove the grain. On the following night the Saint appeared to him in a vision, holding in his hand a fork, which he pointed at the throat of the baron, saying to him: "If thou dost not immediately leave my house which thou hast occupied, I shall put thee to a miserable death." Awaking in a violent alarm, the baron instantly gave orders for doing what was required of him, declaring publicly that he had seen the

Saint in a vision. A variety of miracles are daily performed there, such as the healing of those who are sick or deformed.

The Christians who have the care of the church possess groves of those trees which produce the Indian nuts, and from these they get their living; paying, as a tax to one of the royal brothers, a groat monthly for each tree.

It is related that the death of this most holy Saint took place in the following manner. Having retired to a hermitage, where he was engaged in prayer, and being surrounded by a number of pea-fowls, with which bird the country abounds, an idolater of the tribe of the Gaui, before described, who happened to be passing that way, and did not perceive the holy man, shot an arrow at a peacock, which struck the Saint in the side. Finding himself wounded, he had time only to thank the Lord for all his mercies, and into His hands he resigned his spirit.

In this province the natives, although black, are not born of so deep a dye as they afterwards attain by artificial means, esteeming blackness the perfection of beauty. For this purpose, three times every day, they rub the children over with oil of sesame. The images of their deities they represent black, but the devil they paint white, and assert that all the demons are of that colour. Those amongst them who pay adoration to the ox, take with them, when they go to battle, some of the hair of a wild bull, which they attach to the manes of their horses, believing its virtue to be such, that every one who carries it about with him is secure from all kind of danger. On this account the hair of the wild bull sells for a high price in these countries.

Chapter 19

OF THE KINGDOM OF MURPHILI OR MONSUL

THE kingdom of Murphili is that which you enter upon leaving the kingdom of Maabar, after proceeding five hundred miles in a northerly direction. Its inhabitants worship idols, and are independent of any other state. They subsist upon rice, flesh, fish, and fruits.

In the mountains of this kingdom it is that diamonds are found.* During the rainy season the water descends in violent torrents amongst the rocks and caverns, and when these have subsided the people go to search for diamonds in the beds of the rivers, where they find many. Messer Marco was told that in the summer, when the heat is excessive and there is no rain, they ascend the mountains with great fatigue, as well as with considerable danger from the number of snakes with which they are infested. Near the summit, it is said, there are deep valleys, full of caverns and surrounded by precipices, amongst which the diamonds are found; and here many eagles and white storks, attracted by the snakes on which they feed, are accustomed to make their nests. The persons who are in quest of the diamonds take their stand near the mouths of the caverns, and from thence cast down several pieces of flesh, which the eagles and storks pursue into the valley, and carry off with them to the tops of the rocks. The men immediately ascend, drive the birds away, and recovering the pieces of meat, frequently find diamonds sticking to them. Should the eagles have had time to devour the flesh, they watch the place of their roosting at night, and in the morning find the

---

* The Great Mogul, Orloff, Koh-i-nor, and other large diamonds, have all come from this province.

stones amongst the dung and filth that drops from them.*
But you must not suppose that the good diamonds come
among Christians, for they are carried to the Great Khan,
and to the kings and chiefs of that country.

In this country they manufacture the finest cottons that
are to be met with in any part of India. They have cattle
enough, and the largest sheep in the world, and plenty of
all kinds of food.

Chapter 20
OF THE PROVINCE OF LAC ❧ LOAC ❧ OR LAR

LEAVING the place where rests the body of the glorious
Saint Thomas, and proceeding westward, you enter the
province of Lar, from whence the Bramins, who are spread
over India, derive their origin.

These are the best and most honourable merchants that
can be found. No consideration whatever can induce them
to speak an untruth, even though their lives should depend
upon it. They have also a hatred for cheating or of taking
the goods of other persons. They are likewise remarkable
for the virtue of being satisfied with the possession of one
wife. When any foreign merchant, unacquainted with the
usages of the country, introduces himself to one of these,
and commits to his hands the care of his merchandise, this
Bramin undertakes the management of it, disposes of the
goods, and renders a faithful account of the proceeds, attending scrupulously to the interests of the stranger, and

---

* This story is told by Sindbad the Sailor in the *Arabian Nights,* and is also found
with variations in Chinese and other Eastern literatures. Henri Cordier, in Yule's *Ser
Marco Polo,* says that the earliest record of this legend concerns the twelve jewels in the
breastplate of the high Hebrew Priest. It is also believed that the legend originated in
the Indian practice of sacrificing animals to the gods at the time a new mine was
opened. Birds of prey collected about the dead flesh to which diamonds adhered. This
interpretation is without much foundation.

not demanding any recompense for his trouble. The owner, however, grants him a profit of what he pleases to bestow.

They eat meat, and drink the wine of the country. They do not, however, kill any animal themselves, but get it done by the Mahometans. The Bramins are distinguished by a certain badge, consisting of a thick cotton cord, which passes over the shoulder and is tied under the arm, in such a manner that the thread appears upon the breast and behind the back.

The king is extremely rich and powerful, and has much delight in the possession of pearls and valuable stones. When the traders from Maabar present to him such as are of superior beauty, he trusts to their word with respect to the estimation of their value, and gives them double the sum that each is declared to have cost them. Under these circumstances, he has the offer of many fine jewels.

The people are gross idolaters, and pay great attention to signs and omens. When they are about to make a purchase of goods, they immediately observe the shadow cast by their own bodies in the sunshine, and if the shadow be as large as it should be, they make the purchase that day.

Moreover, when they are in any shop for the purpose of buying anything, if they see a tarantula, of which there are many, they take notice from which side it comes, and regulate their business accordingly. Again when they are going out of their houses, if they hear any one sneeze, they return into the house, and stay at home.

They are very abstemious in regard to eating, and live to an advanced age. Their teeth are preserved sound by the use of a certain vegetable which they are in the habit of masticating. It also promotes digestion, and conduces generally to the health of the body.

Amongst the natives of this region there is a class

peculiarly devoted to a religious life, who are named Chughi [Jogi], and who in honour of their divinities lead most austere lives. They go perfectly naked, not concealing any part of their bodies, and say there can be no shame in that state of nudity in which they came into the world. With respect to what are called the parts of shame, they observe that, not being conscious of the sins of the flesh, they have no reason to blush at their exposure.

They pay adoration to the ox, and carry a small figure of one, of gilt brass or other metal, attached to their foreheads. They also burn the bones of oxen, reduce them to powder, and with this make an ointment for the purpose of marking various parts of the body, which they do in a reverential manner. If they meet a person with whom they are upon cordial terms, they smear the centre of his forehead with some of these prepared ashes.

They do not deprive any creature of life, not even a fly, a flea, or a louse, believing them to be possessed with souls; and to feed upon any animal they would consider as a heinous sin. They even abstain from eating vegetables, herbs, or root, until they have become dry, holding the opinion that these also have souls. They make no use of spoons nor of plates, but spread their food upon the dried leaves of the Adam's apple, called likewise apples of paradise. They live to a great age, some of them even to a hundred and fifty years, enjoying health and vigour, although they sleep upon the bare earth. This must be attributed to their temperance and chastity. When they die, their bodies are burned, in order that they might not breed worms, who in time would die, and the spirit of the body would bear the sin of their death.

Chapter 21

OF THE CITY OF KAEL

KAEL is a considerable city, governed by Astiar, one of the four brothers, kings of the country of Maabar, who is rich in gold and jewels, and preserves his country in a state of profound peace. On this account it is a favourite place of resort for foreign merchants, who are well received and treated by the king. Accordingly all the ships coming from the west—as from Ormus, Chisti, Aden, and various parts of Arabia—laden with merchandise and horses, make this port, which is besides well situated for commerce. The prince maintains in the most splendid manner not fewer than three hundred women.

All the people of this city, as well as the natives of India in general, are addicted to the custom of having continually in their mouths the leaf called tembul; which they do, partly from habit, and partly from the gratification it affords. Upon chewing it, they spit out the saliva to which it gives occasion. Persons of rank have the leaf prepared with camphor and other aromatic drugs, and also with a mixture of quick-lime. I have been told that it is extremely conducive to health. If it is an object with any man to insult another in the grossest and most contemptuous manner, he spits the juice of this masticated leaf in his face. Thus insulted, the injured party hastens to the presence of the king, states the circumstances of his grievance, and declares his willingness to decide the quarrel by combat. The king thereupon furnishes them with arms, consisting of a sword and small shield; and all the people assemble to be spectators of the conflict, which lasts till one

of them remains dead on the field. They are, however, forbidden to wound with the point of the sword.

Chapter 22

OF THE KINGDOM OF KOULAM

UPON leaving Maabar and proceeding five hundred miles
towards the south-west, you arrive at the kingdom of
Koulam. It is the residence of many Christians and Jews,
who retain their proper language. The king is not tributary
to any other.

Much good dye-wood grows there, and pepper in great
abundance, being found both in the woody and the open
parts of the country. It is gathered in the months of
May, June, and July; and the vines which produce it are
cultivated in plantations. Indigo also, of excellent quality
and in large quantities, is made here. They procure it
from a certain herb, which is taken up by the roots and
put into tubs of water, where it is suffered to remain till it
rots; when they press out the juice. This, upon being
exposed to the sun, and evaporated, leaves a kind of paste,
which is cut into small pieces of the form in which we
see it.

The heat during some months is so violent as to be
scarcely endured, yet merchants come here from various
parts of the world, such, for instance, as the kingdom of
Manji and Arabia, attracted by the great profits they obtain
both upon the merchandise they import, and upon their
returning cargoes.

Many of the animals found here are different from those
of other parts. There are tigers entirely black; and various
birds of the parrot kind, some of them as white as snow,
with the feet and the beak red. Other birds have a mixture

K O U L A M

CHAP. 23 *MARCO POLO* 303

of red and azure, and still others of a diminutive size. The peacocks also are handsomer and larger than ours, as well as of a different form, and even the domestic fowls have a peculiar appearance. The same observation will apply to the fruits. The cause of such diversity, it is said, is the intense heat that prevails in these regions.

Wine is made from the sugar yielded by a species of palm. It is extremely good, and inebriates faster than the wine made from grapes. The inhabitants possess abundance of everything necessary for the food of man excepting grain, of which there is no other kind than rice; but of this the quantity is very great. Among them are many astrologers and physicians, well versed in their art.

All the people, both male and female, are black, and, with the exception of a small piece of cloth attached to the front of their bodies, they go quite naked. Their manners are extremely sensual, and they take as wives their relations by blood, their cousins, and the widows of their deceased brothers. But this, as I have been informed, is the state of morals in every part of India.

Chapter 23

OF KOMARI

Komari [Cape Comorin] is a province where a part of our northern constellation, invisible at Java, and to within about thirty miles of this place, may be just seen, and where it appears to be the height of a cubit above the horizon. The country is not much cultivated, being chiefly covered with forests, which are the abode of a variety of beasts, especially apes, so formed, and of such a size, as to have the appearance of men. There are also long-tailed monkeys,

very different from the former in respect to magnitude.
Tigers, leopards, and lynxes, abound.

Chapter 24

OF THE KINGDOM OF DELY

LEAVING the province of Komari, and proceeding westward three hundred miles, you reach the kingdom of Dely,
which has its proper king and peculiar language. It does
not pay tribute to any other state. The people worship
idols. There is no harbour for shipping, but a large river
with a safe entrance.

The strength of the country does not consist in the multitude of its inhabitants, nor in their bravery, but in the difficulty of the passes by which it must be approached, and
which render its invasion by an enemy nearly impossible.

It produces large quantities of pepper and ginger, with
many other articles of spicery. Should a vessel be accidentally driven within the mouth of its river, not having
intended to make that port, they seize and confiscate all
the goods she may have on board, saying: "It was your intention to have gone elsewhere, but our gods have conducted
you to us, in order that we may possess your property."
The ships from Manji arrive here before the expiration
of the fine-weather season, and endeavour to get their
cargoes shipped in the course of a week, or a shorter time
if possible, because of sand-banks along the coast, which
often prove dangerous, however well provided they may be
with large wooden [iron-wood] anchors calculated for
holding against hard gales of wind. The country is infested
with tigers, and many other ferocious animals.

Chapter 25

OF MALABAR

MALABAR is an extensive kingdom of the Greater India, situated towards the west, concerning which I must not omit to relate some particulars. The people are governed by their own king, who is independent of every other state, and they have their proper language.

In this country the north star is seen about two fathoms above the horizon. Here as in the kingdom of Guzzerat, which is not far distant, there are numerous pirates, who yearly scour these seas with more than one hundred small vessels, seizing and plundering all the merchant ships that pass that way. They take with them to sea their wives and children of all ages, who continue to accompany them during the whole of the summer's cruise. In order that no ships may escape them, they anchor their vessels at the distance of five miles from each other; twenty ships occupy a space of a hundred miles. Upon a trader's appearing in sight of one of them, a signal is made by fire or by smoke; when they all draw closer together, and capture the vessel as she attempts to pass. No injury is done to the crew, but as soon as they have made prize of the ship, they turn them on shore, recommending to them to provide themselves with another cargo, which, in case of their passing that way again, may be the means of enriching their captors a second time.

In this kingdom there is vast abundance of pepper, ginger, cinnamon, and Indian nuts. The finest and most beautiful cottons are manufactured that can be found in any part of the world.

The ships from Manji bring copper as ballast. Besides this they bring gold brocades, silks, gauzes, gold and silver bullion, together with many kind of drugs not produced in Malabar, and these they barter for the commodities of the province. There are merchants on the spot who ship the former for Aden, from whence they are transported to Alexandria.

Having now spoken of the kingdom of Malabar, we shall proceed to describe that of Guzzerat, which borders on it. Should we attempt to treat of all the cities of India, the account would be too long, and prove tiresome.

Chapter 26

OF THE KINGDOM OF GUZZERAT

THE kingdom of Guzzerat, which is bounded on the western side by the Indian Sea, is governed by its own king, and has its peculiar language. The north star appears from hence to have six fathoms of altitude.

This country affords harbour to pirates of the most desperate character. When in their cruises they seize upon a travelling merchant they immediately oblige him to drink a dose of sea-water which produces violent purging. In this way they discover whether he has swallowed pearls or jewels.

Here there is great abundance of ginger, pepper, and indigo. Cotton is produced in large quantities from a tree that is about six yards in height, and bears during twenty years; but the cotton taken from trees of that age is not adapted for spinning, but only for quilting. Such, on the contrary, as is taken from trees of twelve years old, is suitable for muslins and other manufactures of extraordinary fineness.

Great numbers of skins of goats, buffaloes, wild oxen, rhinoceroses, and other beasts are dressed here, and vessels

are loaded with them, and bound to different parts of
Arabia.　Coverlets for beds are made of red and blue
leather, extremely delicate and soft, and stitched with gold
and silver thread, upon these the Mahometans are accustomed to repose.　Cushions also, ornamented with gold
wire in the form of birds and beasts, are the manufacture
of this place; and in some instances their value is so high
as six marks of silver.　Embroidery is here performed with
more delicacy than in any other part of the world.　Proceeding further, we shall now speak of the kingdom named
Kanan.

Chapter 27

OF THE KINGDOM OF KANAN

KANAN [Bombay] is a large and noble kingdom, situated
towards the west.　We say towards the west, because Messer
Marco's journey being from the eastern side, he speaks
of the countries in the direction in which he found them.

It is governed by a prince, who does not pay tribute to
any other.　The people are idolaters and have a peculiar
language.　Neither pepper nor ginger grows here, but the
country produces a sort of incense, in large quantities, which
is not white, but on the contrary of a dark colour.

Many ships frequent the place in order to load this drug,
as well as a variety of other articles.　They likewise take
on board a number of horses, to be carried for sale to different parts of India.

Chapter 28

CONCERNING THE KINGDOM OF KAMBAIA

KAMBAIA [Cambay] is an extensive kingdom, situated
towards the west, governed by its own king, who pays no
tribute to any other, and having its proper language.　The

people are idolaters. In this country the north star is seen still higher than in any of the preceding, in consequence of its lying further to the north-west.

The trade carried on is very considerable, and a great quantity of indigo is manufactured. There is abundance of cotton cloth, as well as of cotton in the wool. Many skins well dressed are exported from hence, and the returns are received in gold, silver, copper, and tutty [zinc]. There not being anything else deserving of notice, I shall proceed to speak of the kingdom of Servenath.

Chapter 29

OF THE KINGDOM OF SERVENATH

SERVENATH, likewise, is a kingdom lying towards the west, the inhabitants of which are idolaters, are governed by a king who pays no tribute, have their peculiar language, and are a well-disposed people.

They gain their living by commerce and manufactures, and the place is frequented by a number of merchants, who carry thither their articles of merchandise, and take away those of the country in return. I was informed, however, that the priests who serve in the temples of the idols are the most cruel in the world. We shall now proceed to speak of the kingdom named Kesmacoran.

Chapter 30

OF THE KINGDOM OF KESMACORAN

THIS is an extensive country, having its proper king and its peculiar language. Some of the inhabitants are idolaters, but the greater part are Saracens.

They subsist by trade and manufactures. Their food is rice and wheat, together with flesh and milk, which they have in abundance. Many merchants come here, both by sea and land.

This is the last province of the Greater India, as you proceed to the north-west; for, as it begins at Maabar, so it terminates here. In describing it, we have noticed only the provinces and cities that lie upon the sea-coast; for were we to deal with those situated in the interior, it would render our work too long.

We shall now speak of some of the Indian Islands. One of them is termed the Island of Males, and the other, the Island of Females.

Chapter 31

OF THE ISLANDS OF MALES AND OF FEMALES ❦ AND WHY THEY ARE SO CALLED

DISTANT from Kesmacoran about five hundred miles toward the south, in the ocean, there are two islands within about thirty miles from each other. One of these is inhabited by men, without the company of women, and is called the Island of Males; and the other by women, without men, which is called the Island of Females.

The inhabitants of both are of the same race, and are baptized Christians, but hold the law of the Old Testament. The men visit the Island of Females, and remain with them for three successive months, namely, March, April, and May, each man occupying a separate habitation along with his wife. They then return to the male island, where they live the rest of the year, without the society of any female.

The wives retain their sons with them until they are of the age of twelve years, when they are sent to join their fathers. The daughters they keep at home until they become marriageable, and then they bestow them upon some of the men of the other island. This mode of living is occasioned by the peculiar nature of the climate, which does not allow of their remaining all the year with their wives, unless at the risk of sacrifice. They have their bishop, who is subordinate to the see of the island of Soccotera.

The men provide for the subsistence of their wives by sowing the grain, but the latter prepare the soil and gather in the harvest. The island likewise produces a variety of fruits. The men live upon milk, flesh, rice, and fish, of which they catch an immense quantity, being expert fishermen. Both when fresh taken and when salted, the fish are sold to the traders of the island, but whose principal object is to purchase ambergris, which is collected there.

Chapter 32

OF THE ISLAND OF SOCCOTERA

UPON leaving these islands, and proceeding five hundred miles in a southerly direction, you reach the island of Soccotera, which is very large, and abounds with the necessaries of life. The inhabitants find much ambergris upon their coasts, which comes from the entrails of whales.

Being an article of merchandise in great demand, they make it a business to take these fish; and this they do by means of a barbed iron, which they strike into the whale so firmly that it cannot be drawn out. To the iron harpoon a long line is fastened, with a buoy at the end, for the purpose of discovering the place where the fish, when dead, is to be found. They then drag it to the shore, and proceed to extract the ambergris from its belly, whilst from its head they procure several casks of oil.*

---

* "It will have been seen that the Heidelburg Tun of the Sperm Whale embraces the entire length of the entire top of the head . . . attend now, I pray you, to that marvellous and—almost fatal operation whereby the Sperm Whale's great Heidelburg Tun is tapped. . . . In this business he proceeds very heedfully, like a treasure-hunter in some old house, sounding the walls to find where the gold is masoned in. . . . A large whale's case generally yields about five hundred gallons of sperm." *Moby Dick.*

All the people, both male and female, go nearly naked, having only a scanty covering before and behind, like the idolaters who have been described. They have no other grain than rice, upon which, with flesh and milk, they subsist. Their religion is Christianity, and they are duly baptized, and are under the government, as well temporal as spiritual, of an archbishop, who is not in subjection to the Pope of Rome, but to a patriarch who resides in the city of Baghdad, by whom he is appointed. Or sometimes he is elected by the people themselves, and their choice is confirmed.

Many pirates resort to this island with the goods they have captured, and which the natives purchase of them without any scruple, justifying themselves on the ground of their being plundered from heathens and Saracens. All ships bound to the province of Aden touch here, and make large purchases of fish and of ambergris, as well as of various kinds of woven cotton goods manufactured on this island.

The inhabitants deal more in sorcery and witchcraft than any other people, although forbidden by their archbishop, who excommunicates them for the sin. Of this, however, they take little account. If any vessel belonging to a pirate should injure one of theirs, they do not fail to lay him under a spell, so that he cannot proceed on his cruise until he has repaid the damage. Even should he have had a fair and leading wind, they have the power of causing it to change, and obliging him, in spite of himself, to return to the island.

They can, in like manner, cause the sea to become calm, and at their will can raise tempests, occasion shipwrecks, and produce many other extraordinary effects, that need not be mentioned. We shall now speak of the island of Madagascar.

Chapter 33

OF THE GREAT ISLAND OF MADAGASCAR

LEAVING the island of Soccotera, and steering a course between south and south-west for a thousand miles, you arrive at the great island of Madagascar, which is one of the largest and most fertile in the world. In circuit it is three thousand miles.

The inhabitants are Saracens, or followers of the law of Mahomet. They have four sheikhs, which in our language may be expressed by "elders," who divide the government amongst them. The people subsist by trade and manufacture, and sell a vast number of elephants' teeth, as those animals abound in the country, as they do also in that of Zenzibar, from whence the exportation is equally great.

The principal food eaten at all seasons of the year is the flesh of camels. Flesh of other cattle serves also for food, but the former is preferred, as being both the most wholesome and the most palatable of any to be found in this part of the world.

The woods contain many trees of red sandal, and, in proportion to the plenty in which it is found, the price of it is low. There is also much ambergris from the whales, and as the tide throws it on the coast, it is collected for sale.

The natives catch lynxes, tigers, and a variety of other animals, such as stags, antelopes, and fallow deer, which afford much sport; as do also birds, which are different from those of our climates.

The island is visited by many ships from various parts of the world, bringing assortments of goods consisting of brocades and silks of various patterns, which are sold to the merchants of the island, or bartered for goods in return. They make large profits.

Ships do not visit other numerous islands lying further south; this and the island of Zenzibar alone being frequented. This is because of the sea current that runs with such force towards the south that it renders their return impossible. The vessels that sail from the coast of Malabar for this island, perform the voyage in twenty or twenty-five days, but in their returning voyage are obliged to struggle for three months; so strong is the current of water, which constantly runs to the southward.

The people of the island report that at a certain season of the year, an extraordinary kind of bird, which they call a rukh, makes its appearance from the southern region. In form it is said to resemble the eagle, but it is incomparably greater in size; being so large and strong as to seize an elephant with its talons, and to lift it into the air, in order to drop it to the ground and in this way kill it. When dead the bird feasts upon the carcase.

Persons who have seen this bird assert that when the wings are spread they measure sixteen paces in extent, from point to point; and that the feathers are eight paces in length, and thick in proportion.*

Messer Marco Polo, conceiving that these creatures might be griffins, such as are represented in paintings, half birds and half lions, particularly questioned those who reported their

---

* "Until a very recent epoch there flourished in Madagascar huge birds . . . which laid enormous eggs, and not unnaturally recall the mythical 'roc' that figures so largely in Arabian tales." See "Fossil Birds," *Encyclopædia Britannica*. A giant egg is now in the British Museum. Its capacity would be about two-and-a-third gallons.

having seen them as to this point; but they maintained that their shape was altogether that of birds, or, as it might be said, of the eagle.

The Great Khan having heard this extraordinary relation, sent messengers to the island, on the pretext of demanding the release of one of his servants who had been detained there, but in reality to examine into the circumstances of the country, and the truth of the wonderful things told of it. When they returned to the presence of his Majesty, they brought with them, so I have heard, a feather of the rukh, positively affirmed to have measured ninety spans, and the quill part to have been two palms in circumference. This surprising exhibition afforded his Majesty extreme pleasure, and upon those by whom it was presented he bestowed valuable gifts.

They were also the bearers of the tusk of a wild boar, an animal that grows to the size of a buffalo, and it was found to weigh fourteen pounds. The island contains likewise giraffes, asses, and other wild animals, very different from these of our country. Having said what was necessary on this subject, we shall now proceed to speak of Zenzibar.

Chapter 34

OF THE ISLAND OF ZENZIBAR

BEYOND the island of Madagascar lies that of Zenzibar, which is reported to be in circuit two thousand miles. The inhabitants worship idols, have their own peculiar language, and do not pay tribute to any foreign power. They are large in stature, but their height is not proportioned to the bulk of their bodies. Were it otherwise, they would appear gigantic.

They are, however, strongly made, and one of them is

R   U   K   H

capable of carrying what would be a load for four of our
people. At the same time, he would require as much food
as five. They are black, and go naked, covering only the
private parts of the body with a cloth. Their hair is so
crisp, that even when dipped in water it can with difficulty
be drawn out. They have large mouths, their noses turn
up towards the forehead, their ears are long, and their
eyes so large and frightful, that they have the aspect of
demons. The women are equally ill-favoured, having wide
mouths, thick noses, and large eyes. Their hands, and also
their heads, are large and out of proportion.

There are in this island the most ill-favoured women
in the world. Their large mouths and thick noses, and
ill-favoured breasts are four times as large as those of
other women. They feed on flesh, milk, rice, and dates.
They have no grape vines, but make a sort of wine from
rice and sugar, with the addition of some spicy drugs, very
pleasant to the taste, and having the intoxicating quality
of the other.

In this island elephants are found in vast numbers, and
their teeth form an important article of trade.

In this country is found also the giraffe, which is a handsome beast. The body is well-proportioned, the fore-legs
long and high, the hind-legs short, the neck very long, the
head small, and in its manners it is gentle. Its prevailing
colour is light, with circular reddish spots. Its neck, including the head, is three paces.

The sheep of the country are different from ours, being
all white excepting their heads, which are black; and this
also is the colour of the dogs. The animals in general have
a different appearance from ours.

Many trading ships visit the place, which barter the goods
they bring for elephants' teeth and ambergris, of which

much is found on the coasts of the island, in consequence
of the sea abounding with whales.

The chiefs of the island are sometimes engaged in warfare with each other, and their people display much bravery
in battle and contempt of death. They have no horses, but
fight upon elephants and camels. Upon the backs of the
former they place castles, capable of containing from fifteen
to twenty men, armed with swords, lances, and stones,
with which weapons they fight. Previously to the combat
they give draughts of wine to their elephants, supposing
that it renders them more spirited and more furious in the
assault.

In treating of the provinces of India, I have described
only the principal and most celebrated; and the same has
been done with respect to the islands, the number of which
is quite incredible. I have heard, indeed, from mariners
and eminent pilots of these countries, and have seen in the
writings of those who have navigated the Indian seas, that
they amount to no fewer than twelve thousand seven hundred, including the uninhabited with the inhabited islands.

The division termed the Greater India extends from
Maabar to Kesmacoran, and comprehends thirteen large
kingdoms, of which we have enumerated ten. The Lesser
India commences at Ziampa, and extends to Murfili, com-
prehending eight kingdoms, exclusive of those in the islands,
which are very numerous. We shall now speak of the
Second or Middle India, which is called Abascia.

Chapter 35

TREATING OF THE GREAT PROVINCE NAMED ABASCIA ◂ OR MIDDLE INDIA

ABASCIA [Abyssinia] is an extensive country, termed the
Middle or Second India. Its principal king is a Christian.

Of the others, who are six in number, and tributary to the first, three are Christians and three are Saracens.

I was informed that the Christians of these parts, in order to be distinguished as such, make three signs or marks, namely, one on the forehead, and one on each cheek, which are imprinted with a hot iron.   This may be considered as a second baptism with fire, after the baptism with water. The Saracens have only one mark, which is on the forehead, and reaches to the middle of the nose.   The Jews, who are likewise numerous here, have two marks, and these upon the cheeks.

The capital of the principal Christian king is in the interior of the country.   The dominions of the Saracen princes lie towards the province of Aden.   The conversion of these people to the Christian faith was the work of the glorious apostle, St. Thomas, who having preached the gospel in the kingdom of Nubia, and converted its inhabitants, afterwards visited Abascia, and there, by the influence of his discourses and the performance of miracles, produced the same effect. He subsequently went to abide in the province of Maabar, where, after converting an infinite number of persons, he received, as we have already mentioned, the crown of martyrdom, and was buried on the spot.

These people of Abascia are brave and good warriors, being constantly engaged in hostility with the Soldan of Aden, the people of Nubia, and many others whose countries border upon theirs.   In consequence of this unceasing practice in arms, they are accounted the best soldiers in this part of the world.

In the year 1288, as I was informed, this great Abyssinian prince adopted the resolution of visiting in person the holy sepulchre of Christ in Jerusalem, a pilgrimage that is every year performed by vast numbers of his subjects.   He was, however, dissuaded from it by the officers of his government, who represented to him the dangers to which he would be exposed in passing through so many places belonging to the Saracens, his enemies. He then determined upon sending a bishop as his representative, a man of high reputation for sanctity, who, upon his arrival at Jerusalem, recited the prayers and made the offerings which the king had directed. Returning, however, through the dominions of the Soldan [Sultan] of Aden, the latter caused him to be brought into his presence, and endeavoured to persuade him to become a Mahometan. Upon his refusing to abandon the Christian faith, the Soldan, making light of the resentment of the Abyssinian monarch, caused him to be circumcised, and then suffered him to depart. Upon his arrival, and making a report of the indignity and violence to which he had been subjected, the king immediately gave orders for assembling an army, at the head of which he marched, for the purpose of exterminating the Soldan. The Soldan, on his part, called to his assistance two Mahometan princes, his neighbours, by whom he was joined with a very large force. In the conflict that ensued, the Abyssinian king was victorious, and having taken the city of Aden, he gave it up to pillage, in revenge for the insult his bishop had sustained.

The inhabitants of this kingdom live upon wheat, rice, flesh, and milk. They extract oil from sesame, and have abundance of all sorts of provisions. In the country there are elephants, lions, giraffes, and a variety of other animals, such as wild asses, and monkeys that have the resemblance of men, together with many birds, wild and domestic. It is extremely rich in gold, and much frequented by merchants, who obtain large profits. We shall now speak of the province of Aden.

Chapter 36

OF THE PROVINCE OF ADEN

THE province of Aden is governed by a king, who bears the title of Soldan [Sultan]. The inhabitants are all Saracens, and utterly detest the Christians. In this kingdom there are many towns and castles, and it has the advantage of an excellent port, frequented by ships arriving from India with spices and drugs. The merchants who purchase them with the intention of conveying them to Alexandria, unlade them from the ships in which they are imported, and distribute the cargoes on board of other smaller vessels or barks. With these they navigate a gulf of the sea for twenty days, more or less, according to the weather they experience.

Having reached their port, they then load their goods upon the backs of camels, and transport them overland, thirty days' journey, to the river Nile. Here they are again put into small vessels, called *jerms*, in which they are conveyed by the stream of that river to Kairo, and from thence, by an artificial canal, named Kalizene, at length to Alexandria.

This is the least difficult, and the shortest route the merchants can take with their goods, the produce of India, from Aden to that city. In this port of Aden, likewise, the merchants ship a great number of Arabian horses, which they carry for sale to all the kingdoms and islands of India, obtaining high prices for them, and making large profits.

The Soldan of Aden possesses immense treasures, arising from the taxes he lays, both on the merchandise that comes from India, and that which is shipped in his port as the returning cargo, this being the most considerable mart in all that quarter for the exchange of commodities, and the place to which all trading vessels resort.

I was informed that when the Soldan of Babylon led his army the first time against the city of Acre, and took it, this city of Aden assisted him with thirty thousand horses and forty thousand camels. So great is the hate borne against the Christians. We shall now speak of the city of Escier.

Chapter 37

OF THE CITY OF ESCIER

THE ruler of this city Escier [Shehr, Arabia] is a Mahometan, who governs it with justice, under the superior authority of the Soldan of Aden.

Its distance from thence is about forty miles to the south-east. Subordinate to it there are many towns and castles. Its port is good, and it is visited by many trading ships from India, which carry back a number of excellent horses, highly esteemed in that country, and sold there at considerable prices.

This district produces a large quantity of white incense of the first quality, which distils, drop by drop, from a certain small tree that resembles the fir. The people occasionally tap the tree, or pare away the bark, and from the incision the frankincense gradually exudes, which afterwards becomes hard. Even when an incision is not made a dripping is perceived to take place, in consequence of the excessive heat of the climate.

There are also many palm-trees, which produce good dates in abundance. No grain excepting rice and millet is cultivated in this country, and it becomes necessary to obtain supplies from other parts. There is no wine made from grapes; but they prepare a liquor from rice, sugar, and dates, that is a delicious beverage. They have a small breed of sheep, the ears of which are not situated like those in others of the species; two small horns growing in the place of them, and lower down, towards the nose, there are two orifices that serve the purpose of ears.

These people are great fishermen, and catch the tunny in such numbers, that two may be purchased for a Venetian groat. They dry them in the sun, and as by reason of the extreme heat, the country is in a manner burnt up, and no sort of vegetable is to be seen, they accustom their cattle, cows, sheep, camels, and horses, to feed upon dried fish, which being reguarly served to them, they eat without any signs of dislike.

The fish used for this purpose are of a small kind, which they take in vast quantities during the months of March, April, and May; and when dried, they lay up in their houses for the food of their cattle. These will also feed upon the fresh fish, but are more accustomed to eat them in the dried state.

In consequence also of the scarcity of grain, the natives make a kind of biscuit of the substance of the larger fish, in the following manner: they chop it into very small particles, and moisten the preparation with a liquor rendered thick and adhesive by a mixture of flour, which gives to the whole the consistency of paste. This they form into a kind of bread, which they dry and harden by exposure to a burning sun. A stock of this biscuit is laid up to serve them for the year's consumption.

The frankincense before mentioned is so cheap in the country as to be purchased by the governor at the rate of ten gold ducats the quintal, who sells it again to the merchants at forty bezants. This he does under the direction

of the Soldan of Aden, who monopolizes all that is produced in the district at the above price, and derives a large
profit from the re-sale. Nothing further presenting itself
at this place, we shall now speak of the city of Dulfar.

Chapter 38

OF THE CITY OF DULFAR

DULFAR is a large and respectable city or town, at the
distance of twenty miles from Escier, in a south-easterly
direction. Its inhabitants are Mahometans, and its ruler also
is a subject of the Soldan of Aden. This place lies near the
sea, and has a good port, frequented by many ships.

Arabian horses are collected here from the inland country, which the merchants buy up and carry to India, where
they gain considerably by disposing of them. Frankincense
is likewise produced here, and purchased by the merchants.
Dulfar has other towns and castles under its jusirdiction.
We shall now speak of the gulf at Kalayati.

Chapter 39

OF THE CITY OF KALAYATI

KALAYATI is a large town situated near a gulf which has
the name of Kalatu, distant from Dulfar, about six hundred miles towards the south-east. The people are followers of the law of Mahomet, and are subject to the
Melik of Ormus, who, when he is attacked and hard
pressed by another power, has recourse to the protection
afforded by this city, which is so strong in itself, and so
advantageously situated, that it has never yet been taken
by an enemy.

The country around it not yielding any kind of grain,

it is imported from other districts. Its harbour is good, and many trading ships arrive there from India, which sell their piece-goods and spices to great advantage, the demand being considerable for the supply of towns and castles lying at a distance from the coast. These likewise carry away freights of horses, which they sell advantageously in India.

The fortress is so situated at the entrance of the gulf of Kalatu, that no vessel can come in or depart without its permission. Occasionally it happens that the Melik of this city, who is under certain engagements with, and is tributary to the king of Kermain, throws off his allegiance in consequence of the latter's imposing some unusual contribution. Upon his refusing to pay the demand, and an army being sent to compel him, he departs from Ormus, and makes his stand at Kalayati, where he has it in his power to prevent any ship from entering or sailing. By this obstruction of the trade the king of Kermain is deprived of his duties, and being thereby much injured in his revenue, is constrained to end the dispute with the Melik.

The strong castle at this place constitutes, as it were, the key, not only of the gulf, but also of the sea itself, as from thence the ships that pass can at all times be discovered. The inhabitants in general of this country subsist upon dates and upon fish, either fresh or salted, having constantly a large supply of both; but persons of rank, and those who can afford it, obtain corn for their use from other parts. Upon leaving Kalayati, and proceeding three hundred miles towards the north-east, you reach the island of Ormus.

Chapter 40

OF ORMUS

Upon the island of Ormus there is a handsome and large city, built close to the sea. It is governed by a Melik, which is a title equivalent to that of lord. He has many towns and castles under his authority.

The inhabitants are Saracens, all of them professing the faith of Mahomet. The heat that reigns here is extreme; but in every house they are provided with ventilators, by means of which they introduce air to the different floors, and into every apartment, at pleasure. Without this resource it would be impossible to live in the place. We shall not say more of this city, as in a former book we have given an account of it, together with Kisi and Kerman.

Having thus treated sufficiently at length of those provinces and cities of the Greater India which are situated near the sea-coast, as well as some of the countries of Ethiopia, termed the Middle India, I shall now, before I bring the work to a conclusion, step back, in order to notice some regions lying towards the north, which I omitted to speak of in the preceding Books.

BOOK IV

THE WARS AMONG THE
TARTAR PRINCES AND SOME
ACCOUNT OF THE NORTHERN
COUNTRIES

Chapter 1

OF GREAT TURKEY

IN GREAT TURKEY THERE IS A king called Kaidu, who is the nephew of the Great Khan, for he was son of the son of Zagataï, who was brother to the Great Khan. He possesses many cities and castles, and is a very great lord. He is Tartar, and his men also are Tartar, and they are good warriors, which is no wonder, for they are all men brought up to war; and I tell you that this Kaidu never gave obedience to the Great Khan, without first making great war.

And you must know that this Great Turkey lies to the north-west when we leave Ormus, by the way already mentioned. Great Turkey is beyond the river Ion, and stretches out northward to the territory of the Great Khan.

This Kaidu has already fought many battles with the people of the Great Khan, and I will relate to you how he came to quarrel with him. You must know for a truth that Kaidu sent word one day to the Great Khan that he wanted his part of what they had obtained by conquest, claiming a part of the province of Cathay and of that of Manji. The Great Khan told him that he was quite willing to give him his share, as he had done to his other sons, if he, on his part, would repair to his court and attend his council as often as he sent for him; and the Great Khan willed further that he should obey him like the others his sons and his barons. On this condition the Great Khan said that he would give him part of their conquest of China.

Kaidu, who distrusted his uncle the Great Khan, rejected this condition, saying that he was willing to yield him obedience in his own country, but that he would not go to his court for he feared he would be put to death. Thus originated the quarrel between the Great Khan and Kaidu, which led to a great war, and there were many great battles between them. And the Great Khan posted an army round the kingdom of Kaidu, to prevent him or his people from committing any injury to his territory or people. But, in spite of all these precautions, Kaidu invaded his territory, and fought many times with the forces sent to oppose him. Now King Kaidu, by exerting himself, could bring into the field a hundred thousand horsemen, all good men, and well trained to war and battle. And moreover he has with him many barons of the lineage of the emperor, that is of Chinghis Khan, who was the founder of the empire.

We will now proceed to narrate certain battles between Kaidu and the Great Khan's people; but first we will describe their mode of fighting. When they go to war, each is obliged to carry with him sixty arrows, thirty of which are of a smaller size, intended for shooting at a distance, but the other thirty are larger, and have a broad blade. These they use near at hand, and strike their enemies in the faces and arms, and cut the strings of their bows, and do great damage with them. And when they have discharged all their arrows, they take their swords and maces, and give one another heavy blows with them.

Chapter 2

OF BATTLES THAT WERE FOUGHT BY KING KAIDU AGAINST THE ARMIES OF HIS UNCLE THE GREAT KHAN

IN the year 1266, this King Kaidu, with his cousins, one of whom was called Jesudar, assembled a vast number of people, and attacked two of the Great Khan's barons, who also were cousins of King Kaidu, though they held lands of the Great Khan. One of these was named Tabai or Ciban. They were sons of Zagataï, who had received Christian baptism, and was own brother to the Emperor Kublai.

Kaidu with his people fought with these his two cousins, who also had a great army, for on both sides there were about a hundred thousand horsemen. They fought very hard together, and there were many slain on both sides, but at last King Kaidu gained the victory, and did great damage to the others. But the two brothers, the cousins of King Kaidu, escaped without hurt, for they had good horses, which bore them away with great swiftness.

Having thus gained the victory, Kaidu's pride and arrogance increased, and he returned into his own country, where he remained full two years in peace, without any hostilities between him and the Great Khan. But at the end of two years Kaidu again assembled a great army. He knew that the Great Khan's son, named Nomogan, was at Karakoran, and that with him was George the grandson of Prester John, which two barons had also a very great army of horsemen. King Kaidu, having assembled his host, marched from his own country, and, without any occurrence worth mentioning, arrived in the neighbourhood of Karakoran, where the two barons, the son of the Great

Khan and the grandson of Prester John, were with their army.

The latter, instead of being frightened, prepared to meet them with the utmost ardour and courage; and having assembled their whole army, which consisted of not less than sixty thousand horsemen, they marched out and established their camp very well and orderly at a distance of about ten miles from King Kaidu, who was encamped with his men in the same plain. Each party remained in their camp till the third day, preparing for battle in the best way they could, for their numbers were about equal, neither exceeding sixty thousand horsemen, well armed with bows and arrows, and a sword, mace, and shield to each.

Both armies were divided into six squadrons of ten thousand men each, and each having its commander. And when the two armies were drawn up in the field, and waited only for the signal to be given by sounding the nacar, they sang and sounded their instruments of music in such a manner that it was wonderful to hear. For the Tartars are not allowed to commence a battle till they hear the nacars of their lord begin to sound. As soon as the sound of the nacars was heard, the battle began, and they put their hands to their bows, and placed the arrows to the strings. In an instant the air was filled with arrows like rain, and you might see many a man and many a horse struck down dead, and the shouting and the noise of the battle was so great, that one could hardly have heard God's thunder. In truth, they fought like mortal enemies. And truly, as long as they had any arrows left, those who were able ceased not to shoot; but so many were slain and mortally wounded, that neither party gained ground.

When they had exhausted their arrows, they placed the bows in their cases, and seized the swords and maces, and, rushing upon each other, began to give terrible blows with them. Thus they began a very fierce and dreadful battle, with such execution upon each other, that the ground was soon covered with corpses. Kaidu especially performed great feats of arms, and but for his personal prowess, which restored courage to his followers, they were several times nearly defeated. And on the other side, the son of the Great Khan and the grandson of Prester John also behaved themselves with great bravery. In a word, this was one of the most sanguinary battles that had ever taken place among the Tartars. It lasted till nightfall, and in spite of all their efforts, neither party could drive the other from the field, which was covered with so many corpses that it was a pity to see. Many a lady that day was made a widow, and many a child an orphan. And when the sun set, both parties gave over fighting, and returned to their several camps to repose during the night.

Next morning, King Kaidu, who had received information that the Great Khan had sent a very powerful army against him, put his men under arms at daybreak, and, all having mounted, he ordered them to proceed homewards. Their opponents were so weary with the previous day's battle, that they made no attempt to follow them, but let them go without molestation. Kaidu's men continued their retreat, until they came to Samarcand, in Great Turkey.

Chapter 3

WHAT THE GREAT KHAN SAID OF THE INJURIES DONE BY HIS NEPHEW KAIDU

Now the Great Khan was greatly enraged against Kaidu, who was always doing so much injury to his people and his territory, and he said that if he had not been his nephew, he should not have escaped an evil death. But his feelings of relationship hindered him from destroying him and his land, and thus Kaidu escaped from the hands of the Great Khan. We will now leave this matter, and we will tell you a strange history of King Kaidu's daughter.

Chapter 4

OF THE DAUGHTER OF KING KAIDU ❧ HOW STRONG AND VALIANT SHE WAS

You must know, then, that King Kaidu had a daughter named, in the Tartar language, Aigiarm, which means shining moon. This damsel was so strong, that there was no young man in the whole kingdom who could overcome her. She vanquished them all.

Her father the king wished to marry her; but she declined, saying, that she would never take a husband till she met with some gentleman who should conquer her by force, upon which the king, her father, gave her a written promise that she might marry at her own will. She now caused it to be proclaimed in different parts of the world, that if any young man would come and try strength with her, and should overcome her by force, she would accept him for her husband.

This proclamation was no sooner made, than many came from all parts to try their fortune. The trial was made with great solemnity. The king took his place in the principal hall of the palace, with a large company of men and women; then came the king's daughter, in a dress of cendal, very richly adorned, and next came the young man, also in a dress of cendal. The agreement was, that if the young man overcame her so as to throw her by force to the ground, he was to have her for wife; but if, on the contrary, he should be overcome by the king's daughter, he was to forfeit to her a hundred horses. In this manner the damsel gained more than ten thousand horses, for she could meet with no one able to conquer her, which was no wonder, for she was so well-made in all her limbs, and so tall and strongly built, that she might almost be taken for a giantess.

At last, about the year 1280, there came the son of a rich king, who was very beautiful and young. He was accompanied with a very fine retinue, and brought with him a thousand beautiful horses. Immediately on his arrival, he announced that he was come to try his strength with the lady. King Kaidu received him very gladly, for he was very desirous to have this youth for his son-in-law, knowing him to be the son of the king of Pamar. Kaidu privately told his daughter that he wished her on this occasion to let herself be vanquished. But she said she would not do so for anything in the world. Thereupon the king and queen took their places in the hall, with a great attendance of both sexes, and the king's daughter presented herself as usual, and also the king's son, who was remarkable no less for his beauty than for his great strength.

When they were brought into the hall, it was, on account of the superior rank of the claimant, agreed as the conditions of the trial, that if the young prince were conquered, he should forfeit the thousand horses he had brought with him as his stake. This agreement having been made, the wrestling began; and all who were there, including the king and queen, wished heartily that the prince might be the victor, and become the husband of the princess. But, contrary to their hopes, after much pulling and tugging, the king's daughter gained the victory, and the young prince was thrown on the pavement of the palace, and lost his thousand horses. There was not one person in the whole hall who did not lament his defeat.

After this the king took his daughter with him into many battles, and not a cavalier in the host displayed so much valour; and at last the damsel rushed into the midst of the enemy, and seizing upon a horseman, carried him off to her own people. We will now quit this episode, and proceed to relate a great battle which fell out between Kaidu and Argon, the son of Abaga the lord of the east.

Chapter 5

HOW ABAGA SENT ARGON HIS SON WITH AN ARMY

Now Abaga, the lord of the east, held many provinces and many lands, which bordered on the territory of King Kaidu, on the side towards the tree which is called in the book of Alexander, *Arbor Secco*. And Abaga, in consequence of the damages done to his lands by King Kaidu, sent his son Argon with a very great number of horsemen into the country of the Arbor Secco, as far as the river Ion, where they remained to protect the country against King Kaidu's people.

In this manner Argon and his men remained in the plain of the Arbor Secco, and garrisoned many cities and castles thereabouts. Thereupon King Kaidu assembled a great number of horsemen, and gave the command of them to his brother Barac, a prudent and brave man, with orders to fight Argon. Barac promised to fulfil his commandment, and to do his best against Argon and his army. He marched with his army, and proceeded for many days without meeting with any accident worth mentioning, till he reached the river Ion, where he was only ten miles distant from the army of Argon. Both sides immediately prepared for battle, and in a very fierce engagement, which took place three days afterwards, the army of Barac was overpowered, and pursued with great slaughter over the river.

Chapter 6

HOW ARGON SUCCEEDED HIS FATHER IN THE SOVEREIGNTY

SOON after this victory, Argon received intelligence that his father Abaga was dead, for which he was very sad. He set out with all his host on his way to his father's court, a distance of forty days' journey, in order to receive the sovereignty.

Now Abaga had a brother named Acomat Soldan, who had become a Saracen, and who no sooner heard of his brother Abaga's death, than he formed the design of seizing the succession for himself, considering that Argon was at too great a distance to prevent him. He therefore collected a powerful army, went direct to the court of his brother Abaga, and seized upon the sovereignty.

There he found such an immense quantity of treasure as could hardly be believed, and by distributing this very lavishly among Abaga's barons and knights, he won their hearts, and they declared they would have no other lord but him. Moreover, Acomat Soldan showed himself a very good lord, and made himself beloved by everybody. But he had not long enjoyed his usurped power, when news came that Argon was approaching with a very great host. Acomat showed no alarm, but courageously summoned his barons and others, and within a week he had assembled a vast number of cavalry, who all declared that they were ready to march against Argon, and that they desired nothing more than to take him and put him to death.

Chapter 7

HOW ACOMAT WENT WITH HIS HOST TO FIGHT ARGON

WHEN Acomat Soldan had collected full sixty thousand horsemen, he set out on his way to encounter Argon and his people, and at the end of ten days' march he halted, having received intelligence that the enemy was only five days' march from him, and equal in number to his own army. Then Acomat established his camp in a very great and fair plain, and announced his intention of awaiting his enemy there, as a favourable place for giving battle.

As soon as he arranged his camp, he called together his people, and addressed them as follows: "Lords," said he, "you know well how I ought to be lord of all which my brother Abaga held, because I was the son of his father, and I assisted in the conquest of all the lands and territories we possess. I will say no more, for I know that you are wise men and love justice, and that you will act for the honour and good of us all." When he had ended, all the barons, and knights, and others who were there, replied with one accord that they would not desert him as long as they had life in their bodies. After this Acomat and his army remained in their camp, waiting the approach of the enemy.

Chapter 8

HOW ARGON TOOK COUNSEL WITH HIS BARONS

To return to Argon; as soon as he received certain intelligence of the movements of Acomat, and knew that he was encamped with so large an army, he was greatly affected, but he thought it wise to show courage and ardour before his men. Having called all his barons and wise counsellors into his tent, for he was encamped also in a very fair spot,

he addressed them as follows: "Fair brothers and friends,"
said he, "you know well how tenderly my father loved you;
while alive he treated you as brothers and sons, and you
know in how many battles you were with him, and how
you helped him to conquer the land he possessed. You
know, too, that I am the son of him who loved you so much,
and I myself love you as though you were my own body.
And truly every one ought to reckon on victory, since justice is on our side, and our enemies are in the wrong. I
will say no more, but again to implore every one of you to
do his duty."

Chapter 9

HOW THE BARONS REPLIED TO ARGON

WHEN the barons and knights who were present had
heard Argon's address, each resolved that he would prefer
death in the battle to defeat; and while they stood silent,
reflecting on his words, one of the great barons arose and
spoke thus: "Fair sir Argon, fair sir Argon," said he, "we
know well that what you have said to us is the truth, and
therefore I will be spokesman for all your men who are
with you to fight this battle, and tell you openly that we will
not fail you as long as we have life in our bodies, and that
we would rather all die than not obtain the victory."

When this man had ended, all the others declared that
they were of his opinion, and the whole army clamoured to
be led against the enemy without delay. Accordingly, early
next morning, Argon and his people began their march with
very resolute hearts, and when they reached the extensive
plain in which Acomat was encamped, they established their
camp in good order at a distance of about ten miles from
him. As soon as he had encamped, Argon sent two trusty
messengers on a mission to his uncle.

Chapter 10

HOW ARGON SENT HIS MESSENGERS TO ACOMAT

WHEN these two trusty messengers, who were men of very advanced age, arrived at the enemy's camp, they dismounted at Acomat's tent, where he was attended by a great company of his barons, and having entered it, they saluted him courteously. After they had remained seated a short space, one of the messengers rose up on his feet and delivered his message as follows: "Fair sir Acomat," said he, "your nephew Argon wonders much at your conduct in taking from him his sovereignty, and now again in coming to engage him in mortal combat; truly this is not well, nor have you acted as a good uncle ought to act towards his nephew. Wherefore he informs you by us that he prays you gently, as that good uncle and father, that you restore him his right, so that there be no battle between you, and he will show you all honour, and you shall be lord of all his land under him. This is the message which your nephew sends you by us."

Chapter 11

ACOMAT'S REPLY TO THE MESSAGE OF ARGON

WHEN Acomat Soldan had heard the message of his nephew Argon, he replied as follows: "Sir messenger," said he, "what my nephew says is vain, for the land is mine and not his. I conquered it as well as his father; and therefore tell my nephew that if he will, I will make him a great lord, and I will give him land enough, and he shall be as my son, and the highest in rank after me. And if he will not, you may assure him that I will do all in my power to put him to death. Now this is what I will do for my

nephew, and no other thing or other arrangement shall you
ever have from me."

When Acomat had concluded, the messengers asked again,
"Is this all the answer which we shall have?" "Yes," said
he, "you shall have no other as long as I live."

The messengers immediately departed, and riding as fast
as they could to Argon's camp, dismounted at his tent and
told him all that had passed.   When Argon heard his
uncle's message, he was so enraged, that he exclaimed in
the hearing of all who were near him, "Since I have received
such injury and insult from my uncle, I will never live or
hold land if I do not take such vengeance that all the
world shall talk of it!"

After these words, he addressed his barons and knights:
"Now we have nothing to do but to go forth as quickly as
we can and put these faithless traitors to death, and it is my
will that we attack them to-morrow morning, and do our
utmost to destroy them."   All that night they made preparations for battle; and Acomat Soldan, who knew well by his
spies what were Argon's designs, prepared for battle also,
and admonished his people to conduct themselves with
valour.

Chapter 12

THE BATTLE BETWEEN ARGON AND ACOMAT

NEXT morning, Argon, having called his men to arms
and drawn them up skilfully in battle order, addressed them
in an encouraging manner, after which they advanced
towards the enemy.   Acomat had done the same, and the
two armies met on their way and engaged without further
parley.   The battle began with a shower of arrows so thick
that it seemed like rain from heaven, and you might see
everywhere the riders cast from the horses, and the cries

and groans of those who lay on the earth mortally wounded were dreadful to hear. The slaughter was very great on both sides; but at last, though Argon himself displayed extraordinary valour, and set an example to all his men, it was in vain, for fortune turned against him, and his men were compelled to fly, closely pursued by Acomat and his men, who made great havoc of them.

In the flight Argon himself was captured, upon which the pursuit was abandoned, and the victors returned to their camp and tents, glad beyond measure. Acomat caused his nephew, Argon, to be confined and closely guarded, and, being a man given to his pleasures, he returned to his court to enjoy the society of the fair ladies who were there, leaving the command of the army to a chief, with strict orders to keep Argon closely guarded, and to follow him to court by short marches, so as not to fatigue his men.

Chapter 13

HOW ARGON WAS LIBERATED

Now it happened that a great Tartar baron, who was of great age, took pity on Argon, and said that it was a great wickedness and disloyalty thus to hold their lord a prisoner, and that he would do his best to set him free.

He began by persuading many other barons to adopt the same sentiments, and his personal influence, on account of his age and known character for justice and wisdom, was so great, that he easily gained them over to the enterprise, and they promised to be directed by him. The name of the leader of this enterprise was Boga, and the chief of his fellow-conspirators were named Elcidai, Togan, Tegana, Taga, Tiar Oulatai, and Samagar.

With these, Boga went to the tent where Argon was

THE BATTLE BETWEEN ARGON AND ACOMAT

confined, and told him that they repented of the part they had taken against him, and that in reparation of their error they had come to set him free and take him for their lord.

Chapter 14

HOW ARGON RECOVERED THE SOVEREIGNTY

WHEN Argon heard Boga's words, he thought at first that they came to mock him, and was very angry and cross. "Fair sirs," said he, "you sin greatly in making me an object of mockery, and ought to be satisfied with the wrong you have already done me in imprisoning your rightful lord. You know that you are behaving wrongfully, and therefore I pray go your way and mock me no more."

"Fair sir Argon," said Boga, "be assured that we are not mocking you at all, but what we say is quite true, and we swear to it upon our faith." Then all the barons took an oath that they would hold him for their lord.

Argon on his side swore that he would never trouble them for what was past, but that he would hold them all as dear as his father Abaga had done. And as soon as these mutual oaths had been taken, they took Argon out of prison, and received him as their lord. Then Argon told them to shoot their arrows at the tent in which the chief who had the command of the army was, and they did so, and thus the chief was slain. This chief was named Soldan, and was the greatest lord after Acomat. Thus Argon recovered the sovereignty.

Chapter 15

HOW ARGON CAUSED HIS UNCLE ACOMET TO BE PUT TO DEATH

AND when Argon found that he was assured of the sovereignty, he gave orders to the army to commence its march towards the court. It happened one day that Acomat was at court in his principal palace making great festivity, when a messenger came to him and said: "Sir, I bring you news, not such as I would, but very evil. Know that the barons have delivered Argon and raised him to the sovereignty, and have slain Soldan, your dear friend; and I assure you that they are hastening hither to take and slay you. Take counsel immediately what is best to be done."

When Acomat heard this, he was at first so overcome with astonishment and fear that he knew not what to do or say; but, at last, like a brave and prudent man, he told the messenger to mention the news to no one, and hastily ordered his most trusty followers to arm and mount their horses. Informing nobody where he was going, he took the route to go to the Sultan of Babylonia, believing that there his life would be safe.

At the end of six days he arrived at a pass which could not be avoided, the keeper of which knew that it was Acomat, and perceived that he was seeking safety by flight. This man determined to take him, which he might easily do, as he was slightly attended. He accordingly placed Acomat under a strong guard, and marching with him to the court, arrived there just three days after Argon had taken possession of it, who was greatly mortified that Acomat had escaped.

Chapter 16

HOW ACOMAT WAS SLAIN BY ORDER OF HIS NEPHEW

WHEN, therefore, Acomat was delivered to him a prisoner, he was in the greatest joy imaginable, and commanding the army to be assembled immediately, without consulting with anybody, he ordered one of his men to slay his uncle, and to throw his body into such place as it would never be seen again. This order was immediately executed. Thus ended the affair between Argon and his uncle Acomat.

Chapter 17

THE DEATH OF ARGON

WHEN Argon had done all this, and had taken possession of the principal palace with the sovereignty, all the barons who had been in subjection to his father came to perform their homages as to their lord, and obeyed it as such in everything.

And after this, Argon sent Casan, his son, with full thirty thousand horsemen, to the Arbor Secco, which is in that country, to protect his land and people. Argon thus recovered his sovereignty in the year 1286 of the incarnation of Jesus Christ, and Acomat had held the sovereignty two years. Argon reigned six years, at the end of which he died, as was generally said, by poison.

Chapter 18

HOW QUIACATU SEIZED UPON THE SOVEREIGNTY AFTER THE DEATH OF ARGON

WHEN Argon was dead, his uncle, named Quiacatu, seized upon the sovereignty, which he was enabled to do with the more ease in consequence of Casan being so far distant as the Arbor Secco.

Casan was greatly angered when he heard of the death of his father and of the action of Quiacatu, but he could not leave his post at that moment for fear of his enemies. He threatened, however, that he would find the occasion to revenge himself as signally as his father had done upon Acomat. Quiacatu held the sovereignty, and all were obedient to him except those who were with Casan. He took the wife of his nephew Argon and held her as his own, and enjoyed himself much with the ladies, for he was excessively given to his pleasures. Quiacatu held the sovereignty two years, at the end of which he was carried off by poison.

Chapter 19

HOW BAIDU SEIZED UPON THE SOVEREIGNTY AFTER THE DEATH OF QUIACATU

WHEN Quiacatu was dead, Baidu, who was his uncle, and a Christian, seized upon the sovereignty, and all obeyed him except Casan and the army with him. This occurred in the year 1294.

When Casan learned what had occurred, he was more furious against Baidu than he had been against Quiacatu, and, threatening to take such vengeance on him as should be talked of by everybody, he resolved that he would delay no longer, but march immediately against him. He accordingly provisioned his army, and commenced his march.

When Baidu knew for certain that Casan was coming against him, he assembled a vast number of men, and marched for ten days, and then encamped and waited for him to give battle.

On the second day Casan appeared, and immediately there

began a fierce battle, which ended in the entire defeat of
Baidu, who was slain in the combat. Casan now assumed
the sovereignty, and began his reign in the year 1294. Thus
did the kingdom of the Eastern Tartars descend from
Abaga to Casan, who now reigns.

Chapter 20

CONCERNING THE KING OF THE TARTARS WHO RULES THE FAR NORTH

It should be known therefore, that in the northern parts
of the world there dwell many Tartars, under a chief of
the name of Kaidu, who is of the race of Chinghis Khan, and
nearly related to Kublai, the Great Khan. He is not the
subject of any other prince. The people observe the usages
and manners of their ancestors, and are regarded as genuine
Tartars.

These Tartars are idolaters, and worship a god whom
they call Naagai, that is, the god of earth, because they
think and believe that this their god has dominion over the
earth, and over all things that are born of it. To this false
god they make idols and images of felt, as is described in
a former book.

Their king and his armies do not shut themselves up in
castles or strong places, nor even in towns; but at all times
remain in the open plains, the valleys, or the woods, with
which this region abounds. They have no corn of any kind,
but subsist upon flesh and milk, and live amongst each other
in perfect harmony; their king, to whom they all pay implicit obedience, having no object dearer to him than that of
preserving peace and union amongst his subjects, which is
the essential duty of a sovereign. They possess vast herds
of horses, cows, sheep, and other domestic animals. In

these northern districts are found bears of a white colour, and of prodigious size, being for the most part about twenty spans in length. There are foxes also whose furs are entirely black, wild asses in great numbers, and certain small animals named rondes, which have most delicate furs, and by our people are called zibelines or sables. Besides these there are various small beasts of the marten or weasel kind, and those which bear the name of Pharaoh's mice. The swarms of the latter are incredible, but the Tartars employ such ingenious contrivances for catching them, that none can escape their hands.

In order to reach the country inhabited by these people, it is necessary to perform a journey of fourteen days across a wide plain, entirely uninhabited and desert—a state that is occasioned by innumerable collections of water and springs, that render it an entire marsh. This, in consequence of the long duration of the cold season, is frozen over, excepting for a few months of the year, when the sun dissolves the ice, and turns the soil to mud, over which it is more difficult and fatiguing to travel than when the whole is frozen.

For the purpose, however, of enabling the merchants to frequent their country, and purchase their furs, in which all their trade consists, these people have exerted themselves to render the marshy desert passable for travellers, by erecting at the end of each day's stage a wooden house, raised some height above the ground. Here persons are stationed, whose business it is to receive and accommodate the merchants, and on the following day to conduct them to the next station. Thus they proceed from stage to stage, until they have effected the passage of the desert.

In order to travel over the frozen surface of the ground, they construct a sort of vehicle, not unlike that made use of

by the natives of the steep and almost inaccessible mountains in the vicinity of our own country, and which is termed
a *tragula* or sledge.   It is without wheels, is flat at the
bottom, but rises with a semicircular curve in front, by which
construction it is fitted for running easily upon the ice.   For
drawing these small carriages they keep in readiness certain
animals resembling dogs, and which may be called such,
although they approach to the size of asses.   They are very
strong.   Six of them, in couples, are harnessed to each carriage, which contains only the driver who manages the
dogs, and one merchant, with his package of goods.   When
the day's journey has been performed he returns, together
with the team of dogs.   The merchant returns with furs
that find their way, for sale, to our part of the world.

Chapter 21

OF THOSE COUNTRIES WHICH ARE TERMED THE REGION OF DARKNESS

BEYOND the most distant part of the territory of those
Tartars from whence the skins that have been spoken of are
procured, there is another region which extends to the
utmost bounds of the north, and is called the Region of
Darkness.   During most part of the winter months the sun
is invisible, and the atmosphere is obscured to the same
degree as that in which we find it just about the dawn of
day, when we may be said to see and not to see.

The men of this country are well made and tall, but of a
very pallid complexion.   They are not united under the
government of a king or prince, and they live without any
established laws or usages, in the manner of the brute creation.   Their intellects also are dull, and they have an air
of stupidity.

The Tartars often proceed on plundering expeditions
against these people, to rob them of their cattle and goods.
For this purpose they avail themselves of those months in
which the darkness prevails, in order that their approach
may be unobserved. Being unable to ascertain the direction
in which they should return homeward with their booty,
they provide against the chance of going astray by riding
mares that have young foals at the time, and these foals
they leave behind. When their works of darkness have
been accomplished, and they are desirous of revisiting the
region of light, they lay the bridles on the necks of their
mares, and suffer them freely to take their own course.
Guided by maternal instinct, they make their way directly
to the spot where they had quitted their foals. By these
means the riders are enabled to return in safety.

The inhabitants of this region take advantage of the
summer season, when they enjoy continual daylight, to
catch vast multitudes of ermines, martens, foxes, and other
animals of that kind, the furs of which are more delicate,
and consequently more valuable, than those found in the
districts inhabited by the Tartars. During the summer,
also, these people carry their furs to the neighbouring countries, where they dispose of them in a manner highly
advantageous; and, according to what I have been told, some
of them are transported even as far as to the country of
Russia, of which we shall proceed to speak in this the concluding part of our work.

Chapter 22

OF THE PROVINCE OF RUSSIA ◄ AND ITS PEOPLE

THE province of Russia is of vast extent, is divided into
many parts, and borders upon that northern tract which

THE LAND OF DARKNESS

has been described as the Region of Darkness. Its inhabitants are Christians, and follow the Greek ritual in the offices of their Church.

The men are extremely handsome, tall, and of fair complexions. The women are also fair and of a good size, with light hair, which they are accustomed to wear long. The country pays tribute to the king of the Western Tartars, with whose dominions it comes in contact on its eastern border. Within it are collected in great abundance the furs of ermines, arcolini, sables, martens, foxes, and other animals of that tribe, together with much wax. It contains several mines, from whence a large quantity of silver is procured.

Russia is an exceedingly cold region, and I have been assured that it extends even as far as the Northern Ocean, where, as has been mentioned in a preceding part of the work, falcons are taken in vast numbers, and from here carried to various parts of the world.

Chapter 23

OF THE STRAITS OF CONSTANTINOPLE

At the straits leading into the Great Sea, on the west side, there is a hill called the Faro. But since beginning on this matter I have changed my mind, because so many people know all about it, therefore we will not put it in our description, but go on to something else. And so I will tell you about the Tartars of the Ponent, and the lords who have reigned over them.

Chapter 24

OF THE LORDS OF THE TARTARS OF THE WEST

THE first lord of the Tartars of the West was Sain, who was a very great and powerful king. He conquered Russia, and Comania, and Alania, and Lac, and Mengiar, and Zic, and Gucia, and Gazari. All these provinces were conquered by King Sain. Before this conquest, they were all Comanians, but they were not under one government; and through their want of union they lost their lands, and were dispersed into different parts of the world; and those who remained were all in a state of serfdom to King Sain.

After King Sain reigned King Patu, after him King Berca, next King Mungletemur, then King Totamongu, and lastly Toctai, who now reigns.

Having thus given you a list of kings of the Tartars of the West, we will tell you of a great battle that fell out between Alaù, the lord of the East, and Berca, the lord of the West, as well as the cause of the battle, and its result.

Chapter 25

OF THE WAR BETWEEN ALAU AND BERCA ❦ AND THE BATTLE THEY FOUGHT

IN the year 1261 there arose a great quarrel between King Alaù, lord of the Tartars of the East, and Berca, king of the Tartars of the West, on account of the province which bordered on each of their territories, which both claimed, and each was too proud to yield it to the other. They mutually defied each other, each declaring that he would go and take it, and he would see who dared hinder him.

When things had come to this point, each summoned his followers to his banner, and they exerted themselves to such a degree that within six months each had assembled full three hundred thousand horsemen, very well furnished with all things needed for war.

Alaù, lord of the East, now began his march with all his forces, and they rode many days without meeting with any adventure worth mentioning. At length they reached an extensive plain, situated between the Iron Gates and the Sea of Sarain, in which they encamped in good order, and there was many a rich pavilion and tent. And there Alaù said he would wait to see what course Berca would follow, as this spot was on the borders of the two territories.

Chapter 26
HOW BERCA AND HIS HOST WENT TO MEET ALAÙ

Now when King Berca had made all his preparations, and knew that Alaù was on his march, he also set out on his way, and in due time reached the same plain where his enemies awaited him, and encamped at about ten miles' distance from him.

Berca's camp was quite as richly decked out as that of Alaù, and his army was more numerous, for it numbered full three hundred and fifty thousand horsemen.

Chapter 27
ALAÙ'S ADDRESS TO HIS MEN

WHEN Alaù knew certainly that Berca was come with so great an army, he assembled his chiefs, and addressed them as follows:—"Fair brothers, and sons, and friends," said he, "you know that all my life I have prized you and assisted you, and hitherto you have assisted me to conquer in many battles, nor ever were you in any battle where we failed to obtain the victory, and for that reason are we come here to fight this great man Berca. I know well that he has more men than we have, but they are not so good, and I doubt not but we shall put them all to flight and discomfiture. One thing only I wish to impress upon you, that it is better to die on the field in maintaining our honour, than to suffer discomfiture; so let each of you fight so that our honour may be safe, and our enemies discomfited and slain."

Thus each of the kings encouraged his men, and waited for the day of the battle, and all prepared for it in the best way they could.

Chapter 28

OF THE GREAT BATTLE BETWEEN ALAÙ AND BERCA

WHEN the day fixed for the battle arrived, Alaù rose early in the morning, and called his men to arms, and mar-shalled his army with the utmost skill. He divided it into thirty squadrons, each squadron consisting of ten thousand horsemen; and to each he gave a good leader and a good captain. And when all this was duly arranged, he ordered his troops to advance, which they did at a slow pace, until they came half way between the two camps, where they halted and waited for the enemy.

On the other side, King Berca had drawn up his army, which was arranged in thirty-five squadrons, exactly in the same manner as that of Alaù's, and he also ordered his men to advance, which they did within half-a-mile of the others. There they made a short halt, and then they moved forward again till they came to the distance of about two arbalest shots of each other.

After the two armies had remained a short while in the face of each other, the nacars at length sounded, upon which both armies let fly such a shower of arrows at each other that you could hardly see the sky, and many were slain, man and horse.

The battle continued till dusk, when Berca began to give way, and fled, and Alaù's men pursued furiously, cutting down and slaying without mercy. After they had pursued a short distance, Alaù recalled them, and they returned to their tents, laid aside their arms, and dressed their wounds.

Next morning Alaù ordered the bodies of the dead to be buried, enemies as well as friends, and the loss was so great on both sides that it would be impossible to describe it. After this was done, Alaù returned to his ccuntry with all his men who had survived the battle.

Chapter 29

HOW TOTAMANGU WAS LORD OF THE TARTARS OF THE WEST

You must know that in the west there was a king of the Tartars named Mongletemur, and the sovereignty descended to Tolobuga, who was a young bachelor, and a very powerful man, named Totamangu, slew Tolobuga, with the assistance of another king of the Tartars, named Nogai. Thus Totamangu obtained the sovereignty by the aid of Nogai, and, after a short reign, he died, and Toctai, a very able and prudent man, was chosen king.

Meanwhile the two sons of Tolobuga had grown to be now capable of bearing arms, and they were wise and prudent. The two brothers assembled a very fair company, and went to the court of Toctai, and presented themselves with so much courtesy and humility on their knees that Toctai welcomed them, and told them to stand up.

Then the eldest said to the king, "Fair sir Toctai, I will tell you in the best way I can why we are come to court. You know that we are the sons of Tolobuga, who was slain by Totamangu and Nogai. Of Totamangu, I have nothing to say, since he is dead; but we claim justice on Nogai for the slaughter of our father, and we pray you as a righteous lord to grant it us. This is the object of our visit to your court."

Chapter 30

HOW TOCTAI SENT FOR NOGAI TO COURT

WHEN Toctai had heard the youth, he knew that what he said was true, and he replied, "Fair friend, I will willingly yield to your demand of justice upon Nogai, and for that purpose we will summon him to court, and do everything which justice shall require." Then Toctai sent two messengers to Nogai, and ordered him to come to court to answer to the sons of Tolobuga for the death of their father; but Nogai laughed at the message, and told the messengers he would not go.

When Toctai heard Nogai's message, he was greatly enraged, and said in the hearing of all who were about him, "With the aid of God, either Nogai shall come before me to do justice to the sons of Tolobuga, or I will go against him with all my men and destroy him."

When Nogai knew certainly that Toctai was preparing to come against him with so large a host, he also made great preparation, but not so great as Toctai, because, though a great and powerful king, he was not so great or powerful as the other.

Chapter 31

HOW TOCTAI PROCEEDED AGAINST NOGAI

WHEN Toctai's army was ready, he commenced his march at the head of two hundred thousand horsemen, and in due time reached the fine and extensive plain of Nerghi, where he encamped to wait for his opponent. With him were the two sons of Tolobuga, who had come with a fair company of horsemen to avenge the death of their father.

Chapter 32

TOCTAI AND NOGAI ADDRESS THEIR PEOPLE

NOGAI also was on his march, with a hundred and fifty thousand horsemen, all young and brave men, and much better soldiers than those of Toctai. He arrived in the plain where Toctai was encamped two days after him, and established his camp at a distance of ten miles from him.

Then King Toctai assembled his chiefs, and said to them: "Sirs, we are come here to fight King Nogai and his men, and we have great reason to do so, for you know that all this hatred and rancour has arisen from Nogai's refusal to do justice to the sons of Tolobuga; and, since our cause is just, we have every reason to hope for victory. Be therefore of good hope; but at all events I know that you are all brave men, and that you will do your best to destroy our enemies."

Nogai also addressed his men in the following terms: "Fair brothers and friends," said he, "you know that we have gained many great and hard fought battles, and that we have overcome better men than these. Therefore be of good cheer. We have right on our side; for you know well that Toctai was not my superior to summon me to his court to do justice to others. I will only further urge you to demean yourselves so in this battle that we shall be talked of everywhere, and that ourselves and our heirs will be the more respected for it."

Chapter 33

THE VICTORY OF KING NOGAI

NEXT day they prepared for battle. Toctai drew up his army in twenty squadrons, each with a good leader and captain; and Nogai's army was formed in fifteen squadrons.

After a long and desperate battle in which the two kings, as well as the two sons of Tolobuga, distinguished themselves by their reckless valour, the army of Toctai was entirely defeated, and pursued from the field with great slaughter by Nogai's men, who, though less numerous, were much better soldiers than their opponents. Full sixty thousand men were slain in this battle, but King Toctai. as well as the two sons of Tolobuga, escaped.

Chapter 34 and Last

CONCLUSION

AND now ye have heard all that I can tell you about the Tartars and the Saracens and their customs, and likewise about the other countries of the world as far as my travels and knowledge extend. Only we have said nothing whatever about the Greater Sea and the provinces that lie round it, although we know it thoroughly. But it seems to me a needless task to speak about places which are visited by people every day. For there are so many who sail all about the sea constantly.

Of the manner in which we took our departure from the Court of the Great Khan you have heard at the beginning of the book, in that chapter where we told you of the difficulty that Messer Maffeo and Messer Nicolo and Messer Marco had about getting the Great Khan's leave to go; and in the same chapter is related the lucky chance that led to our departure. And you may be sure that but for that chance, we should never have got away in spite of all our trouble, and never have got back to our country again.

I believe it was God's pleasure that we should get back in order that people might learn about the things that the world contains.

Thanks be to God!   Amen!   Amen!

I N D E X

THE END